Dedicated to

PHILIP E. MOSELY

1905-1972

teacher and friend

FOREWORD

Western scholarship on the Soviet Union has been evolving steadily in recent years, an evolution marked by increasing insight into the Soviet system, a capacity for making significant differentiations, and for placing Soviet studies in a context of broad international developments.

This book is a remarkable example of each of these qualities, and it therefore will be valuable not only to students of Soviet policies, but to all those interested in Third World economic development and the growing interdependence of the world economy.

The great value of the book as a study of an important aspect of Soviet policy stems from Professor Valkenier's ability to combine thoughtful analysis of Soviet writings with a discriminating use of less formal materials. She has demonstrated that a knowledgeable scholar can sift and evaluate information gained from discussions and interviews over many years so that it multiplies synergistically the value of written materials. Methodologically, this represents an important advance in our effort to move toward more realistic insights into the perceptions and policy-making processes of the Soviet Union.

Two singular benefits derive from Professor Valkenier's painstaking scholarship. First, in place of the prevailing tendency to speak of *the* Soviet view on these matters, she has convincingly identified significant differences and contending schools of thought among Soviet and East European analysts of Third World developments. And second, in contrast to the conventional view of Soviet thinking and policies as static, she has traced marked changes over time in the way Soviet Party leadership has perceived the problems of the Third World and sought to adapt its economic policies to an increasingly complex reality.

These insights clarify not only the movement away from the ideologically simplistic formulations of the Khrushchev era to a more differentiated awareness of the complexity of Third World developments but, even more, the movement from the Stalinist doctrine of two antagonistic world markets to a realization of Soviet self-interest in an interdependent global economy. The practical consequence of these changes, Professor Valkenier demonstrates, has been an evolution of Soviet economic policies from simple propagandistic exploitation of Third World grievances to a search for more productive economic relations, one that recognizes Soviet involvement in an interdependent world economy. As the book's title suggests, this search is complicated by the limitations inherent in the Soviet economy and by cross-cutting Soviet political interests, including the USSR's competitive relations with the United States and other countries of the West.

As I have suggested, the book challenges prevailing views — in my judgment, successfully. In doing so, it contributes to our knowledge of Soviet behavior and, no less, to our understanding of problems affecting economic development.

Marshall Shulman

PREFACE

This book describes how the Soviet Union's economic performance, capabilities, and the associated Marxist theory have become the Achilles' heel of Moscow's relations with the Third World. Such was not the situation at the outset of Khrushchev's offensive. In 1955, the USSR challenged the West to economic competition in the former colonies, confident that it alone offered them the correct combination of guidance and aid. Twenty-five years later that confidence appears shaken, for it has become evident that Soviet economic capacity does not match Soviet political aspirations. Moreover, many Soviets recognize that their Marxist theories have failed to keep up with the rapid developments in science and technology affecting international economic relations. Khrushchev's initial assurance and uncompromisingly competitive aims have given way to moderation and a fumbling for new means and rationales in the vastly more complicated world of Brezhnev's last years.

My study is an examination of Soviet scholarly works and polemics, as well as of official statements and statistics. It deals with the conceptual framework in which a range of economic perceptions and relationships operate; it is neither an economic analysis nor a compendium of factual data. It looks at changes in Soviet views and practices to show to what extent economic realities have forced the Soviets to recognize that the developing countries are part of an interdependent world market in which the USSR can exercise no decisive control or leverage. It also describes the groupings in the current debate to demonstrate that no single school of thought guides the making of Soviet foreign policy.

Chapter 1 discusses what led up to the current drive to replace the concessionary aid-trade programs with profitable exchanges. The next chapter traces the acceptance of the notion of the global economy operating over and above the socialist and capitalist systems and the ways of adapting to it. Chapter 3 deals with the rise of moderation in Soviet development theory, and the final chapter analyzes Moscow's reservations about the developing countries' program for a new international economic order. Shifts in these four areas indicate significant departures from Moscow's former belief in a common front with the Third World against imperialism and in its ability decisively to challenge Western economic predominance.

The book's thesis is that the modifications in Soviet theory and practice over the past 25 years have resulted from various disappointments with the initial expectations of easy success for Soviet-type "socialist" policies and institutions in the former colonies. The USSR has had difficulties with generating a satisfactory pattern of trade exchanges with these countries; it can no longer afford the aid they still require; Moscow has become disenchanted with the feasibility of speedy "socialist" remedies for the problems of backwardness; and it has come to face the lack of congruence between the Soviet and the Third World programs for restructuring international economic relations.

This thesis — which rests on the perception that increasingly more Soviets have a sense of the limitations on power — runs counter to prevalent interpretations in some Western quarters. Numerous commentators and analysts assume that: (1) the optimistic and competitive goals formulated by Khrushchev remain unchanged and are still the operational code in the Kremlin; (2) the USSR still intends to and is capable of gaining control over the vast raw material supplies of Asia and Africa; (3) the Soviets possess a magic systemic formula guaranteeing success for socialist revolutions in the developing countries; and (4) they command unlimited resources to buy goodwill or to prop up client regimes.

In offering a description of how economic realities have placed the Soviet Union's original politically based aspirations in a bind, I am not chalking up points on some cold war scoreboard. Instead, I hope that the book will acquaint readers with the evolution in Soviet perceptions of the outside world, which in turn might make it possible to detect nuances and discernment in Soviet policies and proposals. Granted that scholars and researchers do not make foreign policy either in Moscow or in Washington, their analyses, nevertheless, do reflect and contribute to the mental climate in which foreign policy decisions are made.

Many people and institutions have contributed to this book. Foremost, I should acknowledge my debt to Philip E. Mosely, under whose guidance I first began to work on Soviet relations with the newly independent countries some 20 years ago. His insistence on a solid historical approach — of change as it occurs over time — as against facile judgments of the moment, has been a guiding principle. A two-year research grant from the National Council on Soviet and East European Research enabled me to do uninterrupted research and thinking on the subject. The hospitality extended by the W. A. Harriman Institute for Advanced Study of the Soviet Union at Columbia University as well as the interest shown by Marshall Shulman have provided the ideal combination of support, friendly atmosphere, and intellectual stimulation one needs in the long haul of writing a book. Consultations and conversations with numerous U.S., British, Indian, Soviet, Polish, and Hungarian specialists have been invaluable. I am grateful to them all and hope that they will understand the spirit in which this study is offered. And finally I thank my husband, Robert, for his good spirit and editorial advice.

Parts of Chapter 2 first appeared in my article "Development Issues in Recent Soviet Scholarship," *World Politics*, vol. 32, no. 4 (July 1980): 485-508, and the excerpts are reprinted by permission of Princeton University Press.

Elizabeth Kridl Valkenier
New York City, May 1983

CONTENTS

FOREWORD   vii
Marshall Shulman

PREFACE   ix

LIST OF ACRONYMS   xv

1   AID AND TRADE: FROM POLITICS TO ECONOMICS   1

Phase 1: Economic Relations as a Political Weapon (1953-64)   3
Phase 2: The Pursuit of Economic Advantage (1965-74)   11
Phase 3: The Post-1974 Slump   22
Socialist Foreign Economic Policy at Present   26
Notes   33

2   THE WORLD ECONOMY: FROM BIFURCATION
    TO GLOBALISM   37

The "Two World Markets" Theory   39
Academic Research under Khrushchev   40
Analysis in the Early Brezhnev Period   45
Innovations and Groupings since 1976   52
East European and Western Theoretical Inroads   59
The Third World in a Global Perspective   62
Notes   69

3   DEVELOPMENT THEORY: FROM ECONOMIC
    LIBERATION TO INTERDEPENDENCE   73

Development Economics under Khrushchev   74
Economic Factors after 1964   76

The Post-1974 Conceptual Framework 81
Development Issues in a New Light 86
Socialist Orientation and Economic Progress 97
Notes 103

4 **THE NEW INTERNATIONAL ECONOMIC ORDER:
THE PARTING OF THE WAYS** 109

The Fourth and Fifth UNCTAD Sessions and Beyond 111
Reassessment among Soviet Specialists 117
The International Division of Labor at Present 122
East European Views 127
The Third World Looks at Soviet Theory 135
Third World and Soviet Bloc Aims 140
Notes 143

5 **IN CONCLUSION** 147

APPENDIX 151

BIBLIOGRAPHY 161

SUBJECT INDEX 177

COUNTRY INDEX 185

NAME INDEX 187

ABOUT THE AUTHOR 189

LIST OF ACRONYMS

CC	Central Committee
CMEA	Council of Mutual Economic Assistance
CPE	Centrally planned economy
CPSU	Communist Party of the Soviet Union
IMEMO	Institute of World Economy and International Relations
LDCs	Less developed countries
MEMO	*World Economy and International Relations*
NEP	New Economic Policy
NIEO	New International Economic Order
UNCTAD	United Nations Conference on Trade and Development
UNIDO	United Nations Industrial Development Organization
UNITAR	United Nations Institute for Training and Research

Note: Translations of Russian titles appear in the bibliography.

1

AID AND TRADE: FROM POLITICS TO ECONOMICS

In the immediate postwar years, Moscow, burdened with reconstruction and the consolidation of its hegemony in Eastern Europe and the Far East, had deliberately distanced itself from the colonial areas and newly independent states. Resumption of its interests in those regions is commonly associated with the post-Stalin leadership. Freed from Stalin's paranoid obsessions, his successors recognized that the former colonies could be profitably manipulated for Soviet purposes. But in fact a low-keyed economic rapprochement had already been tried 11 months before the dictator's death.

The convocation of the International Economic Conference, held in Moscow in May 1952, indicated that after completing its post-World War II reconstruction the Soviet Union was anticipating an overproduction in capital goods and wanted to find markets in exchange for raw materials. M. V. Nesterov, president of the USSR Chamber of Commerce, spoke about the many opportunities for expanding trade with the countries of Southeast Asia and the Middle East. In return for their exports of cotton, jute, leather, foodstuffs, rubber, and nonferrous metals, the USSR was ready to send 3 million rubles' worth of machinery and equipment within the next two or three years. These businesslike proposals were not couched in any political terms. Nevertheless, Nesterov was careful to separate

1

exchanges with the developing countries from his proposals for the expansion of East-West trade.[1]

By contrast, the East European participants (Oskar Lange, the well-known Polish economist, was the conference chairman) did not observe a compartmentalized or trifurcated approach. Without drawing any systemic distinctions between groups of countries, they stressed that the normalization of world trade had become a necessity for all nations and that the People's Democracies "wanted to take part in an expanded world trade." The difference between the Soviet politically based approach to foreign trade and the East European recognition of objective economic imperatives is worth noting. At the start of the Soviet bloc's entry into the markets of developing countries, it was hardly visible and did not have any policy repercussions. But with time the needs of the East European trade-dependent economies and the innovating initiatives this situation created had considerable influence on Soviet theory and practice.

The offers of trade made in the spring of 1952, as well as the creation of a new agency (Mashinoeksport) to handle exports to the less developed countries (LDCs), did not bring any actual expansion of commercial activity. Only after Stalin's death did the Soviets pass from words to action.

Active courtship of the developing areas began at the United Nations. On July 15, 1953, at the sixteenth session of the Economic and Social Council, the Soviet delegation broke with its postwar record of nonparticipation and financial nonsupport to announce that the Soviet Union would contribute 4 million rubles (equivalent to $1 million at the rate of exchange then) to the Expanded Technical Assistance Program. (Prior to that date, the Soviet Union had used the U.N. forum to attack all existing aid programs as designed to make the developing countries into "raw material appendages" of the United States and other Western powers.) In August 1953 the first trade agreement in Latin America, including the extension of a $30 million credit for the purchase of capital equipment, was signed with Argentina. In December 1953 the USSR and India concluded the first five-year trade pact, which provided for substantial exports of Soviet machinery in exchange for local raw materials. In January 1954 Moscow offered Afghanistan its first postwar credit — $3.5 million for the construction of two grain elevators, a flour mill, and a mechanized bakery. (In October an additional credit of $2.1 million was granted for road building.) And in February 1955

Moscow agreed to provide India with technical assistance for the construction of a steel mill.[2]

By the end of 1955, the Soviet Union had staged trade exhibits in Indonesia, Syria, Morocco, Argentina, and Uruguay and had participated in numerous international fairs. What seemed like a parade of economic missions began to pass between Moscow and various Third World capitals.

Both at that time and later, it was not possible to draw a clear distinction between aid and trade, since the USSR almost never offered outright grants but only low interest loans to cover the purchase of Soviet machinery and services for the projects to be built with Soviet assistance. Similarly, much of the debt repayment could be made through the shipment of traditional exports. Thus there has always been an automatic conversion of what has been loosely termed "aid" (both by the Soviets and Westerners) into trade flows.

Although unprecedented, these actions were reported in the Soviet press in a matter-of-fact way. There was no attempt to make any propaganda claims about their nature, to ascribe to them any special purpose, or to represent them as a new program. Trade promotion was in the hands of foreign trade officials, and the Soviets acted like ordinary salesmen. Hence the alarm that was instantaneously registered in the West centered at first on fears of economic competition. There was apprehension that the Soviet Union's new ability to export surplus capital goods, produced under the rigid discipline of a planned economy, would pose a serious challenge in areas that, in everyone's memory, had been safe preserves for Western business.[3]

PHASE I: ECONOMIC RELATIONS AS A POLITICAL WEAPON (1953-64)

The economic rapprochement soon passed from the hands of trade experts to the supervision of the Soviet leadership and became part and parcel of an all-out political offensive aimed at encouraging the developing countries to nibble away at the territorial, strategic, political, and economic domain of the West.

The first outlines of an aggressive approach emerged in late 1955 during Bulganin's and Khrushchev's Asian tour, which took them to India, Afghanistan, and Burma. The trip started with the Soviet leaders rather diffidently offering to "share" Soviet experience in building industrial enterprises. But it ended with Nikita Sergeevich challenging the West to outright competition. Angered by some press allegations that the USSR would be incapable of providing India with effective technical assistance, the impulsive and combative Khrushchev proclaimed to the unnamed scoffers: "To those who write in this way we say: 'Perhaps you wish to compete with us in establishing friendship with the Indians? Let us compete.'" He then raised the original offer to "share" experience to outright readiness to "assist."[4] In the following days, there were increasingly hostile references in the Soviet leaders' speeches to the West's responsibility for India's backwardness in the past as well as to nefarious plots for future exploitation. There were also increasingly pointed references to India's "wise" decision not to participate in any military groupings.

Soon other events helped to convert the nascent aid-trade program into a political weapon; by the late 1950s, it had become an important component in the competition for the allegiance of the developing countries and for influence on their future course.

When in July 1956 John Foster Dulles withdrew U.S. support for the first stage in the construction of the High Aswan Dam (partly in retaliation for Nasser's arms deal with Czechoslovakia and recognition of mainland China), Moscow stepped in with an offer. The subsequent nationalization of the Suez Canal and the resulting invasion by Britain, France, and Israel during the Soviet invasion of Hungary led to the signing of actual agreements. Significantly, Moscow not only financed the first stage of construction, it also insisted on excluding the West from assisting the subsequent stages as well. Thus the USSR became the sole source of foreign aid for this ambitious project, creating a tangible symbol of Communist support for economic liberation and development in the face of Western opposition.

In September 1956 the Soviets extended a $100 million credit to Indonesia to finance, among other things, the country's first two steel mills. Like Egypt, Indonesia was embroiled in highly acrimonious disputes with the Netherlands and other Western powers. As it happened, the Soviet loan was ratified by the Indonesian Parliament in February 1958, just as the country's economic, military, and political troubles with the West had reached their peak. Similarly, in September 1958, when Guinea rejected de Gaulle's offer of political association and instead chose full national independence, causing a complete rupture with the metropole, the USSR extended diplomatic recognition within two days and a $35 million loan within a few months. Diplomatic and economic ostracism by the West made the Soviet Union the only source of aid for the hard-pressed West African country.

The mounting propaganda campaign accompanying these moves made it plain that the Soviets strove not to expand trade so much as to score political victories. Nor would they stint on whatever was necessary; in fact, Khrushchev liked to boast that in promoting the economic liberation of the developing countries the Soviet Union eschewed the notion of "mutual advantage" and knowingly followed policies that were "disadvantageous to us commercially."[5] Such assertions, together with his confident predictions that socialism was bound to prevail over capitalism within the foreseeable future, created the impression that Moscow regarded the developing world as the most promising area for advancing its goals to weaken, or (to use Khrushchev's phrase) to "bury," the West.

Khrushchev's ascendancy to full power, certified at the 21st Party Congress in early 1959, reaffirmed what had become the predominant line in Soviet policy toward the developing nations. In the speeches extolling Khrushchev's victory over Malenkov, Bulganin, and Molotov, it was revealed that "in foreign affairs" his rivals had "opposed or energetically hindered . . . the development of economic relations with and aid . . . to the underdeveloped and dependent countries of Asia and the Near East. They behaved like narrow nationalists." The same congress marked the adoption of the ambitious Seven Year Plan geared in part to winning the economic competition in the former colonial areas. By 1965, it was claimed, the Socialist camp would produce more than half the world's industrial output and this would enable the USSR to expand assistance to the developing countries. Accordingly, Otto Kuusinen, a prominent theoretician of the international Communist movement, informed the delegates that whereas in the past "there was a period when we had nothing to share, having [now] grown richer, we shall help our friends." In addition, Academician Konstantin Ostrovitianov made extravagant claims for the Soviet trade potential resulting from the fulfillment of the Seven Year Plan: "The Soviet ruble will soon start to enter the world market, there progressively supplanting the dollar."[6]

Under Khrushchev, the aid-trade program had three overarching political purposes. First, economic assistance served to cement close association with radical, anti-Western regimes. In general, aid was not extended to the moderate, pro-Western governments. The circumstances associated with granting the first large-scale credit to Egypt (after it became embroiled with the West) set the pattern for other deals. The USSR cultivated such poor and relatively insignificant countries as Guinea and Mali, which were vociferously at odds with France, while ignoring the intrinsically more important, but pro-Western, Nigeria. Similarly, aid was extended to Ghana, which sought to organize the radical states in opposition to the more moderate Casablanca group. Iraq qualified for Soviet aid only after the July 1958 revolution that resulted, among other things, in the country's withdrawal from the Baghdad Pact. In Asia, Sukarno's strongly anti-Western "positive neutralism" earned Indonesia substantial amounts of aid (almost $400 million). Even larger aid was extended to India (over $800 million) to fortify its more evenhanded version of neutralism.

Second, aid grants were part of a strategy to promote tension between the LDCs and the West and among the pro- and anti-Western newly independent countries. For instance, there was no attempt to moderate Sukarno's irredentist claims in New Guinea against the Dutch. On the contrary, during his February 1960 visit to Indonesia, Khrushchev not only granted Sukarno another large loan — $250 million — but also punctuated speeches with expressions of support and sympathy for the Indonesian people's "just struggle" to regain West Irian, plus pointed remarks that it would be "naive" to suppose that the "colonialists would relinquish their positions voluntarily."[7] Similarly, Afghanistan and India, both among Moscow's largest Asian aid recipients, received outspoken Soviet support in their respective territorial claims (Pushtoonistan and Kashmir) against pro-Western Pakistan.

Finally, Soviet aid went hand in hand with fostering neo-Marxist ideology, designed to forge an alliance between the Socialist camp and the former colonies. During the months between the Moscow Meeting of 81 Parties in December 1960 and the 22nd CPSU Congress in October 1961, the middle-class leaders of the newly independent countries were raised in status to "revolutionary democrats" who would transcend the limits of bourgeois revolutions. (At the same time, the Communist parties of the Third World were instructed either to dissolve or to moderate their platforms accordingly.) The economic programs of the revolutionary democrats, specifically their industrialization and nationalization drives, received approbation as progressive protosocialist policies. And Soviet credits were heralded as making a substantial contribution to that endeavor.

The aims and terms of Soviet aid were unabashedly anti-Western. Credits were earmarked to support import-substitution industrialization and the expansion of the state sector, both goals being conceived in the framework of the highly emotional vocabulary of "economic liberation" rather than in the more neutral matrix of economic development per se. Industrialization was represented as the economic lever for transforming developing countries into independent actors on the world market and for ending Western domination, which relegated them to the role of raw material producers. The public sector was the institutional lever for eliminating the exploitative Western presence as well as the retrogressive capitalist elements of private business. From the start, the direction and content of Soviet policies were presented as antithetical to Western ways. To quote from a typical assessment:

> The distinctive feature of [Soviet] credits is that they are designated to develop key branches of the economy of the recipient countries. . . . While the Soviet Union's aid promotes the building up of an independent national economy in the former colonies and dependent countries, the terms of capitalist credits are such as to preserve their economic dependence. . . . Soviet credits above all promote the development of the state sector of the national economy which represents the strongest basis for the genuine independence of underdeveloped countries. The credit policy of the Western imperialist circles is diametrically opposite in nature. Its chief purpose is to reinforce the dominating positions held by foreign monopoly capital in these countries.[8]

The terms of Soviet aid were also structured as an alternative to Western practice. The Soviets made it a point not to give outright grants (in the late 1950s, almost one-quarter of U.S. aid consisted of grants), since that was considered a condescending gesture. Instead they offered loans that carried interest rates of 2.5 to 3 percent and were repayable over a period of 8 to 15 years, beginning one year after completion of the project or deliveries of the machinery. Moreover, repayments could be made in local currencies or in the form of traditional exports, a feature that was especially welcome to developing countries due to their balance-of-payment problems. In addition, the selection of the specific projects was not dependent on Moscow's views concerning the most efficient local allocation of resources; the final decision was left to the recipient. This feature was responsible not only for the notorious stadiums but also for the prestige-enhancing, though not always economically viable, projects in heavy industry. Finally, Moscow always emphasized that whatever was built with Socialist aid became the full property of the recipient nation; the Soviet Union never sought any equity or share of the profits or participation in the management of the project built with its assistance. Upon completion, Soviet-aided projects became the partner's full property.

The fact that the amounts of aid were substantial only served to reinforce the political threat. Starting with the $5.6 million credit to Afghanistan in 1954, Soviet aid reached the annual level of over $800 million by 1959. Thereafter the total declined but again climbed close to $1 billion in 1964. Even though the sum was nowhere near the Western totals, the concentration of Moscow's credits in a few strategically important countries and on ambitious projects lent considerable luster to the program. By 1964 the USSR was extending credits to some 30 countries, but 8 states received about 80 percent of the total: "progressive" Egypt, Ghana, Iraq, Syria, Algeria, Indonesia, and the staunchly neutral India and Afghanistan. Moreover, in some countries the Soviets had committed themselves to a larger dollar volume than the United States had. This was the case in Afghanistan, Mali, Guinea, and Indonesia. In the United Arab Republic and in sub-Saharan Africa, Soviet offers just about matched U.S. aid. In India Soviet and Bloc credits were only about one-third the amount of U.S. aid, but being associated with high visibility projects like the Bhilai steel mill, they created the impression of being larger than the actual sums spent by the United States.

The Soviets also made inroads into foreign trade patterns. Between 1955 and 1964, the share of the LDCs in Soviet trade rose from 4.6 to 10.3 percent, with rates of growth rising accordingly. Whereas from 1956 to 1965, the average annual rate of growth for Soviet trade as a whole was 3.2 percent and for trade with the West was 4.8 percent, the rate for Soviet-LDC exchanges averaged 20 percent. A harmonious complementarity seemed to obtain between the Communist and Third World economies. The simple mass-produced capital goods answered to the pressing needs of the developing countries. This held true both for tractors and for technologically unsophisticated steel mills. Moreover, they were offered at rates cheaper than for Western machinery and on terms that favored the developing countries. (Moscow was willing to take in exchange large quantities of Burmese rice, Egyptian cotton, Ghanaian cocoa, or Brazilian coffee at a time when, following the end of the Korean War, there was a sharp fall in commodity prices.)

Although the overall trade of the Third World did not register as significant a shift as did the Soviet trade (by 1964 the LDCs conducted only about 5 percent of their trade with the Soviet Bloc), the figures for some countries were quite dramatic. For example, Guinea was getting 44 percent of its imports from the Soviet Union and its European allies; Afghanistan conducted 30 percent of its trade with the Bloc, the United Arab Republic, 20 percent, India and Indonesia, 10 percent.

Khrushchev's manner of entry into the former colonial areas produced an appropriately shocked response in the West. It is instructive now to look at U.S. commentaries at the time to see how both diplomats and scholars inclined toward the worst possible interpretations. Under Secretary of State Douglas Dillon declared that "the Soviet economic offensive is a means for carrying the struggle against us in its economic aspects to the most vulnerable sector of the free world. The ultimate objective of Soviet leaders continues to be the downfall of the West."[9] More temperate academic observers concluded that "the present profile of international affairs has been strongly affected by Soviet Third World policies, and that among these policies foreign aid is without doubt the most influential."[10] The more alarmist argued that "postwar expansion of Soviet aid programs supports the thesis that a long-range goal of Soviet socialism is the gradual economic infiltration of all the so-called underdeveloped countries of Africa, Asia and Latin America." These analysts maintained that in a short period of time ("in ten years?") the Soviet "planning commission will have detailed blueprints of the economic steps necessary to gain control of the countries involved."[11] On the contrary, Joseph Berliner, one of the earliest and most perceptive analysts of Soviet aid, argued that even if the USSR were to increase its programs to match the U.S. level it would still be unable to force the hand of the recipient countries. Yet this was certainly not a widely shared view at the time.[12]

There was an almost universal credence in not only the effectiveness of Moscow's economic offensive but also the unlimited capacity of the Soviet Union to expand its operations. Some scholars predicted that the USSR would soon be ready to "send almost unlimited economic aid abroad." Others argued that it was entirely feasible that the Soviet Bloc, which by 1960 accounted for 3 to 4 percent of the LDCs' total trade turnover, could take up as much as 10 to 15 percent of Third World trade within the next ten years.[13] Even when the small size of the actual Soviet operations was acknowledged, its purposeful political thrust seemed to give it power and prospects of unlimited proportions. The State Department's Bureau of Intelligence and Research argued that although total Soviet trade with non-Bloc countries in 1960 amounted to only about $2.9 billion (comparable in volume to Denmark's trade) even such a magnitude in the "hands of state monopoly" could give significant support to Moscow's political designs by opening its vast market to countries with surplus commodities and balance-of-payments problems.[14] Similarly, the Soviet purchase of Indonesian rubber, although it constituted but 2 percent of Jakarta's sales in 1959, was interpreted as marking a shift in Indonesia's foreign trade from Western to Eastern markets.[15]

It is important to have a sense of the alarmist reactions in the West to the Soviet economic entry into the Third World arena. Khrushchev's claims and actions were so ideologically motivated, so optimistic, and so cocksure that they created a profound impression abroad that there was little or no economic rationale behind the Soviet aid and trade drive. Western analysts presumed that the Soviets would spare no efforts to cut the West off from the sources of its industrial power. Such impressions persist to this day. Despite much change in the Soviet mode of operations and a scaling down of expectations on Moscow's part, many Western observers still labor under the shock produced some 25 years ago when Khrushchev first espoused the colonial cause as a major element in his strategy to "bury" the capitalist system. They continue to cite the practices and pronouncements in the years 1955-65 as the Kremlin's operational code, which remains as valid today as it was when the Soviets first bombastically stepped onto the scene.

However, another observation should be made. No matter how excessive Western fears proved to be in the longer run, there is no gainsaying that the first phase of Soviet economic operations in the

Third World — to the extent that it was politically motivated — achieved its objectives. Internationally, the Soviet Union succeeded in denying capitalist states the monopoly of influence in the Third World, contributed to quickening a self-assertive consciousness among the LDCs, and identified the USSR with the liberationist aspirations of these states.

As far as the internal policies of the developing countries were concerned, the Soviet rapid modernization model, the nature of Soviet aid, plus the incessant propaganda about the exploitative nature of ties with the West helped to popularize the import-substitution industrialization drive based on public ownership. These aspirations existed before Moscow's entry on the scene, but its vociferous espousal of domestic measures necessary either to curb or to eliminate the Western presence certainly helped step up the pace of nationalization, industrialization, planning, and other measures meant to strengthen the economic independence of the new states.

In the area of economic assistance, the Soviet example helped alter Western practices in favor of the LDCs. The United States not only gave considerably more aid from 1955 to 1965 than it had in the preceding decade, but Western nations and institutions lowered loan rates in response to the Soviet challenge. Similarly, the Soviet insistence on respecting the developing countries' sovereignty over their natural resources and on emphasizing the importance of industrialization as the spur to indigenous development had an impact on Western firms and donors. Firms became more willing to settle for service contracts rather than outright concessions, and donors became better disposed toward assisting industrial projects. In all these respects, the Western economic posture became less imperious.

PHASE 2: THE PURSUIT OF ECONOMIC ADVANTAGE (1965-74)

Even before his ouster, there were reservations about Khrushchev's penchant for promoting Soviet and socialist causes in the Third World through generous aid handouts without much regard for the costs entailed. Attempts to give the Soviet aid program an economic rationale preceded the actual reversal after October 1964.

Anastas Mikoyan, speaking before the 22nd Party Congress in October 1961, informed his audience that it "will be necessary to make wide use of foreign trade as a factor in economizing on current production expenditure and in capital investment."[16] Although he did not refer specifically to exchanges with the LDCs, there were signs that these transactions were of concern to the government and to specialists. At about this time, the Presidium of the Academy of Sciences set up a research group in the Institute of the Economy of the World Socialist System to devise indexes to measure the effectiveness of economic relations with the newly independent countries. General articles appeared suggesting that "the advantages of the international division of labor" should govern trade within the Bloc and beyond in order to speed up domestic development.[17] A general assessment of the actual administration of aid also became evident. Soviet assistance credits, having consistently climbed since the inception of the program, decreased for the first time in 1962, falling by 58 percent below the previous year's level from $555 million to $233 million). Moreover, high officials began to visit the larger aid recipients to inspect the implementation and progress of the entire Soviet program.

Not only at home was the haphazard character of Soviet economic activities a matter of concern; it was not much to the liking of the developing countries either. At the first session of the United Nations Conference on Trade and Development (UNCTAD), held in early 1964, the developing nations formally requested the USSR to make firm commitments for future purchases of various commodities to make it possible to plan their production and trade.

But so long as Khrushchev remained in command, there could be no thoroughgoing reorientation of the aid and trade program, for this would have undermined its political thrust. Despite the evidence of other ways of thinking, the First Secretary's optimistic faith in the efficacy of ruble diplomacy remained the distinguishing characteristic of Soviet operations until his fall from power. Circumstances that contributed to Khrushchev's ouster neatly sum up his style and policy. In a euphoric mood at the completion of the first stage of the High Aswan Dam in May 1964, the Soviet leader offered the United Arab Republic an additional $277 million credit for its second development plan. It was a grand gesture to underscore Soviet support for the United Arab Republic's drive for economic independence. But the First Secretary made his offer without previously consulting the Politbureau. Later, Khrushchev's personal largesse with Soviet funds was counted among those "hare-brained" schemes that were responsible for his removal from office in October 1964.[18]

Beginning in 1965, Soviet economic relations with the Third World began to shed their ad hoc and predominantly political character. The pursuit of economic advantage became an important criterion, and the necessary ideological justification for the shift was supplied by the new leadership at the 23rd Party Congress in the spring of 1966. In contrast to the pronouncements made at the 21st Congress in 1959, when the speakers confidently expounded the Soviet ability and obligation to help others, Leonid Brezhnev asserted that the successful buildup of the Soviet economy was the chief "international duty" of the USSR. "The more quickly our country moves forward in building the new society, the more successfully will our international tasks be resolved." He also thanked "our foreign friends" for having agreed that the "successful building of Communism in the Soviet Union constitutes the main support for their revolutionary struggle." More specifically, Kosygin remarked upon the practical results of the aid and trade program, stating that cooperation with the LDCs enabled the USSR to "make better use of the international division of labor."[19] That claim was certainly premature, but it indicated a changed perception of the nature of economic relations between the Soviet Union and the Third World.

Informed commentary, which began to appear soon after the 23rd Congress, specified how the new relationship was supposed to operate. The first article, based on the findings of the research group working on the effectiveness of Soviet economic relations with the developing countries, was published in February 1965. Other articles and at least two monographs followed in the next 18 months. One book discussed the planning of foreign trade and its profitability when financed through long-term credits. Another book, written by researchers at the Institute of the Economy of the World Socialist System, recommended stabilizing and expanding ties with the developing countries through closer economic integration.[20]

Basically, these works proposed a precise economic rationale for Soviet transactions with the developing countries by integrating the allocation of aid with the expansion of trade. They viewed giving aid primarily as an alternative to domestic investment and argued that it would be cheaper for the USSR to import certain goods and materials than to produce them at home. Also, it would be more economical to have the East European states replace some of the raw materials they obtained from the Soviet Union by imports from Africa and Asia.

Rendering aid on such principles would commit the USSR to planning with the developing countries the joint extracting or processing of various natural resources and the joint production of some goods, all agreements being based on long-term aid and trade commitments. The list of suitable raw materials most frequently included iron ore, lead, copper, zinc, aluminum, and petroleum; the list of manufactures was much shorter and less explicit, usually starting with cotton fibers or textiles and quickly trailing off into unspecified consumer products and processed goods.

This new emphasis on the primacy of domestic needs over the Soviet Union's perceived international obligations was directly reflected in the reorientation of its assistance programs. Although aid commitments more than doubled during the second phase (the average annual pledge rose from $310 million to $677 million), they were apportioned to make economic relations with the LDCs less of a drain on the Soviet economy. To turn them into a net gain, more stringent procedures were adopted to tighten up the existing aid programs. There was a shift to more promising partners, and new administrative procedures and new forms of cooperation were introduced.

In the reassessment of the existing programs, economic rationality became the criterion. Of course, a sharp eye was kept open for possible political and strategic opportunities. However, where radicalism had become an excessive burden — as was the case with Mali, Ghana, Indonesia, and Burma — the USSR declined to shore up ailing economies. For about five years, the Soviets concentrated on putting their aid program into some rational order. They made feasibility studies before granting loans; they would often propose to finance the expansion or modernization of existing facilities rather than agree to underwrite another new large venture; they turned down requests; and they began to insist on repayment.

The response to the United Arab Republic's second development plan epitomizes the post-Khrushchev attitude. Although the new Soviet leaders promised to honor the former First Secretary's pledge (formalized in a credit agreement of September 1964), they stated that Soviet support was contingent on a more "realistic" assessment. As it happened, Moscow's reconsiderations coincided with Cairo's doubts about the advisability of further industrial expansion. First, the ambitious Five Year Plan was stretched out to seven years. Finally, in October 1966 it was scrapped altogether in favor of a three-year consolidation plan. While these changes were being weighed, numerous Soviet missions visited Cairo to revise the 1964 agreement. According to Western press reports, the Soviets were as much opposed to new grandiose projects and in favor of stabilization as were the experts of the International Monetary Fund (IMF) who were also being consulted.[21]

Economic rationality was as evident in the efforts to expand economic relations beyond the narrow circle of radically oriented countries. States with a moderate pro-Western outlook that could boast of a solvent or dynamic economy as well as a sizable domestic market were no longer scorned as the pliant objects of imperialist machinations. Both on the diplomatic and the economic fronts, Moscow began to pursue a more evenhanded policy wherein state-to-state relations were based more on the obvious needs and capabilities of the two partners than on revolutionary calculations. In Africa, Morocco and Nigeria received Soviet credits for the first time in 1966. In the Near East, Iran attracted Moscow's interest and in 1965 was granted a credit of $290 million — the second largest sum extended by the USSR to a developing country in a single agreement. In the Far East, after 1966, Malaysia, Singapore, and the Philippines were actively wooed in a Soviet trade drive accompanied by the extension of air services and shipping lines. And in Latin America, to overcome the reluctance of many Western Hemisphere states to accept project-type aid, the Soviets began to offer trade credits.

Several new departures in aid administration were introduced to create more organic links between the Soviet Union and its partners. Planning was initiated on various levels. Although at the first UNCTAD in 1964, Nikolai Patolichev had not responded to developing countries' pleas for more details on Soviet planning, at the second session in 1970 he stated that increased imports from these states would be taken into consideration in drawing up Soviet plans.[22]

No hard evidence exists on how the Soviets carried out that promise. However, the practice of reselling on the world market large quantities of Egyptian cotton, Burmese rice, or Ghanaian cocoa (a fairly common procedure during the first phase to judge from the frequent complaints of the injured parties) ceased in the second period. These commodities were absorbed domestically; evidently, Kosygin's promise at the 23rd CPSU Congress in 1966 to bring about "structural" adjustments in Soviet economic exchanges with the LDCs was being carried out.

Bilateral planning was also undertaken. Permanent commissions were set up with major aid recipients and trade partners, not only with such longstanding ones as India, the United Arab Republic, Algeria, and Afghanistan, but also with newer clients like Iran and Morocco. The consultations of these joint commissions were not pro forma. Their sessions, composed of high officials and experts who met regularly and alternately in Moscow and the partner's capital, could last as long as two weeks, wherein details were hammered out, future commitments discussed, and supplementary documents signed.

Long-term agreements were projected and negotiated. In 1968 Moscow and Teheran agreed to work out a 12- to 15-year projection for increased economic collaboration and trade based on their natural resources as well as other economic potentials. Such arrangements went far beyond the simple Soviet commitment to provide machinery and services for specified projects in a country's forthcoming plan, as had been the case hitherto. They now called for a measure of economic integration, based on coordinating relevant aspects of the Soviet Five Year Plan with those of the LDC partner.

The process of planning and coordination was further extended, being introduced on the Council of Mutual Economic Assistance (CMEA) level in 1971. The economic integration plan, announced by the Bloc in August of that year, included provisions for the gradual adoption of the transferable ruble to settle accounts between Communist countries as well as with the developing states. In January 1974, CMEA set up an International Investment Bank with a one billion transferable ruble fund to promote economic and technical assistance to developing countries. And a year later, acting as an open international organization, CMEA signed economic cooperation agreements with Iraq and Mexico.

By the early 1970s, the workings of a new pattern of economic relations, which Kosygin had prematurely proclaimed in 1966, was discernible. The Soviets called it the "international division of labor." This, they claimed, ensured a reliable flow of goods — and, incidentally, guaranteed the repayment of credits. There were some grounds at the CPSU Congress in 1971 for Kosygin to state that "our trade and economic relations with many [developing countries] are entering a stage at which one can begin to speak of stably founded, mutually advantageous relations."[23]

A characteristic feature of the new pattern was the "joint production scheme." Under this pay-back arrangement, Soviet credits for extracting or processing of raw materials, or for the manufacture of a finished product, were repaid by shipments of a share of the project's output. Only one such arrangement had been made under Khrushchev. After Soviet geologists had discovered rich natural gas deposits in northern Afghanistan, an agreement was signed in October 1963 to deliver a large part of the output to the Soviet Union in repayment for aid in extracting the gas and constructing the pipeline to the Soviet border. In the following decade, however, production cooperation came to typify the new Soviet program. It was introduced either to recoup losses sustained in the first stage or to initiate new, more profitable relations. Guinea exemplifies the former case, Iran the latter.

Throughout the Khrushchev period, the USSR and its East European allies had supported Guinea's radical domestic policies. They had supplied more than 60 percent of the foreign exchange for Guinea's Three Year Development Plan, which ended in 1964. The Socialist Bloc claimed that its aid was the catalyst for progressive political and economic change. Relations changed drastically after 1964. Despite President Keita's repeated assurances that the USSR would contribute generously to the forthcoming Seven Year Plan (and especially to the ambitious project for developing the Koncouré River basin), the expected aid never materialized. Instead, in August 1966 Moscow granted credits for additional geological surveys that led in 1969 to the conclusion of an agreement for exploiting the bauxite deposits in Kindia. Under its product-pay-back provisions, Guinea agreed to start shipping in 1971, for the next 30 years, most of the mine's annual 2.5 million tons of high-grade output to the USSR. The deal was beneficial to the Soviet Union in relieving its shortage of high-grade ore. Significantly, the aluminum industry was a sector singled out in the 10th Five Year Plan (1976-80) for expansion and modernization by means of foreign trade exchanges. According to the calculations of Western experts, 20 percent of Moscow's total bauxite supply came from the LDCs, and Guinea was practically the sole supplier.[24]

Iran furnishes an example of the Soviet search for new, more advantageous joint schemes. The USSR did not help in prospecting natural resources there but was eager to accept raw materials in exchange for other aid. Under the terms of the agreement signed in January 1966, the USSR undertook to construct Iran's first steel mill (at Isfahan) and a variety of smaller projects to be repaid by natural gas deliveries from 1970 to 1985. Included in the package was the joint construction of a 1,000-kilometer pipeline from the Kuzhistan fields in the south to the Soviet border. At the start, the annual volume was about 6 billion cubic meters, but deliveries were to increase to the full capacity of 10 billion cubic meters by 1974. This level would be maintained until expiration of the agreement. Although natural gas deliveries from Iran, at their peak in 1977, constituted but 3.2 percent of (the apparent) Soviet consumption, they formed a much higher percentage in Transcaucasia, accounting for as much as 50 percent in some districts and sectors of the industry. There was the further advantage that Iranian imports cost less than Soviet domestic production.[25]

Cooperation in industrial production and manufacturing has had a slower and more difficult start. It has largely taken the simple form of repayment in finished products from the plants set up with Soviet assistance and credits. In this manner, the USSR was supplied with canned meats and vegetables from Guinea and with long-staple cotton yarn from the United Arab Republic and Uganda. Similarly, Indian factories have been producing shoes to Soviet specifications.

The Soviet Union has also tried to institute more intricate cooperation schemes. In 1967 negotiations were begun with India for more complex, intrabranch specialization. Since then, all the major long-term agreements between the two countries have specified further consultations on joint production and specialization between Soviet and Indian enterprises. But by the end of the second stage, the Soviet press had not reported any major breakthrough that would indicate a transfer of part of the Soviet production cycle. Soviet-assisted projects in India kept exporting such finished goods as surgical instruments, pharmaceuticals, electric motors, and aluminum cables. By contrast, the East Europeans had proved to be more flexible and enterprising. Both East Germany and Hungary had made provisions in their national plans to transfer part of the labor-intensive textile production to the LDCs. Hungary, for example, started exporting cotton to India for conversion into textiles.[26]

Purely commercial transactions — pushing cash sales — both with newly affluent Third World countries and old aid recipients were another innovation. Elaborating on new forms of cooperation with the LDCs, Semyon Skachkov, the Soviet aid administrator, included "business-like relations on a commercial basis" among his proposals in January 1966.[27] That same year, after having concluded the natural gas/steel mill barter agreement, Moscow sold Iran a number of industrial installations. Likewise in the United Arab Republic, equipment for geological surveying and for a vocational school was delivered under the terms of a commercial contract and not as part of an aid agreement.

The granting of credits to both foreign governments and firms for the purchase of Soviet equipment and know-how became more frequent to promote regular trade instead of aid. (Until 1966 sales of Soviet machinery were almost exclusively financed by inter-governmental loan agreements.) Though quite concessionary by Western standards, the new loans carried harder terms than the customary "aid" credits (at 2.5 percent interest and repayable in 10 to 12 years after completion of the project). Of the two commercial credits extended to Latin America in 1967, a 4-year $100 million loan to Brazil was at 4 percent interest, and the $15 million loan to Chile was repayable at 3 percent over an 8-year period. Commentary in the Soviet press singled out these deals as examples of new, purely commercial contracts that should be concluded more frequently. Here again the East Europeans have proved to be much more commercially active than the Soviets. In addition to tapping petrodollars through extensive cash sales, they have also invited Arab investment in their countries. Thus the construction of the Adria pipeline from the Mediterranean ports of Yugoslavia to Czechoslovakia was in part financed with Kuwaiti and Libyan funds.

The creation of joint equity firms was another business-oriented practice introduced after 1964. According to CIA figures, by the end of the second phase (in 1975), there were 15 such ventures, both in the public sector and with private companies. The joint shipping lines in Singapore and the Philippines, or the mixed trading companies in Nigeria and Ethiopia (set up to promote the sales of Soviet motor vehicles), were the typical form of Soviet investment. Significantly, the USSR was careful to confine its business forays to trade and to avoid investment in production. Ideological tenets prevented Moscow from acquiring any other direct assets on the territory of another country. For this reason, joint fishing companies are the only joint production ventures that the Soviet Union has been actively pursuing. (By 1976 there were about 20 already in operation or under negotiation.) Presumably, the offshore nature of fishing rebuts any accusations of behavior inconsistent with socialist principles. By contrast, starting in the early 1970s, the East European states, not burdened with the responsibility of maintaining exemplary socialist principles, became very active in setting up equity-based coproduction schemes that ranged from sugar refineries to copper mining.[28]

Political Competition Remains

Despite the practical turn, the refurbished trade and aid program did not jettison political intent. The Soviets continued to claim that their economic relations with the Third World were to be distinguished on principle from those sought by the West. The lure of economic gain did not outweigh the felt need to uphold the image of the leading Socialist country pursuing qualitatively different, "disinterested" economic policies. Hence, articles advocating more advantageous deals with the LDCs always specified that the Soviet Union sought only "fair" returns, in contrast to the onerous, exploitative conditions imposed by Western states and companies.

The sense of competition with the capitalist world and the systemic assertiveness continued unabated. Although there was a certain letup in encouraging socialist or protosocialist (that is, noncapitalist) institutions in the LDCs, the promotion of a separate socialist economics was shifted to the international level. The Soviets began to claim that the aim of their new, more organically linked policies was to change the operation of the world market, that is, to replace the Western-dominated system with a more equitable socialist international division of labor. In other words, Moscow still interpreted its economic relations with the Third World in terms of political rivalry with the West for the allegiances and resources of the developing countries. The competitive spirit imparted to the program at the outset had not disappeared. Thus, when the Special Fund was set up in CMEA's International Investment Bank to offer loans for Bloc projects in the LDCs, this step was hailed as an effective counterpart to the IMF and the World Bank. The Third World was being urged to make a choice, with the new forms of cooperation offered by the USSR represented as a novel type of integration that would eventually supplant the existing system dominated by the rapacious West.

Given the claims that accompanied Moscow's post-1964 policies, Western fears of a Soviet economic takeover were scarcely diminished. The persistence of politically combative slogans challenging capitalist control of the world market made the emergence of a coordinated and economically sound policy look like an even more formidable threat. Moscow's optimism about the efficacy and success of the new, more pragmatic procedures tended to be taken at face value, especially since many aspects of this policy were in keeping with the needs and aspirations of the developing countries. The professed Soviet willingness and seeming ability to extend long-term aid, to correlate aid with trade, to intermesh planning and to import manufactured goods, to guarantee stable and long-range purchases of raw materials (at a time when world prices tended to fluctuate wildly or to decline) responded to the needs of the new nations for continuous programming, for stable raw material prices, and for expanding markets for their nascent industries.[29]

It is not surprising, then, that some Western specialists have characterized the second phase of Soviet economic relations with developing countries as a new anti-Western strategy. These analysts believed that the expanding stable division of labor between the Socialist Bloc and the developing countries would bring vast areas of the Third World, especially regions contiguous to the USSR's southern borders, into the Soviet economic sphere of influence. In Richard Lowenthal's formulation, the Soviets had launched "a new Third World strategy . . . with the aim not just of winning political or ideological influence in the Third World, but of strengthening the Soviet Bloc's economic base and reducing the economic superiority of the West."[30]

It was not merely the tenor of Soviet commentary that lent credence to such an interpretation. Some economic indicators seemed to substantiate Moscow's optimistic claims of success in its grand design. The LDC's share in the total Soviet turnover rose from 10.3 percent in 1964 to 14.6 percent in 1974. In the same period, deliveries of machinery rose from 21 to 25 percent of Soviet exports to the Third World. Moreover, by the early 1970s Moscow and its East European allies began to convert trade accounts from bilateral clearing to settlement in convertible currencies. These developments seemed to confirm general expectations that the USSR could launch a viable program wherein it supplied the LDCs with the products of its heavy industry in return for raw materials and other goods that were either in short supply or too expensive to produce at home.

However, what was overlooked was the fact that neither the USSR nor CMEA managed to make a significant breakthrough on the Third World markets. By 1975 the LDCs conducted only 6 percent of their trade with the Socialist countries — a rise of about 1 percent since 1964 — and their machinery imports from the Bloc constituted less than 7 percent of the total. Although the Communist nations could claim considerable gains in absolute terms, in relative terms their progress was hardly significant.

PHASE 3: THE POST-1974 SLUMP

The dynamism engendered during the second phase began to dissipate in the mid-1970s. Several factors undermined the post-Khrushchev plans and expectations. The steep rise in fuel prices enabled some partners to increase imports from the West and, more importantly, made unprofitable the once advantageous long-term barter arrangements with Moscow. Other partners registered general economic advances that diminished their need for the type of assistance and technological level of equipment that the Soviet Union could supply. Third, the worsening terms of trade made the poorer clients more dependent on larger amounts of aid; and that occurred at a time when the USSR, because of the slowing tempo of domestic growth and the growing demands of the Socialist community, had fewer resources available for foreign assistance.

Starting with 1975, there was a downturn in Soviet-Third World trade. By 1980 it amounted to 12.7 percent of the USSR total turnover, and its annual rate of growth had declined from 23.8 percent in 1974 to 3.8 percent in 1977. (In contrast, East-West trade began to flourish. From 21.3 percent of the total in 1970, it climbed to 31.3 percent in 1974 and inched up to 32.1 percent in 1979.)

Although Soviet aid increased in absolute figures, it declined in relative terms. Thus the share of CMEA in the total aid receipts of the developing countries fell from 8 percent in the early 1970s to only 2 percent in 1977. And as the assistance of the centrally planned economies (CPEs) declined, so did their exports of machinery and transport equipment; their share of the total fell from 15.5 percent in 1970 to 13.7 percent in 1977. (Turnkey plants in Soviet exports declined from 3.9 percent of the total in 1970 to 3.1 percent in 1980.)[31] All these indicators showed that an expanding trade — the object of an entire decade of effort — had failed to materialize. Instead of boasting about the ever-climbing indicators, official commentary tends now to state dryly that this particular trade has "stabilized" at the level of around 12 percent of the Soviet total.

The story of two major failures in the long-term association that the Soviets had projected helps illustrate some reasons behind the general slowdown. The outcome of Soviet Bloc-Iraqi compensation agreements shows how unexpected changes in the world economy have undone long-range barter plans. In order to increase and diversify their sources of oil supply, the CPEs became readily and extensively involved in assisting Iraq first to exploit the North Rumelia area for the nascent national petroleum company and later to dispose of the nationalized product. Under the terms of the $248 million credit the USSR and its European allies granted Iraq in 1969, the equipment and services for surveying, drilling, pumping, and refining oil, as well as for some other industrial installations, were to be repaid by oil shipments during the following five to six years. When Baghdad nationalized its oil resources in 1972 and met with a general boycott on Western markets, the barter arrangements with the Soviet Bloc were expanded through further loans: by 1973 CMEA credits came to some $900 million, with the USSR providing almost half.

The Iraqis readily acknowledge the Socialist help in enabling them "to ensure sovereignty over Iraq's natural resources and to carry out development programs." But when the initial barter agreements ran out in 1974, Iraq took advantage of the high prices it could get on the world market and shifted to importing mainly from the West. Consequently, the CMEA's share in Iraqi imports fell from 28 percent of the total in 1972 to 7.9 percent in 1975. Moreover, Baghdad began accepting assistance from Socialist countries only on a noncompensatory, contractual basis. Clearly, the USSR had no leverage or power either to entice or persuade Iraq to continue with the swap arrangements.[32]

Soviet relations with Algeria have had an ironic outcome. Although the recipient of extensive Soviet planning assistance, Algeria has not intermeshed or even adjusted its production and trade for the donor's benefit. Until 1978 Algeria was the second largest recipient of Soviet aid to Africa. Much of the aid went for organizing a nationwide planning system, starting up oil production, and establishing a national petroleum company. (At present, a quarter of the oil produced by the Algerian national oil company, Sonatrach, comes from Soviet-aided projects.) Yet only 4 percent of Algerian oil exports go to Eastern Europe, and almost none go to the USSR. Neither the Soviets nor the East Europeans have been able to secure long-term agreements for oil despite having contributed substantially to the creation of an infrastructure for Algerian production.

Ironically, it is wine that regularly constitutes a large share of Algerian exports to the Soviet Union — as much as 80-90 percent of the total. This pattern is a telling survival from the first, generous phase of Moscow's economic penetration of the Third World. In keeping with their professed aim of supplanting the former metropoles, the Soviets offered to pick up this particular export item after Algeria lost the French market in the postindependence acrimonies. Despite the coordinated and well-executed assistance program that followed the initial entry and seemed to create promising conditions for the conversion of aid into appropriate trade flows — the goal of phase two — the scheme failed to materialize once the situation on the world market came to favor the oil producers.

Despite the demonstrable setbacks and difficulties, Soviet and East European planners project increased trade with the Third World for the 1980s and beyond. The draft guidelines for the 11th Five Year Plan (1981-85), published in December 1980, specified the need to utilize foreign trade to supply the nation with raw materials and other goods, and the intention to expand trade with the LDCs. Similar intentions were expressed in the final communiqué of the thirty-sixth CMEA session held in June 1982. No specific targets have been stated in any of these documents. But in the calculations of the Hungarian Institute of World Economics, the share of the LDCs in Soviet imports is expected to increase during 1978-90 from 8 percent to 18-20 percent and in exports from 15.8 percent to 17-20 percent. (For other European members of CMEA, the corresponding figures are for increases from 7.6 percent to 15-17 percent for imports and from 12.2 percent to 14.5-16.5 percent for exports.)[33]

The pronouncements of Soviet leaders, lesser officials, and specialists indicate an ever-growing interest in seizing the advantages to be gained from foreign trade. Speaking to the Central Committee in November 1981, Brezhnev said that "the carefully weighed, well-thought-out development of foreign economic relations [is] a considerable resource for improving the efficiency of our economy." According to Skachkov, the role for the LDCs in this scheme is to help the USSR not only to meet fuel and some raw material needs but also to alleviate food shortages. Other officials have no qualms these days in stating that whereas "strict observance of the principle of equality and mutual advantage" governed the development of economic relations with the developing countries during the 10th Five Year Plan (1976-80), there will be more stress during the 11th Plan on developing "cooperation on a commercial basis."[34] Economists present similar arguments, for example:

> The interest enhancing the effectiveness of capital investments in and of meeting more fully the CMEA countries' requirements in power and raw material resources, makes it expedient to increase CMEA imports from countries outside the region, above all, from the developing countries. This will account for a considerable growth of trade turnover between these groups in the 1980s and, obviously, in the following decade.[35]

How is the envisioned expansion of trade with the LDCs to be carried out in view of the evident slowdown (especially in the sale of Soviet machinery) that Soviets regard as the best indicator of success? Official statements and writings do not yield much information beyond stressing the mounting urgency to make economic relations with the developing countries "more effective." Thus far the most notable change in the pattern of trade has been the marked rise in the sale of military equipment. The 1970s witnessed a quantum jump in commercial transactions over the traditional method of transfer of weapons on concessionary terms. Regardless of whether political or economic motives predominate in the Soviet arms trade, there is no doubt that it has netted vast profits for Moscow. According to CIA figures, this lethal commerce has enabled the USSR "to cover large deficits in . . . trade with the less developed countries and supplement Soviet hard currency earnings." The reason is that at least 55 percent of the $16.5 billion purchases from 1974 to 1978 were made by Algeria, Iraq, and Libya and by other customers whose orders were financed by the rich Arab states.[36]

Success with military sales, however, has in no way lessened Soviet preoccupation with its faltering civilian trade. Moscow's evident failure to engender a well-functioning socialist international division of labor has led to another reexamination of economic operations in the Third World. At the heart of the current phase lies the realization that the USSR and its Bloc cannot manage alone. For what has emerged since 1975 is an implicit, if not explicit, admission in government circles and the academic community that the establishment of an alternate, worldwide economic order, patterned on integration arrangements set up in the CMEA, is both an impossible and an impractical proposition. To one extent or another, Soviet officials and scholars now admit that the Socialist countries have to act in a world that resists bifurcation. On the official level, the realization is evident in the increasingly frank pursuit of policies that make more sense in terms of economics than of ideology. As for the specialists, they not only approve of the trend, but also furnish theoretical justifications for the advantages to be derived from a greater opening up to, and participation in, the world market. The degree to which a global outlook has come to modify the separatist socialist theories among various groups in the USSR is discussed in the next chapter. What is germane here is the story of how the failure of unilaterally conceived plans for a socialist international division of labor has prompted yet another search for new departures.

SOCIALIST FOREIGN ECONOMIC POLICY AT PRESENT

What is singular about the current reassessment advanced in many specialized writings is the spirit of frankness and objectivity. These publications discuss: the slow, almost static, tempos of growth in trade; the rising and persistent excess of exports over imports; the wide fluctuations by country and by year; the excessive concentration on a few partners; and the marked preference of most developing countries for flexible, short-term arrangements. This pessimistic and sober tone contrasts with the hitherto upbeat argumentation. Another novelty is the paucity or absence of references to the "exemplary" nature of Soviet-Third World relations as being qualitatively different from imperialist exploitation. Many economists have given up trying to square "socialist" aspirations and obligations with "advantageous" economic policies. Concentrating on the latter problem, they propose that the USSR adopt new, more flexible policies to turn foreign economic operations to advantage. Given this preoccupation, the traditional normative assumptions and goals assume secondary importance. Their arguments have more to do with the realities of international economic life — the widening differentiation among the LDCs and the erosion of complementarity between the Bloc and the developing countries — than with traditional ideological tenets.

Significantly, the most articulate critical evaluation and practical proposals for the future originate mainly from the same specialists who furnished the economic rationale for the second phase. To judge by the pattern of the past, their analyses might well provide a basis for revitalizing lagging Soviet-Third World economic relations. Despite the persisting rhetoric, many official statements already display a similar neorealist bent, and some recent trends in Soviet overseas operations coincide with these economists' recommendations. On both levels, the separation of economics from ideology — something that the Soviets were at pains to avoid during the second phase — has acquired a more consistent and more open aspect during the current third phase.

Indicative of the new outlook is the commentary of reform-minded economists on the practical implications of the changing economic profile of the Third World — its stratification into countries that have reached relatively advanced levels and those that remain backward. These economists note that the situation creates both opportunities and dilemmas. There is much apprehension that most countries that had chosen the socialist orientation also happen to be among the least developed. The implication is that these states need large amounts of aid, which the USSR is no longer able to supply. Many specialists no longer intone the Bloc's obligation to aid these states in the name of socialist solidarity. Instead, they stress the advantages the USSR could gain by concentrating on dealing with the richest LDCs. In other words, in the face of mounting economic difficulties, considerations of actual return have become the overriding criterion among those experts who since the early 1960s have been working on improving the operations of the aid-trade programs.

Much is made of the fact that the CPEs conduct one-third of their LDC trade with members of OPEC, although these countries comprise less than one-tenth of the developing world. The ensuing suggestions for improving terms of trade, as well as economic exchanges in general, center on expanding contacts with the oil producers. Given this approach, if these specialists mention the socialist international division of labor at all, it is not as an alternate system that challenges Western domination but as a mutually advantageous policy that leaves developing countries free to deal with the West as they see fit and, most important of all, permits the CPEs

> to raise the effectiveness of the world socialist economy, to satisfy more quickly and fully the needs of the national economy and of the population in those goods whose production is either impossible because of climatic conditions or . . . more expensive than . . . in the developing countries.[37]

The reform-minded and skeptically inclined economists also question the assumption of the conflict-free scenario on which the socialist international division of labor was based. That assumption underestimated the strength of the Western position; it overestimated the demand for Soviet machinery; and it discounted the rise of competition from the LDCs. Instead of dwelling on the persisting evils of neocolonial exploitation as assuring the USSR a secure economic presence, they discuss dispassionately how capitalist firms have been able to expand their exports due to market analysis, a wide assortment of products, efficient servicing, favorable loans and insurance terms, and effective advertising. The absence of these conditions and qualities in the Bloc's export and trade practices has led to the decline in machinery sales. So has the industrialization of many developing countries, which has made them self-sufficient in the products the CPEs had become used to exporting. More than that, the more advanced Soviet aid recipients are increasingly able to export basic industrial goods and technical assistance they used to obtain from the USSR to other, less developed Third World countries.[38]

Proposals to overcome the slump are not limited to purely technical remedies, such as upgrading and refining the assortment of Soviet capital goods exports and their servicing. They also include new procedures that would introduce better business practices and cooperation with the LDC partners, that is, substantive changes that would remove many of the ideologically conditioned traits that have distinguished the Soviet aid-trade program from its inception in 1953. For example, specialists suggest that production cooperation should be revitalized through equity participation. The practice of limiting mixed ventures to trading and joint fishing companies is now said to work against Soviet interests. If the USSR were to invest in the production of raw materials or semifinished industrial goods, it would be better assured of return flows by the virtues of ownership and a voice in management.

Moreover, Soviet economists no longer argue that the socialist partner should realize a smaller profit than a capitalist investor would in order to make the very concept palatable with socialist claims and morality. Profit as such is now represented as a legitimate part of the entire transaction. For some, it is no longer the symbol of exploitation, but a monetary expression of value, a universal norm of accounting that ensures efficient operations. "Without profitability, i.e., gain, no economy can exist and develop effectively."[39] Similarly, there are critical voices urging that the Soviets stop or modify their practice of handing over complete designs and documentation. Instead, they should institute licensing that would secure a return. In other words, cooperation should not be based on concessionary handouts but on good business practices that transcend systemic definitions.

Suggestions for improving foreign operations include, in addition, proposals for domestic reforms based on the introduction of modified market forces. Specialists argue that the "solution of institutional problems hampering the development of relations with the developing countries" should require "better stimulation of foreign activity of socialist enterprises, their increased interest and responsibility, improvement of procedures for concluding agreements on specialization and cooperations, etc."[40]

Tripartite cooperation is another much discussed new method that cannot possibly bear an exclusive "socialist" trademark. It is advocated on two levels. More commonly, tripartite proposals envision East-West-South collaboration wherein Western firms provide the most advanced technology and equipment, the Eastern Bloc furnishes the intermediate level of machinery and know-how, while the LDCs would supply labor and raw materials. The interest in this form of cooperation recognizes that the CPEs have not maintained that dynamic and innovative momentum that would induce the LDCs to commit themselves to an exclusive relationship.

More recently, the concept of trilateral cooperation has been expanded, testifying to Soviet vulnerability on Third World markets to other competitors. Specialists are suggesting that the USSR also team up with the more advanced LDCs for the design or construction of industrial projects, the extraction of raw materials, and provision of consulting services in other developing states. This new form of collaboration is seen as offering "greater financial" prospects and as "opening up new markets to the organizations of the socialist countries."[41]

Some new departures in the economic cooperation programs coincide with the line of change suggested by the specialists. Actual overseas operations also reveal a search for increased profits and maneuverability through multilateralization. On the political level, the USSR would undoubtedly prefer to penetrate the Third World economies on its own or in partnership with other Socialist states. Not only has this proved to be difficult if not impossible, but Moscow increasingly finds that the economic advantages of teaming up with the West outweigh ideological strictures.

The changing arrangements of the Soviet-Iranian natural gas agreements illustrate how economic circumstances dictate departures from bilateralism. The 20-year agreement signed in 1966, providing for the repayment of Soviet plants, equipment, and machinery with Iranian natural gas, was supplemented in 1975. Moscow entered into a tripartite "swap" agreement with a West European consortium representing Austrian, West German, and French gas utilities. Under the terms agreed upon, the Soviets were to take delivery, in consignment to the consortium, of 13.4 billion cubic meters of gas per year at the Soviet-Iranian border and then furnish 11 billion cubic meters of gas to West German and Austrian border points. Shipment was to begin in 1981, after construction of another pipeline from southern Iran to the Soviet border. But following the overthrow of the Shah, the agreement was unilaterally abrogated in the summer of 1979.

Although at this writing there is no definite word about the final outcome, what is significant is the enlargement of a bilateral agreement into a trilateral one. Obviously, this was considered to be in Moscow's favor. The USSR was to be paid transit fees in hard currency although no actual transshipment of Iranian gas was involved (the gas was to be used in Transcaucasia and the roughly equivalent amounts were to be delivered from Soviet fields closer to Europe). In addition, Moscow obtained the extension of the hard currency equivalent of 650 million rubles in Western credits for the purchase of Western equipment for construction of the pipelines in the Soviet Union.[42]

The operations of the Adria pipeline furnish another instance of circumstances that forced the transition from the second to the third phase. Begun in 1970 by Czechoslovakia, Hungary, and Yugoslavia, with the support of Arab investment, the line was to facilitate imports of crude oil from the Near East and North Africa where the East European states had been busy making bilateral swap deals for fuel. However, when it was completed in 1978, the barter agreements had expired and world market prices were too high for the CMEA members to avail themselves of this facility. To resolve the impasse, Hungary offered to construct a spur to the Austrian border, thereby enabling Austria to import oil from the Mediterranean through the Adria pipeline and Hungary to collect needed hard currency from transit fees.[43]

The trilateral form of cooperation has become a fixed and expanding feature of CPE overseas operations. By 1980, 226 such agreements had been signed by socialist foreign trade organizations, Western firms, and Third World partners.[44] Before 1975, the East Europeans were the most active in signing tripartite contracts; since then, however, there has been a marked rise in Soviet activity. Provisions for joint cooperation in third countries have been part of all the recent long-term cooperation agreements that the USSR has concluded with major capitalist countries. According to Soviet sources, these clauses refer specifically to the LDCs and are expected to enlarge and diversify Soviet operations.[45] Moscow has also taken steps to make similar arrangements with its most advanced Third World partners. For example, the 10-15 year pact for economic and technical cooperation signed with India in March 1979 provides for collaboration in designing and constructing industrial projects in third countries.[46]

Even more indicative than the conclusion of tripartite agreements is the evolution of the tripartite cooperation itself. At the start, in the early 1970s, East-West-South cooperation amounted to fortuitous ad hoc arrangements, the result of bidding, and were hardly more than subcontracting procedures. At the decade's end, this cooperation has not only acquired more permanence through inter-state agreements for joint activities in third countries, it has also been institutionalized as a regular business practice through the formation of joint East-West companies. In 1977 Moscow for the first time contracted to participate in two such firms. Technicon Spa, established in Genoa as a joint Soviet-Italian company for the construction of steel and tinplate plants in third countries, is a 50-50 partnership between Italpiamti, a subsidiary of an Italian state engineering group, and Litsensintorg, a Soviet foreign trade organization. Another foreign trade association, Emergomasheksport, formed a consortium with the Japanese giant in heavy electrical engineering, Hitachi, to supply large-scale electric power plants to developing countries.[47]

These instances of what is now considered to be the desirable direction in economic relations with the Third World are reflected in the general pattern of Soviet operations. As perhaps the clearest example of the extent to which economic motivation has replaced the political and ideological approach, one can compare the nature of Soviet aid and trade activities in Africa in the years after 1954 (when Africa went through the first wave of decolonization) with those after 1974 (when there was again the turmoil of decolonization upon the collapse of the Portuguese empire). In both periods, the continent experienced a similar anti-Western political upheaval, providing a similar background for entirely different Soviet responses. The comparison graphically illustrates the distance Soviet economic policies have traveled during the past 25 years.

From 1956 to 1964, the continent absorbed 45 percent of total Soviet credits granted to the LDCs, and in some countries the Soviets committed themselves to a volume equal to or even larger than that granted by the United States. The radical, noncapitalist states (Egypt, Algeria, Ghana, Mali, and Congo Brazzaville) ranked as top recipients. Of those, Egypt, whose revolutionary course under Nasser received Soviet approbation as being nearly socialist, obtained $1 billion of the $1.7 billion total. Generous credits were granted for large, visible projects in the state sector to promote import-substitution industrialization and to facilitate the adoption of anticapitalist institutions.

From 1974 to 1979, Africa received only 33 percent of Soviet credits. Moreover, Moscow not only directed proportionately less aid to a continent with a heightened national liberation struggle, but it no longer favored the radical states. Thus, of the $2.7 billion in aid granted to Africa from 1975 to 1979, $2 billion were earmarked for the development of phosphate deposits in Morocco, to be shipped to the USSR to increase the production of critically needed fertilizers. And only one-third of a billion was granted to sub-Saharan Africa, where the former Portuguese colonies and the majority of the states with a socialist orientation are located. Thus far, despite urgent requests from these countries, the pattern of aid and trade agreements demonstrates no Soviet readiness to shift economic operations and assistance from the more advanced North to the needy South. Likewise, there are no indications that the Soviets are attempting to develop viable public sector industries, other than the joint fishing companies, which offer a ready and valuable source of food, cash, and strategic information. For the rest, the Soviets have confined their offers of assistance to modest programs in agriculture, irrigation, technical training, and geological surveys.

Significantly, the conclusion of the largest economic project by late 1982 — the hydroelectric power station and irrigation system on Angola's Cuanza River — was not announced with any loud claims about Soviet support for economic liberation or independent development. Neither costs nor terms of payment were mentioned, which suggests that the terms are not concessional. Even more significantly, the USSR did not undertake the project alone but in collaboration with the Brazilian engineering firm, Oderbrecht. It is neither an aid project nor a bilateral agreement — a fact that testifies to how far Soviet economic relations with the radical states have departed from the ideological systemic approach at the outset of the Soviet offensive. The pattern is being duplicated in Soviet activities elsewhere in the Third World.

NOTES

1. Conference proceedings, *New Times* no. 15 (April 9, 1952): Supplement.

2. Excellent factual information on Soviet aid and trade agreements is offered by Marshall Goldman, *Soviet Foreign Aid* (New York: Praeger, 1967) and Charles B. McLane, *Soviet-Third World Relations*, 3 vols. (London: Central Asian Research Center, 1973-74). Unless otherwise specified, all figures, statistics, and facts used in this chapter are taken from the following sources: *Vneshniaya torgovlia SSSR za ... god. Statisticheskii obzor* (Moscow: Vneshtorg,

annual); *Vneshniaya torgovlia*, the monthly foreign trade magazine; and the Central Intelligence Agency's annual publication, *Communist Aid to the Less Developed Countries* (Washington, D.C.: CIA).

3. David Scott, "Soviet Interest in Under-developed Countries," *New Commonwealth* (August 31, 1953): 221-22 and (September 14, 1953): 275-76.

4. *Pravda*, November 22, 1955, p. 2.

5. Ibid., July 13, 1958, p. 4.

6. M. Z. Saburov's speech, *Vneocherednoi XXI S'ezd KPSS. Stenograficheskii otchet* 3 (Moscow: Gospolitizdat, 1959), p. 290. See also Kuusinen's and Ostrovitianov's speeches, ibid., p. 160 and p. 377, respectively.

7. *Pravda*, February 27, 1960, p. 1.

8. V. Rymalov, "Soviet Assistance to Underdeveloped Countries," *International Affairs* (September 1959): 24-25.

9. U.S. Department of State, *Communist Economic Policy in the Less Developed Areas* (Washington, D.C.: Government Printing Office, 1960), Foreword.

10. Charles McLane, "Foreign Aid in Soviet Third World Policies," *Mizan* 10 (November-December 1968): 43.

11. Louis Dupree, "Two Weeks in Soviet Tajikistan and Uzbekistan," *American Universities Field Staff Reports Service* (October 20, 1959): 26.

12. Joseph Berliner, *Soviet Economic Aid* (New York: Praeger, 1958), p. 183.

13. Dupree, "Two weeks," p. 15. K. Billerbeck, *Soviet Bloc Foreign Aid to the Underdeveloped Countries* (Hamburg: Hamburg Archives of World Economy, 1960), p. 95.

14. *The Sino-Soviet Economic Offensive* (Washington, D.C.: Department of State, 1962), p. 20.

15. W. A. Hannah, "Bung Karno's Indonesia," *American Universities Field Staff Reports Service* (December 14, 1959): 3.

16. *Pravda*, October 22, 1961, p. 8.

17. S. Stepanov, "Sotsialisticheskoe vosproizvodstvo i vneshniaya torgovlia," *Vneshniaya torgovlia* (January 1962): 3-10.

18. Uri Ra'anan, "Moscow and the Third World," *Problems of Communism* 14 (January-February 1965): 22-31.

19. Brezhnev's report, *Pravda*, March 30, 1966, pp. 2-3; Kosygin's speech, ibid., April 6, 1966, p. 6.

20. L. Zevin, "Vzaimnaya vygoda ekonomicheskogo sotrudnichestva sotsialisticheskikh i razvivayushchikhsia stran," *Voprosy ekonomiki* (February 1965): 72-83; B. S. Vaganov, ed., *Vneshniaya torgovlia sotsialisticheskikh stran: voprosy teorii* (Moscow: Mezhdunarodnye otnosheniya, 1966); G. M. Prokhorov, *Problemy sotrudnichestva sotsialisticheskikh i razvivayushchikhsia stran* (Moscow: Nauka, 1966).

21. Hedrick Smith, "Cairo, Squeezed, Slashes Budget," *New York Times*, October 11, 1966, p. 37. For a positive Soviet appraisal of the three-year plan, G. Mirsky, "UAR: Home Front," *New Times* no. 50 (December 18, 1968): 8-10.

22. *New Times* no. 15 (April 17, 1968): 9.

23. *Pravda*, April 7, 1971, p. 7.

24. *Minerals' Yearbook, 1971* 3 (Washington, D.C.: Government Printing Office, 1973), p. 822; T. Shabad, "Raw Material Problems of the Soviet Aluminum Industry," U.S. Congress, Joint Economic Committee, *Soviet Economy in a New Perspective* (Washington, D.C.: Government Printing Office, 1976), p. 672.

25. C. H. McMillan and J. B. Hannigan, "The Soviet-Iranian Relationship," Carleton University, Institute of Soviet and East European Studies, *Studies in the Soviet Union's International Energy Arrangements* (November 1969): 13; J. B. Hannigan and C. H. McMillan, "CMEA Trade and Cooperation with the Third World in the Energy Sector," paper prepared for the 1981 NATO Colloquium on *CMEA: Energy 1980-1990*, Brussels, April 8-10, 1981, pp. 22-24; L. Zevin, "Voprosy povysheniya ustoichivosti i effektivnosti ekonomicheskikh sviazei SSSR s razvivayushchimisia stranami," *Planovoe khoziaistvo* (July 1971): 23.

26. For detailed information about the extent and forms of East European aid, see M. Radu, ed., *Eastern Europe and the Third World: East vs. South* (New York: Praeger, 1981).

27. *Vneshniaya torgovlia* (January 1966): 6.

28. Central Intelligence Agency, *Soviet Commercial Operations in the West* (Washington, D.C.: CIA,1977); C. H. McMillan, "Growth of External Investment by the Comecon Countries," *The World Economy* 2 (September 1979): 363-86.

29. For a positive assessment from the developing countries' viewpoint, see D. Nayyar, ed., *Economic Relations Between Socialist Countries and the Third World* (London: Macmillan, 1977).

30. R. Lowenthal, "Soviet 'Counterimperialism,'" *Problems of Communism* 25 (November-December 1976): 52.

31. *Vneshniaya torgovlia* (March 1981): 3.

32. Hannigan and McMillan, "CMEA Trade and Cooperation," p. 17; N. Harchan, "Prospects for Expanding Economic Relations Between Iraq and the European Socialist Countries," in *Economic Cooperation Between Socialist and Developing Countries*, ed. Istvan Dobozi (Budapest: Hungarian Scientific Council for World Economy, 1978), pp. 213-14.

33. I. Dobozi and A. Inotai, "Prospects of Economic Cooperation between CMEA Countries and Developing Countries," in *East-West-South. Economic Interaction between Three Worlds*, ed. Christopher T. Saunders (New York: St. Martin's Press, 1981), pp. 61-62.

34. *Pravda*, November 17, 1982, p. 2; S. A. Skachkov, "Ekonomicheskoe sotrudnichestvo Sovetskogo Soyuza s zarubezhnymi stranami," *Vneshniaya torgovlia* (March 1981): 4 and (June 1982): 4; N. S. Patolichev, "Razvitie vneshnei torgovlii SSSR i perspektivy rasshireniya sovetsko-indiiskikh torgovykh otnoshenii," ibid. (October 1981): 3.

35. Oleg Bogomolov, "The CMEA Countries and the New International Economic Order," in *East-West-South. Economic Interaction between Three Worlds*, ed. Christopher T. Saunders (New York: St. Martin's Press, 1981), p. 254.

36. Orah Cooper and Carol Fogarty, "Soviet Economic and Military Aid to Less Developed Countries, 1954-78," in *Soviet Policy in Developing Countries*,

ed. W. Raymond Duncan (Huntington, N.Y.: Robert E. Krieger, 1981), pp. 19, 21.

37. R. Andreasian, "Sotsialisticheskoe sodruzhestvo i razvivayushchiesia strany: ekonomicheskoe sotrudnichestvo," *Narody Azii i Afriki* (March-April 1981): 6.

38. For best discussion, see *Sotrudnichestvo sotsialisticheskikh i razvivayushchikhsia stran: novyi tip mezhdunarodnykh otnoshenii* (Moscow: Nauka, 1980).

39. Andreasian, "Sotsialisticheskoe sodruzhestvo," p. 11.

40. Bogomolov, "The CMEA Countries," pp. 252-53.

41. *Strany SEV v mirokhoziaistvennykh sviaziakh* (Moscow: Nauka, 1978), pp. 128-29. See also L. Zurawicki, "Prospects for Tripartite Cooperation," *Intereconomics* 12 (July-August 1978): 184-87; L. Zevin, "Concepts of Economic Development of the Developing Nations and Problems of Tripartite Cooperation," in *East-West-South. Economic Interaction between Three Worlds*, ed. Christopher T. Saunders (New York: St. Martin's Press, 1981), pp. 295-302.

42. J. B. Hannigan and C. H. McMillan, "The Soviet Energy Stake in Afghanistan and Iran: Rationale and Risk of Natural Gas Imports," Carleton University, Institute of Soviet and East European Studies, *East-West Commercial Relations Series* (August 1981): 45-47.

43. Hannigan and McMillan, "CMEA Trade and Cooperation," pp. 19-20. At present the Hungarian project is in abeyance.

44. Patrick Gutman, "Tripartite Industrial Cooperation and Third Countries," in *East-West-South. Economic Interaction between Three Worlds*, ed. Christopher T. Saunders (New York: St. Martin's Press, 1981), p. 337.

45. Yuri Krasnov, "Soviet-West German Trade," *New Times* no. 5 (January 1978): 24-25.

46. *Economic Times* (Bombay), March 17, 1979.

47. Gutman's "Tripartite Industrial Cooperation" provides lists of agreements, pp. 340-41, 362-64.

2

THE WORLD ECONOMY: FROM BIFURCATION TO GLOBALISM

Throughout their several stages, Soviet aid and trade have functioned within a context of explicit doctrinal assumptions about the nature of the international economy and its effects on the developing countries. For some 20 years after Stalin's death in 1953, when the Soviets first turned their attention to seizing the opportunities in the Third World, there was a coherent ideological explanation. Its major tenet was that the socialist and capitalist systems behaved in diametrically opposite ways in their foreign economic relations.

The initial, politically aggressive stage had its underpinning in the theory of two separate and competing world markets. The following, economically motivated stage brought the perception of a single world market operating above the two systems that comprised it, but not changing their essence. It justified détente and East-West trade without, however, invalidating the concept of a separate socialist market which could successfully devise its own terms for dealing with the Third World, that is, establish the socialist international division of labor. Until the mid-1970s, these assumptions assured a congruence of Soviet political and economic aims, posited a shared interest between the USSR and the LDCs, and fed hopes of detaching the Third World and its resources from the capitalist camp.

Since then, mounting difficulties and the loss of momentum in Soviet-Third World economic relations have called into question the former cosmology. While still invoked in Soviet diplomacy, the traditional Manichean view of world economics appears less germane for guiding or justifying Soviet economic policies. That view — according to which the socialist and the capitalist camps compete with opposed sets of economic relationships and prescriptions — is being questioned and revised. In many quarters, and for different reasons, it is seen as no longer applicable to the contemporary world.

Global problems — starting with ecology, overpopulation, and energy resources and progressing on to underdevelopment — inexorably demanded consideration. The attention given them in the late 1970s best exemplifies the nature of the recent conceptual ferment and seriously alters the outlook entailed by the preceding concept of a single world economy. The new awareness recognizes that these insistent worldwide problems transcend systemic (antagonistic) interpretations and require cooperative solutions.

It is not an easy matter to describe the recent evolution in perceptions. Theoretical problems are no longer settled by *ex cathedra* pronouncements, as was the practice under Stalin and Khrushchev. The theory of two world markets had been promulgated by fiat; in contrast, the subsequent recognition of a single world economy did not take place with the same unequivocal finality. As a result, various logical consequences of that awareness have not been fully elucidated or incorporated into the working vocabulary of Soviet leaders and scholars. What is going on at present is an intense debate over the degree to which the all-inclusive, global aspects of a single world economy should be accommodated in general theory and incorporated into Soviet policies.

Given the inconclusiveness of the debate and its evident intensity, my method for demonstrating the changing theoretical outlook on the economic position of the LDCs is to analyze its evolution in the work of academic experts against the background of changing Party directives to the research institutes of the Academy of Sciences. The Party's role in directing academic research has not been constant. Over the time period covered by this book, as international relations have become more complex and the leadership faces many more unprecedented issues, Party authorities have become less ready to tell the academic community how to formulate answers and more dependent on expertise unencumbered by a priori definitions. As noted in the Introduction, academic experts do not make policy. But the increasingly articulate expression of independent opinion by specialists does provide an insight into the problems, dilemmas, and alternatives faced by the leadership in trying to improve the functioning both of the Soviet domestic economy and of foreign trade in a situation where global interdependence is as important a factor as systemic competition.

The outcome of the debate on how to respond to the imperatives posed by a single world economy confronted with global problems is not clear in 1983. But the fact that it takes place and that the leadership is seeking advice from experts on how to reformulate dysfunctional ideological tenets on the economic position and role of the LDCs indicates that objective economic factors are forcing reassessments in theory at the same time as they are changing Soviet aid and trade policies.

THE "TWO WORLD MARKETS" THEORY

Khrushchev made his name by denouncing Stalin and devising neo-Marxist categories to revivify Soviet policies. Although he revised Stalinist theory on the position of the former colonies in world politics, he did not discard Stalin's views on international economics. The late dictator's doctrine of two world markets remained intact, for it furnished the justification for the economic offensive his successor launched in the Third World. The Stalinist formulation supported Khrushchev's reasoning that generous loans for steel mills or dams, plus a good deal of rhetoric about economic liberation, would turn the newly independent countries against their former metropoles and bring them into the socialist orbit.

The theory of two world markets was elaborated by Stalin in late 1951 in his comments on a textbook of political economy. He postulated that as a consequence of World War II and the appearance of the "powerful socialist camp," the "single, all-embracing world market" had disintegrated and been replaced by separate socialist and capitalist markets independent of one another.[1]

Neither the place nor the role of the colonial and dependent countries was specified in this scheme. Nevertheless, the new doctrine had three components that guided Soviet perceptions and actions until the early 1970s. For one, it interpreted the activities of the Socialist countries as a destabilizing challenge to the West. Their expanding industrial production and search for outlets for surplus products were seen as putting an end to the "relative stability" of the international market. Second, the doctrine drew a sharp distinction between the operational methods of the two camps. The "exploitation of the world's resources" by the major capitalist countries was contrasted with the harmonious "cooperation" practiced by the Socialist camp, based as it was on a "sincere desire to help one another and to promote the economic progress of all." Third, the doctrine placed the operations of the two markets in the general scheme of global competition between the two systems. While the socialist market would expand, that of its opponent would contract. "The opportunities for sale on the world market [by the major capitalist countries] will deteriorate, and their industries will be operating more and more below capacity. That in fact is what is meant by the deepening of the general crisis of the world capitalist system in connection with the disintegration of the world market."

While these assumptions enticed the USSR into militant and unilateral actions and promised success, Stalin's commentary included another component that could justify a reversal in course, if necessary. According to this fourth component, the imposition of the Western blockade on the USSR, Eastern Europe, and China was responsible for the emergence of the socialist market. Naturally, Stalin made a virtue out of necessity, prescribing the special role for the Socialist states and predicting eventual victory. Still, by giving this particular cause for the disintegration of the single world market, the argument admitted the logical possibility of some other situation wherein more relaxed East-West economic relations might obviate the need for an aggressive counterstrategy by the Socialist camp. That prospect never arose during Khrushchev's years in power, and with characteristic confidence he proceeded to challenge the West in the Third World.

ACADEMIC RESEARCH UNDER KHRUSHCHEV

Soviet activism in the newly independent countries after 1953 brought a resurgence in academic research. The 20th Party Congress in 1956 heard Khrushchev upgrade the newly independent countries to the status of a "vast zone of peace," destined to play a positive role in international affairs on the side of the Socialist camp. It also marked the start of a new era in foreign area studies. Anastas Mikoyan alleged that scholars at the Oriental Studies Institute — the sole learned institution devoted to research on the "East" (the traditional Soviet term for the colonial world) — had been slumbering while the contemporary world passed them by.[2] Thus the same congress that heralded a more active Soviet response to opportunities in the former colonies also directed the specialist community to contribute its share to the implementation of the new diplomacy. From then on there was an ever more lively interaction between the growing body of academic expertise and foreign policy requirements. At the start, the parameters for research (regarding both issues and their interpretation) were set mainly by Party authorities.

Various measures followed to mobilize the "somnolent" profession for the new mission. The first All-Union Conference on Oriental Studies was convened in June 1957 to reiterate in specific detail the directive that scholars readjust their focus from the detached historical to the topical plane of contemporary politics. To facilitate the change, the venerable and prestigious Institue of Oriental Studies was restructured. While research on the classical oriental languages and literatures was left undisturbed in the original Leningrad headquarters, a branch was created in Moscow for the new orientalism, aggressively political and centered on contemporary problems.[3]

During the next five years, the institutional framework was enlarged to meet the needs of the new diplomacy. The resultant structure has not changed since 1961, although the subjects of research and the status of specialists have altered considerably. In 1959, after the formation of several radical African states, the Institute of Africa was created. Similarly in 1961, after the victory of the Cuban revolution, the Latin American Institute was organized. In addition to these regional centers, the Institute of World Economy and International Relations (IMEMO) was set up in 1956 to study the international situation on a global rather than regional basis. At the time, IMEMO could not be regarded as a resuscitation of Eugene Varga's Institute of World Economy and World Politics, which was closed down in 1947 concurrently with the final rupture between the USSR and the West. For one, the opening of IMEMO was not attended by any vindication of Varga's theories about the possibilities of genuine compromise between the two world systems (an idea that was still anathema). Second, the Institute of the Economy of the World Socialist System was set up to underscore the separate position and operations of the Soviet Bloc.

The first issue of the bimonthly journal published by the refurbished Institute of Oriental Studies expressed the goal of the profession as follows: "It is a matter of honor for our orientalists that they should produce works . . . to promote the foreign policy of the Soviet Union with the countries of the East" as well as to popularize "the extraordinary importance of the world system of socialism for the fate of humanity."[4] This goal was pursued on two levels: through the publication of journals, general symposia, and specialized monographs; and the preparation of intelligence reports.

Obviously, the intelligence reports the institutes produced for the government remain a closed book. But from the very beginning scattered references indicate that commercial information was part of the job. From the start, IMEMO worked on collecting and processing industrial and trade intelligence, as well as on providing analyses of political and social trends. In 1961, as already noted, the Presidium of the Academy of Sciences set up a research group in the Institute of the Economy of the World Socialist System to devise indexes of the effectiveness of economic relations with the newly independent countries. In the same year, an economic section was added to the African Institute.

The open work of the research centers was most readily available in the journals they started publishing. The African and the Oriental Studies Institutes have been putting out a joint bimonthly, *Narody Azii i Afriki* (*Peoples of Asia and Africa*), as the original journal *Problemy vostokovedeniya* (*Problems of Orientology*) was renamed in 1961. The third regional center has its own bimonthly, *Latinskaya Amerika* (*Latin America*). Both journals print articles on current affairs as well as on history and culture. The monthly organ of IMEMO, *Mirovaya ekonomika i mezhdunarodnye otnosheniya* (*World Economy and International Relations*), deals solely with current events. The popular illustrated monthly, *Aziya i Afrika segodnia* (*Asia and Africa Today*), started in 1956 as purely a propaganda sheet. But since the late 1970s, in keeping with the rise in professional standards, it has been presenting some substantive articles and discussions.

In addition to numerous specialized monographs, IMEMO and the Oriental Studies Institute have each published three compendiums synthesizing the research and interpretation on the Third World as of 1966, 1974, and 1981. These successive editions, discussed below, serve as a good barometer of change.

During the Khrushchev era, little factual information and substantive analysis appeared in open publications. What was offered to the public served chiefly to provide an elucidation and scholarly imprimatur for views and policies laid down in Party pronouncements or official decrees. The regime furnished the correct assessment of the course of history, defined it in textbooks on communist theory, and expected professionals to operate within these limits. In 1959 Stalin's basic ideological text, *Problems of Leninism*, was replaced with *Fundamentals of Marxism-Leninism*. This was a comprehensive volume, covering everything from dialectics to the place of the newly independent countries in the ongoing competition between the two systems. Three years later, in 1962, it was reissued in a thoroughly revised edition, indicating how ideological readjustment was proceeding.[5] But the academic world played no visible role in the reassessment. The open publications of the various institutes provided analysis that kept within the bounds set by the Party authorities; they did not suggest revisions.

Reflecting the status, as well as the state, of the academic profession during the Khrushchev era, published works had a predominantly political orientation. They dealt almost exclusively with the disintegration of the colonial system, the emergence of the new states, their class structure, and their expanding relations with the USSR — all seen through the prism of the "national liberation revolution," which was accepted as an integral part of the worldwide socialist revolution. In that scheme, the primary purpose was to determine what class and what policies were in step with the inevitable advent of socialism and to what degree.

Economic issues were decidedly slighted. To the extent that the economic situation in developing countries was noticed, it was dealt with not as a problem per se but as a function of the competition between the two camps. The 1961 CPSU Program defined their position as follows:

> The young sovereign states do not belong either to the imperialist system or to the socialist system. But the overwhelming majority have not yet broken away from the world capitalist economy, although they occupy a special place in it. They constitute that part of the world

that is still being exploited by the capitalist monopolies. As long as they do not put an end to their economic dependence on imperialism, they will play the role of the 'world countryside' and will remain objects of semi-colonial exploitation.[6]

The prevalent tone was to analyze economic policies and institutions not in terms of their effect on the GNP or some other neutral indicator of development but in terms of their anti-imperialist and anticapitalist content. Thus Soviet experts attending the first U.N. conference on programming for economic development, held in Delhi in the fall of 1961, were highly critical of its working papers because for the most part they discussed the public sector as supplying the impetus to growth rather than as initiating systemic changes.[7]

As for Soviet aid, economists saw it not only as the catalyst of economic liberation but also as the factor that would transform the nature of international economic relations:

Within the framework of the world socialist system the basis for a new world system is being created in which the capitalist relations of oppression and exploitation of the weak nations by the strong will be finally liquidated. Relations of genuine equality and mutual aid will be established. An important role in the struggle for the creation of such a world-wide [vsemirnoe] economy is bestowed on the constantly expanding aid of the socialist states to the underdeveloped countries.[8]

During the Khrushchev period, there was no open debate on theoretical economic issues that might in any way question or undermine this schema of the nature and outcome of the two systems' competition.[9] Optimism prevailed. A fairly typical example is a book by V. L. Tiagunenko, a leading specialist on developing countries at IMEMO. Entitled *Problems of the Contemporary National Liberation Revolution*, it built on the assumption that the prevailing tendency in the postcolonial world was the growing anticapitalist trend in both the economic and the sociopolitical life of the new nations and that the "transition to socialism was possible for any country, independent of its level of development." On the political side, because the world socialist system existed, Marxist-Leninist leadership did not necessarily have to arise from a strong working-class party but could come from other progressive forces representing the interests of the nation. On the economic side, things looked equally promising. The elimination of foreign and local exploiters, though it might lead to a temporary decline in production, was essential for "deepening" the revolution and was bound to result "very soon" in economic advances.[10]

ANALYSIS IN THE EARLY BREZHNEV PERIOD

During the Brezhnev era, the Soviet interpretation of the developing countries' place in world economy passed through two phases. An unchanged politicized approach prevailed roughly to the mid-1970s, despite considerable innovations in economic thought. The recognition of a single world economy and of the role of technology in development that appeared during this period did not directly affect official formulas on the Third World. Since the new ideas were dictated by the decision to modernize with the aid of Western credits and know-how, they were applied only to relations with the capitalist states and were carefully segregated from the traditional views on the Third World. There was confidence that an uncompromising ideological stance regarding the exploited position of the LDCs on the world market promoted Soviet diplomatic and economic goals. Consequently, the Party line in official pronouncements, as in academic research, differentiated between the new depoliticized concepts pertaining to economic relations with the capitalist West and the old normative values governing economic relations with the LDCs. Nevertheless, the new theories on the functioning of the world market and the role of objective factors in engendering change affected Soviet thinking and research on the economic situation in the developing states.

The drive for modernization and technical renovation, initiated by Brezhnev, pointed out the importance of research and development and the concomitant need to eliminate ideological interference. At the outset only the natural sciences were affected — it was the Brezhnev regime that finally put an end to the Lysenko scandal in biology. Objectivity was not extended to the social sciences. Here, political vigilance required that a visible distance be maintained between Marxism-Leninism and bourgeois scholarship. But with time, under pressure from the academic community, Party intervention was attenuated.

Because of its slow and piecemeal progress, the process would be too tedious to unfold by reference to the published sources. But it is a well-known story in Soviet academic circles that as the arguments of reform-minded economists gained acceptance, they began to press for a forthright acknowledgment of the role of science and technology in furthering social evolution. Politically it was a most sensitive issue since it stressed objective, as opposed to class or systemic, factors of change. At first, the Party leadership responded only to the extent of referring to "scientific-technical progress." But the modernizers pressed for a more unequivocal formulation, and finally in 1971 Brezhnev started referring to the "Scientific-Technological Revolution" (STR). This seemingly small yet significant alteration in phrasing was taken by the reformers as endorsing their view of the factors of change, giving it equal status with the hitherto sacrosanct theory that social change or revolution was the motor force of history.

Two aspects of the story are instructive: the importance attached to theoretical formulas, and the manner in which new concepts are now introduced into open discourse, that is, not by *diktat* and fanfare. As a result, two methods of investigation and interpretation, the old and the new, coexist and interact — without, however, revealing clear signs to Western observers concerning which view might predominate and guide Soviet actions.

The internationalization of the Soviet economy, resulting from modernization and East-West trade, produced new thinking on the framework for these expanded and diversified activities. Here too, there was no formal announcement that Stalin's doctrine of the two world markets was no longer valid and that a new theoretical concept justified Soviet trade with the West. Instead, without any overt fuss, a revised entry on the world market appeared in the third edition of the *Great Soviet Encyclopedia*, published in 1974. Written by Viktor Rymalov, a leading expert on international economics at IMEMO, the article defined the concept as

> . . . the aggregate of all national markets, seen as linked through mutual economic and trade relations. In its initial form, the world market was based on the capitalist mode of production and was the world capitalist market. At present, the world market takes in the full international division of labor as practiced betweeen the world's two socio-economic systems. The world market has expanded in scale as social production has become increasingly internationalized.

(The preceding edition, published in 1954, described the world market as an emanation of capitalism that had collapsed after World War II with the appearance of the Socialist camp and the "new type of international economic relations" it brought forth.)[11]

Little is known about the infighting behind the scenes before the new formulation became public. But without question it was a controversial issue, which entailed considerable ideological justification and elucidation. The first article on the world economy embodying this new viewpoint also appeared in 1974. It tried to convince unnamed skeptics that, first of all, Lenin had argued that Soviet Russia after the Revolution would remain in the framework of the world economy. Next, it explained that the present-day speed and extent of scientific and technological change made it imperative for each country to participate extensively in the international division of labor. In sum, the crux of the author's argument (Margarita Maksimova of IMEMO) was that the recent expansion of economic cooperation between the Soviet Union, its Bloc, and foreign countries demanded creative adaptations in Marxist theoretical thinking.[12]

As already stated, the shift to more viable forms of aid and trade, which took place at the same time as the economic rapprochement with the West, did not prompt any theoretical reformulations about the Third World, which continued to figure prominently in the Kremlin's professed aim to curtail the capitalist world market. The designation of developing countries in the 1961 Party Program as occupying a special, transitional position between capitalism and socialism remained in force. Hence the principle of competition between the two world markets in this area and the belief that socialism offered the only workable solution to backwardness remained intact. However, the outcome of competition was no longer presented as a speedy victory of socialism. On that point, the former views on the relative importance of politics and economics in engendering progress altered substantially. Sanguine optimism in political determinism was replaced with an acceptance of the primacy of economic factors. Nonetheless, these economic realities were made to fit into an ideological framework that presented a separate, coherent Marxist explanation. Thus the refurbished aid-trade program was presented as a step toward establishing an alternate, socialist international division of labor. Premier Kosygin explained the theory at the 24th CPSU Congress in April 1971, as follows:

> Our trade and economic cooperation are entering a stage where we may already speak of firmly established mutually advantageous ties. Our cooperation . . . based on principles of equality and respect for mutual interests, is acquiring the nature of a stable division of labor, counter- posed in the sphere of international economic relations to the system of imperialist exploitation.[13]

Since the Party continued to uphold the doctrine of a special, socialist relationship between the Soviet Bloc and the Third World, both the *Encyclopedia* entry and Maksimova's seminal article refrained from placing developing countries on the new grid of international economic relations. While the need for and advantages of expanding business contacts and trade with the West were then, and later, presented in a quite matter-of-fact manner that acknowl- edged the dictates of interdependence, similar pragmatic economic policies with the Third World were not presented with the same candor, or explained in terms of objective processes. Normative values and political explanations persisted in the discussion of that sector of foreign trade. Although the specialists at the Institute of the Economy of the World Socialist System continued to devise new forms of economic cooperation to assure more profitable exchanges with developing countries (even including tripartite cooperation with the West), they made no attempt to go beyond the theoretical explanations provided by Premier Kosygin in 1971. Even if they did not actually argue that the Soviet Union was striving to create a new, socialist, international division of labor, they certainly were circumspect to note that aid and trade with the LDCs were based on different economic laws arising from the very nature of the socialist system.

Thus Leon Zevin's book on new trends in economic cooperation between the Socialist and the developing countries painstakingly argued that joint industrial ventures or mixed companies, when set up by a Socialist country, were qualitatively different from similar arrangements by Western business since neither political advantage nor profit was the primary aim.[14] Similarly, when Margarita Maksimova presented her theories on the operations of a single world market in a popular book written for a wider audience, she carefully explained that since Soviet-Third World relations were based on

Lenin's theories about the Soviet alliance with national liberation movements against all forms of exploitation, "mutual advantage" in Moscow's relations with the Third World was a "deeper, more flexible principle" than mere commercial accounting or the pursuit of profit.[15]

At the time, the authorities seem to have been confident that they could weave ideology and economic necessity, diplomacy, and trade into an advantageous and manageable policy. Their confidence rested on the assumption that dealings with the West and with the South somehow could be kept distinct without compromising the doctrine of the special relationship between the Soviet Union and the former colonies. The persisting importance of ideological factors in economic relations was well summed up by Leonid Brezhnev before the 25th Party Congress in 1976:

> Intertwined in foreign economic relations are politics and economics, diplomacy and commerce, industrial production and trade. Consequently, the approach to them and their guidance must likewise be comprehensive, linking up the efforts of all departments as well as our political and economic interests. This is exactly how this important issue is regarded by the Party Central Committee.[16]

Nevertheless, despite the unaltered overarching theoretical conception of the role of developing countries in the world economy, the facts and circumstances of their domestic economic situation assumed a significance in political analysis and academic research that had been denied and shunted aside under Khrushchev. During the 1967 celebrations marking the fiftieth anniversary of the October Revolution, the customary paeans to the example of Soviet development and the influence of its policies on the course of events in the former colonies were replaced with a sober admonition from Leonid Brezhnev on how "considerable effort . . . to achieve economic self-reliance" was essential for progress in the Third World.[17] In short, the rudimentary concept of economic efficiency had been made a revolutionary requisite. *Fundamentals of Scientific Communism*, which in 1966 replaced the Khrushchev-era *Fundamentals of Marxism-Leninism* as the basic text on communist theory, stressed that the victory of revolutionary forces in the Third World depended to a large extent on the proper management of the economy.[18]

This accommodation to economic determinants resulted in redirecting Party instructions to the research institutes. In August 1967 the Central Committee (CC) issued a decree on the social sciences, which blandly asked for the study of the economic, social, and political problems of the developing countries. Although the formulation was general, the order of priorities was important in itself. That point was made clear in an editorial in *Narody Azii i Afriki*. Scholars were enjoined to relate their work more closely to the practical tasks facing the CPSU and the Soviet Union. Specifically, the editorial stated, it was not sufficient nor terribly relevant merely to study the formation of the state sector. It was necessary to examine how effectively it functioned. Similarly, finding solutions to food shortage problems rather than devising plans for agrarian reform was the more appropriate task for research.[19]

In urging specialists to turn to practical problems of development, the editorial also reassured them that the Party did not impose "ready solutions." It did, however, convey that the shift of focus in research should not be excessive. The developing states should still be regarded as a uniform category, and there could be no "exceptions" (*vychleneniya*). Though not amplified, this was a clear warning that the new objective, factual approach was not to supplant ideological interpretations. Leonid Brezhnev made the point explicit in March 1968. Speaking about the need to further improve the efficacy of research, he called on "scholars and propagandists specializing in the international field" not to "overestimate" the achievements of Western science and thus to weaken the force of "sharp ideological struggle."[20] Party authorities saw the evident need for less politically slanted economic studies to underpin Soviet policies. But they did not want to forego the diplomatic advantages and propaganda value to be gained from saying that all developing countries were at the mercy of the capitalist world market.

The shift to the more practically oriented research that the Party demanded was promptly implemented. Early in 1968 there was a collective stock-taking by the profession at a conference held to discuss the three-volume study by IMEMO, *Classes and Class Struggle in the Developing Countries*. Since it was a synthesis of the first decade of post-Stalinist scholarship, its reassessment pointed out the transition to a new phase, which was motivated by different interests and perceptions.[21]

The participants in the review session directed their criticisms at the excessive reliance on schematic and wishful thinking at the expense of obvious realities. The consensus was that the focus on the components of a preordained political progress had to be superseded by close analysis of the factors contributing to economic development. Accordingly, by 1974 the outdated compendium was replaced by a new study whose very title indicated a departure from the former vocabulary and conceptualization: *The Developing Countries: Regularities, Tendencies, Perspectives.* (The parallel work by the two regional institutes, *National Liberation Movements in Asia and Africa*, was also reissued in a thoroughly revised edition, *The East Beyond Soviet Borders and Contemporary Times.*)[22] To the extent possible at the time, both books attempted to qualify schematic determinism by stressing two aspects of methodology. As the introductions explained, the new publications aimed at correcting the former deductive and deterministic method of analysis in terms of the developing countries' inevitable transition to socialism. To underscore the point, many contributors noted the unresolved nature of various issues. And to curb unfounded generalizations, they urged the wider and more stringent use of statistics.

However, the correctives that were attempted addressed only domestic developments in the developing countries. The elaborate theoretical structure accounting for their international position was not questioned. The two 1974 studies still looked at the world as divided into antagonistic capitalist and socialist systems and at the LDCs as a unit with common problems resulting from that division.

It should be noted, however, that though these works of synthesis conformed to the ideological line, a different kind of research was also being done. Notwithstanding Brezhnev's strictures against excessive objectivity, IMEMO's journal published in late 1970 the preliminary findings of a new study group on the economic indicators of the level of development in nonsocialist countries. The need for introducing a uniform system of analysis for 76 selected states in Europe, North and South America, Asia, the Middle East, and Africa must have been pressing to justify publication in a preliminary form. Here, for the first time were comparative data on national income, the structure of the economy, population makeup, employment patterns, and literacy levels applied under the same rubrics to capitalist and developing countries alike.[23]

Elementary as the procedure may seem, it heralded a basic shift in Soviet studies of the Third World. Henceforth, the best minds in the profession conducted their research on the developing countries less in terms of the socialist-capitalist competition for their political allegiance and economic cooperation and more in terms of their actual position in the world economy and their domestic potentials. Instead of treating the developing states as a uniform category, all equally dependent and exploited, some scholars began to study their heterogeneity. By the late 1970s, their findings were producing insights that could not possibly support the notion of two world economies.

INNOVATIONS AND GROUPINGS SINCE 1976

The apparent equilibrium between old theory and new practices that characterized the first decade of Brezhnev's rule had become quite unbalanced by 1976. Theoretical foundations, which for the previous 20 years had safely buttressed "distinct" Soviet aid and trade policies, began to erode in the wake of the oil crisis, petrodollars, mounting difficulties with the domestic economy, and the failure to establish a socialist international division of labor with the developing countries.

What is singular about the reaction to this situation is a loss of confidence in the cogency of the old theoretical framework. It is evident that the Party authorities are uncertain how to provide an adequate ideological explanation for the fact that the Soviet Union has to operate on the capitalist-dominated world market, over which it can exercise no decisive influence, and in which the developing countries no longer hold that "special" place that would tilt them toward the Socialist Bloc. The need to find a secure theoretical underpinning for universalistic economic laws and appropriate economic policies has created more elbow room for independent expert opinion. As a result, a fairly open-ended debate has ensued on how to reconcile the current understanding of the world economic situation with traditional Marxist concepts about the lot of the former colonial countries in international economic life.

Recent specialized writings on the Third World contain statements to the effect that what is essential is not merely the refinement of analytical tools but the principle of open-ended inquiry itself. Deductive methodology, deterministic schemes, and normative thinking have come under attack before, but never so directly and with such mounting urgency (and with reference not only to an updated Marxism-Leninism but also to the more universal canons of modern science). For example, one book on the theory of development in the Third World was prefaced with remarks about the indeterminate nature of research and invoked the authority of Niels Bohr's principle of complementarity.[24]

With such an outlook emerging in the profession, the Party's current assertion that it does not want warmed-up doctrinal recipes but creative, viable new formulations to meet the challenge of our time acquires a different meaning. True, the authorities have made similar demands on the profession before — ever since 1956 when Mikoyan told the orientalists to wake up. But in the past, circumstances differed in two respects: the Party had the basic forms at hand and wanted them filled with new content; a pliant mood prevailed among the specialists. Now circumstances have changed: the Party is considering how to change the forms, while the profession, with growing independence of mind, now has the skills to create new content.

One cannot as yet speak of a well-formulated and fully articulated new theory on the place of the LDCs in international economy. Conflicting opinions at home and the constraints abroad prevent this from happening, but they do not foreclose the process of search and conceptual change. What is significant for this study is that despite inhibiting political factors, the debate on universalistic concepts regarding the operations of the international economy proceeds nevertheless.

Three broad interest groups are discernible in the ongoing discussion on how to acknowledge that global interdependence transcends systemic solutions and how to extend the notion of a single world market to cover the developing countries. The first group is the Party apparatus, particularly the people charged with maintaining political power and ideological orthodoxy. They would like to have more effective economic relations without introducing sharp discontinuities in doctrine, administrative structure, and foreign policy. They recognize the growing necessity to internationalize Soviet economic life but are reluctant to admit an unqualified global economic interdependence since this would undercut the ideological and diplomatic competition. Thus Brezhnev started to enumerate various global problems in 1976 (ranging from the environment to food and raw materials) and to talk about the need for "constructive cooperation of all countries" to solve them without, however, proposing any theory to account for the changed nature and operation of the world economy. In 1981, at the 26th Congress, he proposed that the Party Program's formulation on the place and role of the developing countries in international life be altered, again without offering a broader explanation.[25]

The economic ministries constitute the second interest group. Officials and staff in these agencies are concerned not so much with reconciling their activities with ideology as with achieving practical results. Foreign Trade Minister Nikolai Patolichev is very frank about the need to integrate Soviet economy with the world market:

> Today it would perhaps be difficult to find an economic sector in the USSR that is not connected with foreign trade to some extent, or does not receive effective practical aid in its further development. To put it figuratively, foreign trade has become an important artery in the blood circulation of the Soviet Union's economic organism.[26]

Thus the current, eleventh, Five Year Plan stresses the importance of realizing the benefits to be gained from the international division of labor and foreign economic relations in order to spur progress and to satisfy the needs of national production and the Soviet consumer. Similarly, books based on source material from the State Committee on Foreign Economic Relations — the Soviet Union's foreign aid agency — proceed from the assumption that profit is a basic consideration in the drive to improve the forms of cooperation and terms of exchange with the developing countries.[27]

There are two divergent tendencies among the last interest group — the academic specialists. The more conservative technocrats follow a cautious course that combines a hard ideological line with the search for economic rationality. And there are modern-minded innovators who, recognizing the need for extensive reforms in institutions and practices, also press for changes in ideological formulations. While the approach of the conservative experts resembles that of the Party, the outlook of the modernists seems to be closer to that of the ministries. The difference between the two tendencies is best illustrated by the explanations they offer for what led to the appearance of the single world economy, how it works, and how it affects the several components.

The cautiously conservative specialists argue that it was the strength of the Soviet Bloc, together with the exemplary nature of intra-Bloc relations, that were primarily responsible for the emergence of the global economy. They are also prone to stress that the interaction of the two subsystems, though essential and beneficial for the growth of each, does not change their specific modes of production. They define the world economy as a "dialectic unity of opposites in which international economic relations of different social systems are intertwined."[28] This interpretation allows for both competition and interdependence, depending on the circumstances and the audience.

The innovative modernizers provide a depoliticized interpretation. They see the world economy as an objective phenomenon created mainly by the advances in science and technology. It is

> the sum total of not only the national economies of various states but also of the two world systems, socialist and capitalist, each of which develops according to its laws. . . . Despite all the differences and contradictions of the . . . two world markets, they find themselves in a definite mutual interaction. . . . It is possible to take into account not only what divides them, but also a number of common regularities, common tendencies that operate in the world economy as a whole.[29]

To gain a better idea of the ongoing process of theoretical reformulation, it should be noted that this definition is much more universalistic — putting more emphasis on elements that make for interdependence — than the one provided by the same author in 1977. At that time, she stated that the world market was a "sum total of all the separate national economies which find themselves in a situation of complex interaction and mutual dependence," but undercut the importance of "interdependence" by including a long disquisition on the differences in the foreign economic policies of the two systems.[30]

The institutional and ideological boundaries between the three groups should not be drawn too rigidly. One can assume that there is a similar range of opinion among the Party authorities and in the ministries as in the academic community. Moreover, innovations do not originate from any one source; there is considerable and evolving interaction, as well as linkages, between new ideas advanced by the specialists, changes in economic policies, and novel inflections discernible in official pronouncements.

Given the material available to an outside observer, the nature and the course of the recent reassessment can be most easily traced in the writings of the experts. For example, at the 25th Party Congress in 1976, Brezhnev still spoke about the Third World in optimistic terms. Regarding it as unitary, he stressed both the trend toward a progressive domestic course and its positive contribution to international affairs:

> Glancing at the picture of the world today, one cannot help noticing the important fact that the influence of states that quite recently were colonies or semi-colonies has grown considerably. It can be definitely said of most of these states that they are defending with mounting energy their political and economic rights in the confrontation with imperialism. . . . We are united with the overwhelming majority of states that came into being as a result of the breakup of the colonial system by a deep devotion to peace and freedom and an aversion to all forms of aggression and domination, to the exploitation of one country by another. This community of fundamental aspirations is the rich soil on which our friendship will continue to gain strength and flourish.[31]

This upbeat tone was not shared by some specialists. Already on the eve of the 25th CPSU Congress, the Party's theoretical journal, *Kommunist*, published an article by Georgii Mirsky, head of the LDC department at IMEMO, which punctured various certainties about the prospects of socialism in the developing countries and the future of Soviet-Third World relations. The article voiced the traditional diatribes against imperialist exploitation of the former colonies. Nonetheless, it argued with unprecedented candor that imperialism was adapting to the new situation in the Third World and was making enough concessions to the developing countries to retain a meaningful presence; hence, capitalist relations were taking firm root in most LDCs. Moreover, though the article predicted continuing economic conflicts between the West and the Third World, it made absolutely no references to the role of the Soviet Union, its Bloc, or socialism in shaping the course of events. In other words, it implied that in that part of the world economic processes were occurring over which the USSR could exercise no meaningful influence.[32]

This was a startling admission; for 20 years Moscow's claims that it would win the economic competition with the West had been predicated on the belief in the Soviet Bloc's ability to curtail the capitalist world market precisely in the developing countries. At first, this pessimistic outlook was duly countered by the older, conservative, and more important Rostislav Ulianovsky, an academic expert serving as senior official in the international section of the Central Committee.[33] Soon enough, however, doubts paralleling Mirsky's outlook, written by persons as important academically and politically as Ulianovsky, began to gain prominence.

On February 10, 1978, *Pravda* printed a lengthy article by Karen Brutents, another academic expert on the Third World who was working in the Central Committee's international department. It was an unprecedentedly gloomy appraisal (as far as Soviet prospects were concerned) of economic trends in developing countries. Nothing like it had ever been printed in the Party daily before. Entitled "Imperialism and the Liberated Countries," it candidly discussed the success neocolonialism was having in the LDCs by modernizing its methods to fit their demands and changing circumstances. The emphasis was more on the concessions the imperialist powers were granting and on the gains the LDCs were making than on the new methods being a more sophisticated form of exploitation.[34] Since the article was printed under the general heading "Problems of Theory," it was obviously meant to alert readers that at least three correctives in the established Soviet view on the developing countries' position in the world economy were in order: (1) that exploitation and an ever-deepening dependence were not necessarily the only result of Western economic activities in the LDCs; (2) that capitalist relations had taken large strides in these countries; and (3) that no immediate likelihood existed for the Soviet Union to offer these countries a better alternative. (Here, it should be noted that at the 25th Party Congress Brezhnev and Kosygin had conspicuously omitted the customary diatribes against imperialist plunder but did not say anything about the changing nature of colonialism.)

The July 1978 issue of *Kommunist* carried an article, "Some Problems of the Developing Countries," by Evgenii Primakov, director of the Oriental Studies Institute. (Primakov, a trained Arabist with much experience in the Near East as a correspondent, in 1977 succeeded the post-Stalin political appointee, Bobodzhan

Gafurov.) Primakov's article put the main stress on "objective" economic processes, which were increasingly integrating more and more LDCs in an ever-tighter manner with the industrialized capitalist states. Dispensing with the excursus on exploitation, it pointed out that the developing countries readily cooperated with the multinationals on their home territory. More than that, some had grown so rich with petrodollars as to become net exporters of capital to the West, while others, the technically more advanced, had started acting as little "sub-imperialist" islands on the world market. Focusing on objective economic forces and the salient facts of change in the Third World, the article eschewed homilies about economic liberation or the growth of anti-imperialist sentiments and concentrated on demonstrating the mounting wealth of some developing countries and the growing poverty of others. The facts were left to speak for themselves; there was no hint that some points of ideology no longer corresponded to reality or that there was need for theoretical reformulation.[35]

In sum, beginning in 1976, quite unorthodox views about the economic role of developing countries on the world market began appearing with greater frequency and in ever-wider circulation. Contributing to this process was the absence of clear ideological guidelines from the Party combined with continued prodding of the academic community to produce some answers. Insistence on ideological consistency seemed to yield to the urgency of practical problems. Typical of the new atmosphere was Brezhnev's address to a joint meeting of the CMEA Academies of Sciences in February 1977. He spoke about the importance of research for solving various economic problems, stating that some work was still "unrelated" and "useless." Two aspects of his comments were significant: One, there was little reference to Marxism-Leninism but much emphasis on the importance of science and technology — that is, on objective data and methodology. Two, scholars of the Socialist Bloc were urged to work not exclusively on issues connected with the integration (sblizhenie) of their countries but also on "global problems." In other words, they were asked to address issues connected with the greater participation of Socialist states on the world market.[36]

One striking aspect of the wider latitude extended to research is the more open discussion of the loss of momentum in Soviet-Third World relations. As if by coincidence, from 1977 to 1978, several publications and conferences acknowledged erosion in the community of diplomatic, ideological, and economic interests. Although this was quite unprecedented at the time, by the early 1980s it had become a fairly common line of argument.

Three prominent examples can be cited. Rais Tuzmukhamedov, for many years an authoritative commentator on the nonaligned movement, published a book in 1977 that frankly discussed the fact that many Third World organizations and leaders belittled the importance of the Socialist Bloc for developing countries. Nor did the study attempt to maintain the myth of the unity of interests and outlook between the Soviet Union and the nonaligned movement. Next a conference of specialists was convened to discuss the pertinence of the concept of the unity of the Third World. The predominant opinion seemed to be that the concept was inadequate. Politically, the LDCs were not acting in unison in response to Western pressures; ideologically, there was an indefinable conglomeration of ideologies; and economically, fuel prices and petrodollars had transformed some countries into bankers and others into paupers. The conference ended on an inconclusive note, simply taking cognizance of various disagreements and unsettled problems. However, in the profession, the meeting was considered to be something of a landmark, at which numerous theoretical formulations that no longer corresponded to facts had been exposed, thus laying the groundwork for further progress in depoliticizing the field. For example, a number of participants noted that, given the demonstrable economic, political, and ideological differentiation, neither the developing countries nor their "national liberation movements" could be lumped together as a component of the world revolutionary process. Finally, the unity of economic interests also came under critical scrutiny. A symposium, published by the Institute of the Economy of the World Socialist System, attributed the sluggish trade exchanges to the eroding complementarity in the economic potentials and needs of the Soviet Bloc and the developing countries.[37]

EAST EUROPEAN AND WESTERN THEORETICAL INROADS

Two other recent developments indicate the extent to which the field has opened up to fresh ideas: there is frequent reference and recourse to East European economic thought; and the response to Western, especially Social Democratic, writings on underdevelopment is more positive. Both trends add significantly to the current climate of opinion in which important decisions and revisions are under discussion at the same time as there is less normative prodding from the Party. Both attest that other, less dogmatic socialist opinion can now be used to extend and legitimize the bounds of open discourse.

East European economic thought, especially Hungarian and Polish, reflects the viewpoints of countries that are very much trade dependent and where ideological control over research — including contacts with Western scholarship — has not been as rigid and as long-lasting as in the Soviet Union. Consequently, East European experts have been much more objective and original in their views than their Soviet counterparts. For example, the Polish economist Michal Kalecki had maintained early on that sustained, harmonious relations between the Socialist Bloc and the developing countries were problematical since both groups had similar supply-led and investment-hungry economies. In other words, their structures were not sufficiently complementary to offer prospects for a separate, smoothly functioning socialist international division of labor. Accordingly, if the Bloc and the LDCs were to establish viable economic relations, it could not be accomplished on an exclusive East-South basis but had to be fitted into the larger context of the world market. A later, controversial essay by Kalecki stated that the neutral regimes of the Third World behaved "like the proverbial clever calves that sucked two cows."[38] Similarly, the Hungarians, much earlier than the Soviets, turned from preoccupation with the disintegration of the colonial system and rapidly expanding Soviet Bloc-Third World exchanges to the detailed, factual analysis of the actual role and increasing weight of developing countries in the world economy. In the process, they have openly admitted that the ideological guidelines provided by the Party "undoubtedly hindered" productive research and the implementation of "effective policies."[39]

At first, the communication and cooperation between the Soviet and the East European specialists was more indirect than direct. In the early 1960s, many younger Soviet scholars learned Polish (a simple matter for Russian speakers) to gain easier access to a broader spectrum of opinion, that is, not only to Polish publications but especially to the available translations of Western works or the well-informed discussions of the latest developments in Western scholarship. By the 1970s the atmosphere had changed substantially.

The more outspoken and original views of the East Europeans were being translated and published in the Soviet Union, for example, the important work of Tamas Szentes on the political economy of underdevelopment or the Polish economist Jerzy Kleer's study of the world economy. Kleer's book was a forthright and freewheeling argument for the existence of the world market, defined as an interconnected system that determines the functioning and growth of the whole as well as of its constituent parts — a definition far in advance of what was at that time openly mentioned in the Soviet Union. The fact that the book's editor commended it for introducing Soviet readers to such "unfamiliar terms" as "open" and "closed economy," "demonstration effect," and "interdependence" testifies to the general level of information in the USSR.[40]

Another indication that East European views have gained greater weight is the establishment, within the system of cooperation among the CMEA Academies of Sciences, of a joint study group on the economies and politics of the developing countries. To judge from the course of the group's discussions, it is the East Europeans who lead with fresh ideas unencumbered by the traditional ideological baggage. For example, a report prepared by the Hungarian Academy of Sciences for the fourth session in 1977 provoked a lively discussion on whether or not the increased economic and political differentiation of the Third World, delineated in the report, invalidated the theoretical notion of the unity of the developing countries.[41] (As already mentioned, the same idea was broached in the Soviet Union only a year later at a special meeting convened to discuss that topic.)

Recent favorable comments on major Western works on the economic position of the Third World are another indication that an increasing tolerance toward a greater plurality of views parallels the current reassessment of outdated definitions. At first, Scandinavian and Social Democratic publications were thus noticed, marking an important step in attenuating the uniform public hostility toward all non-Marxist-Leninist views. Gunnar Myrdal's *The Asian Dilemma* was published in Russian translation in 1972. By the end of the decade, the Brandt Commission's report, unlike the earlier Pearson report, was given thoughtful and respectful reviews.

The tone of one major review of the Brandt report reveals much about the direction of the most open-minded and innovative thinking among Soviet specialists. It commended the report on three counts:

for its global approach that stressed the interdependence of all issues as well as of countries; for suggesting solutions in terms of constructive dialogue, not of *diktats* or confrontations; and for including the Soviet Bloc in its analysis. It was also emphasized that Brandt himself had made a significant contribution to détente in East-West relations. By implication, he was being commended for trying to do the same in the broader realm of East-West-South economic relations.[42]

A similar positive and receptive tone can be found in many recent comments on Western theories of development. These articles are marked by an absence of the former blanket condemnations that ascribed to Western specialists nothing but the worst intentions, that is, their seeking new and better ways to exploit the Third World. Currently, it is not at all unusual to find reviews of Western books on developing countries that focus on the diversity of opinion among foreign scholars, their controversies, their research on emerging problems, the jettisoning of traditional methods and assumptions, and the search for new modes of analysis. What is more, some review articles suggest that these trends in the West could be valuable for Soviet scholars in reformulating Marxist-Leninist criteria for analyzing the position of the LDCs.[43]

THE THIRD WORLD IN A GLOBAL PERSPECTIVE

The most innovative result to emerge thus far from the post-1976 reassessment is the tendency to look at the Third World from a global viewpoint. Many specialists no longer see the LDCs in a bifurcated world situation, to which only systemic analysis and remedies apply. Instead, these states are viewed as an integral part of a single world economy governed by objective and universalistic economic laws.

Numerous instances of the new outlook indicate that an important conceptual shift has taken place — in some quarters. Among the more telling developments has been the creation, in the summer of 1980, of the Scientific Council on Philosophy and the Social Problems of Science and Technology, with a subsection on global problems. The scientific councils, which are part of the Academy of Sciences, are prestigious bodies that coordinate the work of scholars, ideologues, ministries, and state committees. The establishment of this new council is significant on several counts: One, the fact that the problems raised by science and technology are being discussed within the framework of "philosophy" indicates that matters affecting Marxism-Leninism are being tackled. Two, the practical aspects of its work are equally important, for it collaborates with interdepartmental government committees that deal with foreign economic relations. Three, the topic of backwardness is discussed in the subsection on global problems.

The inclusion of backwardness among matters of global concern marks a big step in the depoliticization of Third World-related issues and the introduction of universalistic terms of discourse. In 1976, when Brezhnev first mentioned global problems, backwardness was not one of them, since the responsibility for underdevelopment was still blamed on the West. At that time, the very concept of global problems (let alone what comprised them) was such a departure from systemic thinking that in a joint article two academics, Vadim Zagladin (a deputy director of the CC's international section) and Ivan Frolov, sounded an unequivocal warning. The recognition of such global issues as ecology or population growth and proposals for dialogue on a "positive solution" of certain related economic problems in no way signified any rapprochement with "bourgeois reformist concepts of globalism, 'world system' models, ideas of 'world-wide humanism,' 'unity of world consciousness,' etc., which . . . serve as pseudo-indicators of 'convergence,' aim at 'de-ideologization,' . . . cosmopolitanism, and try to give global problems a supra-class, supra-social and supra-national character."[44] In short, "globalism" did not signal the imminent demise of the traditional doctrinal interpretations.

The logic of events, however, has a way of overtaking the strictures of ideology. In 1976 Professor Frolov had felt it necessary to issue stern warnings against diluting Marxism-Leninism with alien concepts. But five years later, he spoke of Soviet ideology as facing an entirely different set of problems. As chairman of the global problems subsection of the Scientific Council on Philosophy and Social Problems, he no longer felt obliged to denounce the possible corruption of Marxism-Leninism by "false" universalistic bourgeois concepts. He now pleaded for fresh thinking to update theory. According to Frolov, research on global problems was

incompatible with old stereotyped thinking, with exclusive devotion to old, outdated categories. It is essential to reconstruct [these categories] in the direction of globalism, which should incorporate all aspects of analysis — economic, socio-political and ecological. It is very important to include Marxist-Leninist global concepts in the theory of scientific communism, the basis of our communist world view.

To underscore the need for radical departures, Frolov stated that "we speak not only about the conjunction or coordination of concepts but about the adaptation of the basic categories of scientific communism to the global problems — the new phenomenon of our epoch."[45] (To be sure, he made some comments to the effect that recognition of overarching global problems did not suspend competition between the two systems; in other words, cooperation would never replace the struggle for the final victory of communist relations. But this was a weak argument — an afterthought, really, by comparison with the burden of his remarks.)

The thrust of Frolov's forceful plea shows that there are persons in high circles who propose not merely cosmetic readjustments in theory to meet the global economic challenges but also some serious revisions. The fact that "backwardness" is acknowledged to be a global problem constitutes a reformulation in the traditional Marxist-Leninist cosmology that ascribed underdevelopment to the operations of the capitalist world market. It is a new perception of the world configuration that dispenses with the old demonology; it places backwardness in a nonantagonistic category. If one proceeds logically from there, then the whole superstructure of the malevolent worldwide operations of imperialism no longer has a basis.

Frolov's arguments acquire resonance when placed in the context of what Brezhnev had to say about the Third World at the 26th Party Congress. As could be expected, his remarks were no clear-cut commitment to new interpretations. Yet, when compared with what he said in 1976, a definite change is evident. In 1981 the First Secretary's report was much less assertive about the developing countries. Dispensing with previous claims that certain trends were predominant in the development and activities of these countries, Brezhnev made no sweeping assertions about the triumph of socialism. Instead, he opened that section of his report with an admission of the diversity among the LDCs: "Some pursue a genuine independent policy, others follow policies of imperialism. It is a fairly variegated picture." No customary reference to the "fundamental community of interests" between the Soviet Union and the Third

World as a whole followed this statement. In itself, this particular opening may seem insignificant but not when examined in conjunction with the quite articulate suggestions made by the innovative specialists about the need to come to terms with the fact that what used to be called "the East" — the colonial world or the newly independent countries — no longer formed or acted as a uniform category. Put differently, Brezhnev was countenancing those specialists who were pushing for accepting the diversity of the Third World and for dropping the myth of its unity and special role in the world economy and politics.

That theoretical revisions on the role of developing countries in world economics are under consideration is attested to by Brezhnev's announcement at the congress that the 1961 Party Program needed revisions. The program, he said, "correctly reflects, on the whole, the laws of social development." But still, in the intervening 20 years, much had happened that needed "elucidation," including such "new phenomena in international life" as the "abolition of the colonial system of imperialism" and the "growing role of the new states."[46]

Since that announcement, there have been no further directives from the highest quarters on how to interpret the changed nature of imperialism and the consequent changes in the position of developing countries. Brezhnev's statement, however, has opened a small floodgate: how to proceed with the application of globalism to Third World problems. Thus far two trends can be discerned. As in the past, the Party and the more conservative professionals prefer to go about the depoliticization of international economic relations to accommodate pragmatism without, however, seeking any far-reaching theoretical justifications. Following their own pattern, the modernizers in the academic community are pressing beyond. They offer not only practical recommendations to facilitate Soviet and Bloc participation on the world market but also advocate a larger global vision to depoliticize economic and other issues associated with the Third World to help avert international confrontation.

The directives given to the academic community after the 1981 CPSU Congress obviously accord with the interests and the wishes of the Party. When compared with the directives following the preceding 25th Congress, the change is striking. The indirect acknowledgment of objective (hence universal) economic laws has replaced the former political categorizations.

After the 25th CPSU Congress, economists in the various institutes were instructed to conduct their research on international economic relations under three rubrics: the world socialist system, the developing countries, and contemporary capitalism. Within that framework, they should provide "an intensified analysis . . . of the progressive advances in the economies of the developing countries under the influence of the world socialist system." By contrast, the post-26th CPSU Congress directives placed all research on international economic relations under the single rubric of the "world economy." Specialists were simply asked to "research the role of the Socialist system on the world market, the relations of the Socialist states with the developing and the industrially developed capitalist countries" and make recommendations for broadening the mutually convenient cooperation between the USSR and the LDCs. Significantly, the directive treated backwardness as a global problem.[47]

Thus far, this has been the clearest indication that the former rigid bifurcation or trifurcation of international economic life into geopolitical categories has been jettisoned. In effect, the directives for the profession posit a uniform methodology that acknowledges the operation of objective economic forces.

While Party speakers and conservative experts prefer to restrict the new understanding of the operations of the global economy to practical matters of trade, there is a spate of specialized writing that attempts to turn the official acknowledgment of global problems into a broader reformulation of outdated and dysfunctional theory. Some writers stress that global problems create a situation so unprecedented that it calls for a restructuring of consciousness into "untraditional progressive" methods of thinking, which "demand the destruction of outdated generally-accepted concepts and habits."[48]

Others prefer to be more specific and discuss the implications of globalism not for theory but for policies. They concede that according to Marxism-Leninism the ultimate solution for global problems rests on establishing the social ownership of the means of production. But they find the current situation so pressing that "humanity" cannot simply refrain from acting while waiting for these ideal conditions to mature. A principal trait of global problems is that procrastination exacerbates them — they require immediate attention and action.[49]

Looking at the problems of the Third World from a global perspective has led some specialists to see that underdevelopment can undermine world equilibrium and peace. Two recent authoritative monographs on global problems include sections on the developing countries that discuss backwardness from this viewpoint. One is written by Zagladin and Frolov; the other is a collective volume put out by IMEMO.[50]

The two monographs amply illustrate that the common features of the developing countries acquire an entirely different outline when seen from the new, global perspective. Formerly, the posited unity of the postcolonial areas − accounted for by the backwardness caused by exploitation − was said to incline them to choose progressive domestic and foreign policies that would help alter the worldwide balance of forces. That optimism is gone now; underdevelopment provides an entirely different scenario.

The growing poverty of the majority of the world's population, marked by the widening gap between the LDCs and the advanced industrial countries, has first of all created a sense of "alienation." It has converted anti-imperialist nationalism into a Third World chauvinism and a blind hostility toward all developed nations, both capitalist and socialist.

The second overarching consequence of retarded development is the mounting sense of hopelessness about the situation, resulting in social unrest, which in turn leads to local ethnic or interstate strife. Eventually, given the possibility of great-power involvement, local conflict threatens a global conflagration.

The prospect for resolving either problem looks unpromising, given the steep rise in the Third World's military spending. It diverts scarce resources from more pressing national needs, arresting development and contributing to the further destabilization of an already precarious social and political situation. Furthermore, it fuels local conflict.

Finally, on a world scale, backwardness creates economic burdens and difficulties for the more advanced countries. Not only are they expected to contribute ever-increasing amounts of aid, but because large areas of the world are unproductive, the latter will eventually sap the well-being of the developed states.

Both studies are concerned not so much with the causes of backwardness as with its consequences. They dwell on the extent of underdevelopment and poverty, not to indict imperialism but to warn of the global consequences of substandard living conditions affecting the vast majority of the world's population. The overriding worry of Soviet globalists is that these conditions are like "dynamite." They are the

> destabilizing factor [that] can express itself on the international level in all types of conflict, including conflicts utilizing modern weapons and having at the same time not a progressive but a deeply reactionary character. That type of conflict can become in the future one of the detonators of a world-wide catastrophe.[51]

There is a brighter side to this gloomy outlook. The same experts who see the nonsystemic, worldwide catastrophic aspects of Third World backwardness also express hope that despite the ever-worsening situation,

> those powerful objective tendencies, which have given birth to détente and to the growth of international cooperation in many fields, permit one to expect the possibility of attaining an agreed-upon, wise approach to the solution of the problems connected with overcoming backwardness of the developing countries.[52]

The skeptical reader can retort that such an argument is a meaningless generality or a ploy to lull the West. But there is evidence that the heightened awareness of global issues and imperatives informs policy suggestions that depart from the former confrontational methods. The more daring interpretation of globalism is based on a new and different assumption about the nature of the historical process. It holds that progress depends on society's ability to overcome conflicts arising from the interaction between man and nature.[53] It minimizes or dispenses with the traditional categories of conflict — class struggle and revolutionary change.

Some specific policy recommendations by experts who share this view are revealing. For example, many recent analyses of world resources and the supply of raw materials depart from the hackneyed treatment of the problem mainly in terms of the exploitation of the LDCs by multinational corporations. Instead, they argue that the growing dependence of all states on these commodities has created a world market, which in turn necessitates global regulation to assure the legitimate interests not only of the producing developing countries but also of the consuming industrial states. What underscores the truly global approach of such arguments is the admission that the Soviet Union is not immune to problems affecting all industrialized consumers of raw materials, ranging from production costs to the possible exhaustion of supply.[54]

NOTES

1. J. V. Stalin, *Economic Problems of Socialism* (New York: International Publishers, 1952), pp. 26-27.

2. *XX S'ezd Kommunisticheskoi Partii Sovetskogo Soyuza. Stenograficheskii otchet* 1 (Moscow: Gospolitizdat, 1956), p. 324.

3. For a more detailed description of the institutes, as well as of university faculties and of various publications, see P. Berton and A. Rubinstein, *Soviet Works on Southeast Asia: A Bibliography of Non-Periodical Literature, 1946-1965* (Los Angeles: University of Southern California Press, 1967); Yu. Illyn et al., "African Studies in the USSR: the 1960s and 1970s," *Social Sciences* no. 4 (1979): 64-69; N. A. Kuznetsova and L. M. Kalugina, *Iz istorii sovetskogo vostokovedeniya, 1917-1967* (Moscow: Nauka, 1970).

4. "XXI S'ezd KPSS i zadachi sovetskogo vostokovedeniya," *Problemy vostokovedeniya* (January-February 1959): 18-25.

5. *Osnovy Marksizma-Leninizma* (Moscow: Gospolitizdat, 1959). The second edition has been translated into English: *Fundamentals of Marxism-Leninism* (Moscow: Foreign Languages, 1963).

6. *XXII S'ezd Kommunisticheskoi Partii Sovetskogo Soyuza. Stenograficheskii otchet* 3 (Moscow: Gospolitizdat, 1962), pp. 260-61.

7. "Pervaya konferentsiya OON po problemam ekonomicheskogo planirovaniya v stranakh Azii," *Planovoe khoziaistvo* (February 1962): 91-95.

8. V. Rymalov, "Ekonomicheskoe sorevnovanie dvukh sistem i problema pomoshchi slaborazvitym stranam," *Mirovaya ekonomika i mezhdunarodnye otnosheniya* (February 1960): 42 (hereafter cited as *MEMO*).

9. The one theoretical debate that reached the pages of learned journals concerned the respective political roles of Communists and radical nationalist leaders in the presocialist stages of the national liberation revolution. Reams were written on the subject by academic experts, but the issue was settled by Party decision. The 22nd Party Congress in 1961 recognized the radical middle-class politicians as effective agents of progress. By extension, their economic policies — state capitalism — were also recognized as progressive.

10. *Problemy sovremennykh natsional'no-osvoboditel'nykh revoliutsii* (Moscow: Nauka, 1966), pp. 15, 76ff.

11. *Bol'shaya sovetskaya entsyklopediya*, 16 (Moscow: Sovetskaya entsiklopediya, 1974), pp. 322-23; English translation: *Great Soviet Encyclopedia*, 16 (New York: Macmillan, 1977), p. 676; *Bol'shaya sovetskaya entsiklopediya* 27 (Moscow: Bol'shaya sovetskaya entsiklopediya, 1954), pp. 576-78.

12. M. Maksimova, "Vsemirnoe khoziaistvo i mezhdunarodnoe ekonomicheskoe sotrudnichestvo," *MEMO* (April 1974): 3-16.

13. *Pravda*, April 7, 1971, p. 6.

14. *Economic Cooperation of Socialist and Developing Countries: New Trends* (Moscow: Nauka, 1975), pp. 198ff.

15. *SSSR i mezhdunarodnoe ekonomicheskoe sotrudnichestvo* (Moscow: Mysl', 1977), pp. 112-16; English translation: *USSR and International Economic Cooperation* (Moscow: Progress, 1979).

16. *Pravda*, February 25, 1976, p. 6.

17. Ibid., November 4, 1967, p. 4.

18. *Osnovy nauchnogo kommunizma* (Moscow: Politicheskaya literatura, 1966), p. 179.

19. "Neotlozhymye zadachi dal'neishego razvitiya obshchestvennykh nauk," *Narody Azii i Afriki* (November-December 1967): 5-10.

20. *New Times* no. 14 (April 10, 1968): 37-38.

21. Conference proceedings, *MEMO* (May 1968): 70-104 and (August 1968): 82-96; *Klassy i klassovaya bor'ba v razvivayushchikhsia stranakh* 3 vols. (Moscow: Mysl', 1967-68).

22. *Razvivayushchiesia strany: zakonomernosti, tendentsii, perspektivy* (Moscow: Mysl', 1974); *Natsional'no-osvoboditel'noe dvizhenie v Azii i Afrike* 3 vols. (Moscow: Nauka, 1967-68); *Zarubezhnyi Vostok i sovremennost'* 2 vols. (Moscow: Nauka, 1974).

23. *MEMO* (November 1970): 151-57 and (December 1970): 142-49.

24. L. I. Reisner, ed., *Ekonomika razvivayushchikhsia stran. Teorii i metody issledovaniya* (Moscow: Nauka, 1979), p. 6.

25. Brezhnev first referred to global problems in his report to the 25th Party Congress, *Pravda*, February 15, 1976, p. 5. For expanded comments see his speech on the sixtieth anniversary of the October Revolution, ibid., November 3, 1977, p. 3. See also his report to the 26th Party Congress, ibid., February 24, 1981, p. 9.

26. *Vneshniaya torgovlia* (June 1978): 3.

27. T. V. Teodorovich and V. V. Efanov, *Sotrudnichestvo pri sooruzhenii ob'ektov za rubezhom. Iz opyta sovetskikh organizatsii* (Moscow: Mezhdunarodnye otnosheniya, 1979).

28. O. Bogomolov, "Material'naya osnova prochnogo mira," *Kommunist* no. 2. (January 1978): 96. See also his *Strany sotsializma i mezhdunarodnoe razdelenie truda* (Moscow: Nauka, 1980), pp. 3ff..

29. M. Maksimova, as reported in *MEMO* (January 1982): 138.

30. *SSSR i mezhdunarodnoe*, p. 12.

31. *Pravda*, February 25, 1976, pp. 2-3.

32. "Meniayushchiisia oblik 'tret'ego mira,'" *Kommunist* no. 2 (January 1976): 106-15.

33. "Natsional'no-osvoboditel'noe dvizhenie v bor'be za ekonomicheskuyu nezavisimost'," *Kommunist* no. 14 (September 1976): 112-22.

34. "Imperializm i osvobodivshiesia strany," *Pravda*, February 10, 1978, pp. 3-4.

35. "Nekotorye problemy razvivayushchikhsia stran," *Kommunist* no. 11

(July 1978): 81-91. See also his "Zakon neravnomernosti razvitiya i istoricheskie sud'by osvobodivshikhsia stran," *MEMO* (December 1980); 24-47.

36. *Ekonomicheskaya gazeta* no. 7 (February 1977): 3.

37. R. Tuzmukhamedov, *Razvivayushchiesia strany v mirovoi politike* (Moscow: Mezhdunarodnye otnosheniya, 1977); "Natsional'no-osvoboditel'noe dvizhenie: nekotorye voprosy differentsiatsii," *Aziya i Afrika segodnia* (June 1978): 28-35; *Sotrudnichestvo sotsialisticheskikh i razvivayushchikhsia stran: novyi tip mezhdunarodnykh ekonomicheskikh otnoshenii* (Moscow: Nauka, 1980).

38. M. Paszynski, "Economic Relations between Socialist and Developing Countries in the Changing World," in *Economic Cooperation between Socialist and Developing Countries*, ed. Istvan Dobozi (Budapest: Hungarian Scientific Council for World Economy, 1978), pp. 56-58; M. Kalecki, *Essays in Developing Economies* (Hassock, England: Harvester, 1976), p. 36.

39. T. Szentes, "The Development of Economic, Technical and Scientific Relations between Hungary and the Developing Countries," in *Economic Cooperation between Socialist and Developing Countries*, ed. Istvan Dobozi (Budapest: Hungarian Scientific Council for World Economy, 1978), pp. 143-45.

40. T. Szentes, *'Tret'ii Mir': problemy razvitiya* (Moscow: Progress, 1974); J. Kleer, *Vsemirnoe khoziaistvo. Zakonomernosti razvitiya* (Moscow: Mysl', 1979).

41. *MEMO* (October 1977): 126-36.

42. P. Khvoinik, "Mirovoi kapitalizm i razvivayushchiesia strany," ibid. (October 1980): 44-57.

43. B. I. Slavnyi, "Problemy izucheniya razvivayushchikhsia stran v burzhuaznoi nauke," *Narody Azii i Afriki* (July-August 1976): 136-45; idem, "Nekotorye voprosy formirovaniya obshchei kontseptsii slaborazvitosti v burzhuaznoi nauke," ibid. (July-August 1979): 183-201.

44. "Global'nye problemy sovremennosti," *Kommunist* no. 16 (November 1976): 94-95.

45. "Global'nye problemy nauchno-tekhnicheskoi revoliutsii," *MEMO* (November 1981): 137.

46. *Pravda*, February 24, 1981, pp. 2, 9.

47. "Meropriyatiya po vypolneniyu resheniya XXV S'ezda KPSS v oblasti ekonomicheskoi nauki," *Voprosy ekonomiki* (March 1977): 4-6; "Osnovnye napravleniya raboty otdela ekonomiki AN SSSR po razvitii ekonomicheskoi nauki v svetle reshenii XXVI S'ezda KPSS," ibid. (April 1981): 13-14.

48. A. K. Subbotin, *Mirovye ekonomicheskie problemy: perspektivy resheniya* (Moscow: Mezhdunarodnye otnosheniya, 1980), pp. 180-81.

49. L. Liubimov's review of Subbotin's book, *MEMO* (December 1981): 143-44.

50. V. V. Zagladin and I. T. Frolov, *Global'nye problemy sovremennosti: nauchnyi i sotsial'nyi aspekty* (Moscow: Mezhdunarodnye otnosheniya, 1981); N. N. Inozemtsev, ed., *Global'nye problemy sovremennosti* (Moscow: Mysl', 1981). Unlike the Oriental Studies Institute, IMEMO did not produce an updated version of its 1974 synthesis on the Third World. Therefore, this multi-authored study, which covers the LDCs in terms of underdevelopment, is regarded

as IMEMO's latest word on the subject.

51. Zagladin and Frolov, *Global'nye problemy*, p. 76.

52. Inozemtsev, ed., *Global'nye problemy*, p. 98.

53. Subbotin, *Mirovye ekonomicheskie problemy*, p. 179.

54. S. Glebov, "Problema obespecheniya chelovechestva syr'em i energiei," *MEMO* (October 1980): 30-41. For a similar argument, see also Inozemtsev, ed., *Global'nye problemy*, pp. 138-59.

3

DEVELOPMENT THEORY: FROM ECONOMIC LIBERATION TO INTERDEPENDENCE

Soviet development economics encompasses more than theory. The models elaborated by specialists show a close parallelism in time and emphasis with the actual policies Moscow pursues and the official line on international economy. In tracing development theory through the stages roughly corresponding to changes in Soviet aid-trade policies and views on the world economy, a fundamental shift in perceptions and concerns becomes manifest in three main areas.

Foremost has been the shift from political to economic solutions. At the outset, the speedy, decisive creation of new "progressive" political institutions would (it was proclaimed) engender growth, produce the necessary surplus, and transform social inertia. Over the past 25 years, this Soviet prescription has yielded to gradual reforms governed by economic criteria. In other words, the original systemic formula is being displaced by economic rationality.

Closely related is a parallel change in the perception of capitalist institutions and industrialization. At the start, the extirpation of capitalist relations was proclaimed the prerequisite for economic growth. But as the years passed, Soviet specialists have developed a sober respect for the sequential nature of development, in which capitalist forms of ownership and capitalist work habits fulfill an economically valid (even if historically limited) function.

Similarly, the Soviets no longer are the ardent advocates of import-substitution industrialization. The goal no longer is "economic liberation" and industrial autarky. The Soviets now favor a far less drastic transformation. With a heightened awareness of the global interdependence of economic needs, roles, and mechanisms, they believe that the developing countries should turn to advantage their traditional function as raw material producers.

These changing perceptions and concerns are important for another reason. Initially, Soviet theories on development proposed revolutionary solutions that comported with the aims of many LDCs. More than that, Soviet doctrines helped galvanize and articulate LDC resentments and grievances. Many Third World leaders and theorists, though not themselves Marxist-Leninists, subscribed to premises as phrased by the 1961 CPSU Program:

> Imperialism . . . remains the chief enemy and the chief obstacle to the solution of the national problems facing the sovereign states and all dependent countries. . . . Capitalism is the road of suffering for the people. It will not ensure rapid economic progress nor eliminate poverty.[1]

However, in the past 25 years Soviet understanding of development economics has changed substantially, while radical LDCs have not veered much from the original theory. At a time when the Third World is better organized and able to press its demands, the Soviets have come to prefer a less aggressive and one-sided approach to international economics. Hence the discrepancies between Soviet and Third World thinking on development issues create tensions in their presumed rapport — and in some instances even a bind.

DEVELOPMENT ECONOMICS UNDER KHRUSHCHEV

During the Khrushchev era, specialists viewed the creation of viable national economies almost exclusively through a political prism. The prevailing approach to the economic problems of the former colonies was unrealistically simple. Backwardness, it was

Development Theory / 75

asserted, resulted from colonial rule and persisted because of the survival of capitalist institutions as well as of the unequal relations with the former metropoles. Therefore, curtailing market forces and relations with the West through planning, nationalization, industrialization, and extensive dealings with the Soviet Bloc would produce rapid growth. The almost blind faith in political solutions, grounded on a belief in the efficacy of "economic liberation," was pointed up in the Soviet readiness to grant aid for just about any project proposed by a developing country and rejected by the West, without prior investigation of its economic feasibility.

The subject of the state sector best exemplifies the approach that prevailed at the start. To provide ideological justification for the Soviet involvement in building up nonsocialist economies, a special conference was convened at the Institute of Oriental Studies in 1958. Scholars decided that, unlike the situation in industrially developed states, state capitalism could play an "objectively progressive" role in those newly independent countries where it would be "harmful to the interests of imperialism" and "coincided with the interests of the people."[2]

Although the conference was organized by the institute's economic department, the discussion was couched primarily in political terms. Only a few specialists, for example Aleksei Levkovsky, analyzed the "progressiveness" of state capitalism in terms of what it might do for economic growth. The majority, among whom Rostislav Ulianovsky was prominent, challenged this view, claiming that the utility of state capitalism lay in its "anti-imperialist" tendency. During the next few years, the overriding concern was to demonstrate that programs launched by Moscow's economic clients would eliminate private capitalist relations, as well as dependence on the West, and serve as a transition to socialist institutions. Given this framework, state controls and central planning in India, Egypt, Indonesia, and Burma were seen as bound to succeed since they were directed at gaining economic independence from the West. Conversely, parallel endeavors of Pakistan, the Philippines, or Turkey were derided since these countries were said to be under the domination of monopoly capital and imperialism.

What any set of policies might contribute to increased production was not subject to intensive public discussion at that time. Economic measures were analyzed in terms of what they did to build up the state sector. And until about 1964-65, the performance of the public sector was judged almost exclusively by its size. Thus discussion and investigation centered on four ways of expanding public ownership.

Industrialization and comprehensive planning were regarded as the best methods for endowing a regime with a strong position in the national economy. Only by owning the means of production could the central government exercise proper guidance of a country's economic life. Soviet experts attending the first U.N. conference on programming for economic development advocated the expansion and strengthening of the public sector primarily through industrialization and rigid planning, which were meant to neutralize market forces. Accordingly, they criticized the other working papers that largely saw the public sector in the role of providing a strong impulse to development.[3]

During this period the Soviets favored the nationalization of foreign business and local private enterprise, maintaining that their operations constituted a net deduction from national wealth. The imposition of state ownership was necessary to direct these private funds into development investment. At times more moderate voices would suggest that the state could better increase its resources for capital accumulation by such measures as taxation. But the prevalent mood was to advocate and encourage nationalization without compensation to increase the level of savings. Accordingly, it was regretted that India's second Five Year Plan did not resort to any nationalization to secure additional investment funds, while the expropriation decrees promulgated in Indonesia and Guinea were applauded in the daily and academic press.[4]

The expansion of economic relations with the Soviet Bloc was the fourth method for enhancing the role of the state. Scholars argued that by concentrating assistance on industrial projects in the public domain "Soviet credits above all promote the development of the state sector of the national economy, which represents the strongest basis for the genuine independence of underdeveloped countries."[5] They denounced Western aid for promoting private enterprise and "capitalist relations," for these cemented ties with the West, ensured dependence, and perpetuated backwardness.

ECONOMIC FACTORS AFTER 1964

The shift to more pragmatic aid-trade policies after Khrushchev's ouster encouraged a less politically oriented approach to development problems. In the decade after 1964, the views of Soviet specialists were broadened and refined. More moderate, gradualist opinion – one that acknowledged the advantages of light industry, agriculture, private local and foreign capital, and less comprehensive planning – replaced the former commitment to speedy, radical measures. It became a widely accepted premise that economic growth entailed prerequisites, stages, diversification, and interrelations among the various segments of a national economy. Specialists started paying attention to internal retarding factors and not just to the adverse effects of Western domination. In short, analysis was being based more on economic facts than on political dogma. The new outlook was well summarized by one expert: the more backward an economy, the wider the circle of concrete problems that have nothing to do with either capitalism or socialism but will have to be solved through certain basic practical measures.[6]

The demonstrable failure of excessive state controls in the economies of the Soviet Union's major aid recipients and trade partners spurred the reexamination of former assumptions. Upon the ouster of several radical leaders, beginning with Algeria's Ben Bella in June 1965, the successor regimes invariably cited the chaotic economic conditions, brought about by overambitious government schemes, as a major reason for the coups. Yet the very policies that produced chaos were being extolled at the time in Soviet specialized and popular writings as marking the "correct" and promising choice of the noncapitalist path. Moreover, they had been encouraged with generous aid grants, at least until 1963.

Another contributing factor was that by then Moscow was facing the repayment problem. The Soviets had been especially shrill in claiming that their aid, particularly for the large industrial projects, would be more effective in generating income than Western credits for infrastructure. But, as it happened, Indonesia sought a debt rescheduling as early as 1963; Egypt proved unable to begin repayments in 1964; and Mali's interest payments had to be cancelled and debt repayment deferred in 1965.

Consequently, professional publications began to exhort scholars to examine the performance of the public sector. The editorial in the November-December 1967 issue of *Narody Azii i Afriki* called on specialists to focus on the consequences of expanding public ownership rather than on the expansion itself. Thus the very measures that used to be prescribed as the proper steps to attaining economic liberation and higher levels of development were being criticized, in the late 1960s, for "ultra revolutionary haste," which impeded the solution of complex economic problems. That term covered almost any institutional reform that extended public management and control beyond the state's capacity for efficient administration. During Khrushchev's time, specialists attributed the poor performance of state enterprises to the "penetration of bourgeois elements into higher posts." After 1965 the blame was shunted onto other, less subjective, factors, such as overextension, burdensome bureaucracy, corruption, and deficit operations.[7]

Less rigid planning and a slower rate of nationalization became the most frequently proposed remedies for the malfunctioning of the state sector. The notion that long-range national development plans could be undertaken only when the state owned the basic means of production and neutralized the effects of market forces was challenged by younger, more modern-minded economists. They dubbed it with the term "voluntaristic"; that is, it ignored actual costs and other economic realities.[8] Instead, these economists advocated recourse to more indirect methods such as taxation, tariff rates, and credit policy to steer the economy, and they proposed reliance on "flexible and dynamic policies" based on the "sober consideration of the general state of the market and its possibilities."[9]

In keeping with the reservations on the state's role in fostering development, views on nationalization were similarly transformed. Rostislav Ulianovsky, who earlier favored nationalization as being both politically and economically progressive, now revised his opinions. Writing for *Kommunist* in 1968, he warned against runaway nationalization, conceding that it crippled small and medium-sized industry as well as domestic trade and services.[10] But Ulianovsky and other economists never questioned the principle of eventual state takeover — only its hasty application. Within these bounds, numerous articles drew attention to the fact that nationalization had been too readily adopted by countries that were ill-prepared for the responsibility. Unable to cope, they had to resort to economically unjustifiable steps, which ranged from enlarging the bureaucracy to printing more money.

After 1965 there was also a reassessment of what, precisely, foreign investment and private business contributed to the economic well-being of the new nations. In principle, Soviet hostility to the role of "monopoly capital" in the Third World remained unchanged, but in discussing specific situations and needs the positive role of Western capital in development was acknowledged. Some authors conceded the inability of new states to manage without a Western presence and hence advised against a premature rupture of traditional ties with the former metropoles or the expulsion of foreign capital. Others emphasized the importance of technology transfer and expertise via Western channels. The new consensus was that instead of pursuing radical economic liberation the new states should seek arrangements that would recognize each nation's sovereignty over its natural resources and industry, retaining as large a share of the profits at home as possible. Thus the 1967 settlement between the Belgian Congo and Union Minière was accepted as a wise compromise, not as abject submission. It was explained as such to the Soviet public:

> There is no reason to assume that such agreements are . . . instances of capitulation. Such an approach bears a strong imprint of dogmatism. In the present situation [where the newly independent states are incapable of processing and selling natural resources on their own] they can benefit by making use of foreign capital, provided . . . that it is placed under strict local control and the over-all economic interests of the given country are safeguarded.[11]

A similar change of attitude on the function of the private sector occurred. Of course, no one proposed that the tenet of the leading role of the state be scuttled, only that the state not be overburdened with an unnecessary expansion of functions. The more cautious economists adduced the weakness of the state apparatus to assume excessive burdens, such as the suppression of retail trade. But others were much more positive about private business, finding appropriate quotations from Lenin, who had held in the early 1920s that during the transition from small production to socialism, capitalist relations could and should contribute to increasing output.[12]

Perhaps most significant were the changing perceptions on the relative importance of industry and agriculture. The one-sided preference for industrialization, modeled on the Soviet experience of the early five-year plans, which promised a swift escape from dependence and backwardness, was considerably toned down. A conference on industrialization that was convened at the IMEMO in 1967 heralded a new approach. In a marked departure from earlier theories, it was argued that successful development required a simultaneous and balanced growth in both industry and agriculture.[13]

Significant modifications of the Soviet model also appeared after 1964. The New Economic Policy (NEP) started to overshadow the five-year plans both in official statements and in scholarly work. The CPSU theses for the fiftieth anniversary of the October Revolution referred to the NEP as an advance on the road to communism with special relevance for other countries.[14] Similarly, many economists advancing novel ideas on the importance of foreign investment or private enterprise would buttress their arguments not only with hard figures on the catastrophic performance of the public sector in various developing countries but also with quotations from Lenin's writings in the NEP period on the advantages of strengthening the socialist economy with the infusion of capitalist funds or techniques. Altogether, elements of a mixed economy (with, of course, the state in control of the commanding heights) emerged during the first decade of the post-Khrushchev analysis. Such elements were seen as offering the most efficient way for overcoming backwardness.[15]

It should be remembered, however, that no matter how pragmatic or "liberal" the post-1964 views were by comparison with the former dogmatic prescriptions, they did not affect the overall, political analysis. What changed was the understanding of specific domestic policies in the LDCs, not the interpretation of international economics and how they perpetuated backwardness. No one openly questioned the overarching theories of the bifurcated world economy or the unity of the developing countries, which was defined by their uniform dependence. The changed prescriptions on the tempo of industrialization, on the size of the public sector, and on the role of private enterprise were prompted and justified on the grounds of creating the conditions for the advent of socialism. The ultimate goal of development was still liberation from Western domination and exploitation, as well as the elimination of capitalist relations. Soviet aid and the Soviet-promoted socialist international division of labor were said to play the path-breaking role for attaining the goal.

Though much less confrontational, the socialist model for domestic and international policies was still being proffered as the viable alternative to capitalist relations. In other words, the more moderate outlook in no way impinged on the competition of the two systems for the future economic course of the Third World.

THE POST-1974 CONCEPTUAL FRAMEWORK

In the period since 1974, Soviet views have changed and diversi-fied far more than in the preceding decade. Pragmatic, moderate, economically workable policies remain the objective, but they are increasingly being placed in a different conceptual framework. A single world market and pressing global problems have brought a reinterpretation of development in a wider context, wherein elements of interdependence or universalism often predominate over those of competition and exclusiveness.

The new look bears little resemblance to the model offered by the CPSU Program in 1961: "As long as the [young sovereign states] do not put an end to their economic dependence on imperialism, they will be playing the role of a 'world countryside' and will remain objects of semi-colonial exploitation." To be sure, this understanding still colors many official pronouncements and academic works. But quite different views — significantly departing from or challenging the old tenets — are put forward in academic discussions. Moreover, these views do not remain buried in the pages of specialized publica-tions. They are reflected in the thinking of the Party leadership. Here, it is significant, as already noted, that at the 26th CPSU Congress in 1981 Brezhnev proposed changing the party program to "record such fundamentally important phenomenon of international life as the abolition of imperialism's colonial system."[16]

There is little agreement among Soviet political leaders and specialists on how to adapt what Lenin had to say about conditions in colonial and semicolonial countries early in the century to the vastly changed situation some 65 years later. But the binds and tensions between traditional political theory and the emerging under-standing of development economics in a different international setting have not stopped the discussion. A variety of views is expressed in fairly open debate. One thing is clear: no longer can one speak of a simplistic, monolithic Soviet development theory, holding that the Third World's economic problems can only be solved by extirpating capitalism and joining the Socialist community.

Three new concepts have undermined the traditional Soviet interpretations. First, the recognition of the wide economic differen-tiation among the newly independent countries calls into question the former theory of unrelieved imperialist exploitation. Second, the acceptance of a global division of labor as essential to development undermines the former equation of "economic liberation" with progress. Third, a coming to terms with the fluid, multilevel nature of Third World economies and societies permits scholars to study the complexity and specificity of developing countries with greater attention to their diversity and less adherence to a preordained uniformity.

The collective IMEMO volume on the prospects of developing countries, published in 1974, noted the confusion of criteria used in analyzing development. It called attention to the indiscriminate mixture of sociopolitical and technical-economic categories, as well as the habit of treating the entire Third World as an undifferentiated unit. As a remedy, it proposed a wider and more stringent use of statistics to "separate that gigantic mass of Asian, African and Latin American countries into smaller groups and subgroups" along with a comparative analysis of economic development.[17]

The first purely economic typology of the developing countries, written by a group of mathematicians, economists, and political scientists, appeared in book form in 1976.[18] Reviews praised it for shunning the existing "intuitive-heuristic" approach and using a mathematical, multidimensional taxonomy devised by Rudolph Rummel in the early 1960s and since amplified by Frederick Harbison and others. The novelty, it was noted, consisted not merely in using the most recent computerized analyses but in applying this methodology to all nonsocialist countries alike. No distinction was drawn between the capitalist West and the developing East: the same 31 indicators were applied to all 85 states in the study. Such an approach made possible a more exact analysis of the present-day world where — under the impact of the scientific revolution, the global division of labor, and the evolution of the newly independent countries — a considerable relocation of economic, technological, and political forces had taken place.

As a result, economic typology has gained acceptance on a par with the hitherto prevailing political typology. Different systems of grouping are proposed, but, broadly speaking, four basic categories are recognized: the poorest landlocked countries (mostly in Tropical Africa), the relatively advanced nations of North Africa and Asia, the oil-rich states, and the countries of Latin America. This classification is distinct from the one used to analyze the class nature or foreign policy of Third World regimes. For that purpose, they are now grouped into capitalist-oriented and socialist-oriented countries.

There is no agreement on what constitutes the most reliable system of indicators for including a country in a particular economic grouping. While most of the controversy concerns the components of development – for example, the relative importance of income per capita as against a well-rounded integration of the entire economy – the discussions range further afield than that. They do not stop with the static system of classification established by the 1976 volume on typology but touch upon the dynamics of development or, more specifically, what degree of progress can be acknowledged and what accounts for it.

In this respect the liveliest disputes concern the characterization of capitalist development. The more traditional interpretations hold that the Third World can develop only within the framework of "dependent" capitalism, while the innovators want to dispense with political categories and press for the recognition of "semi-developed capitalism." With recourse to statistics and logic, they argue that objective indicators show the more backward areas of Europe (i.e., Portugal, Greece, and southern Italy) to be on the same level as the more developed countries of Latin America (i.e., Mexico or Brazil) and as such should be grouped together as countries that have reached a level of semideveloped capitalism. By 1980 some experts were pointing out that several LDCs – the net exporters of capital – had become "centers of sub-imperialism," expanding into less developed regions. All these arguments are opposed by the more traditional-minded economists who insist that, despite the enormous differentiation, the Third World nevertheless remains a definable politico-economic category and, no matter how far some countries manage to advance, they can never transcend the limits of dependence.[19]

Only recently have Soviet scholars come to the conclusion that participation in a worldwide division of labor is essential for overcoming economic backwardness. This outlook is a complete reversal: it departs from the former preference for import-substitution policies meant to curtail the Western presence; it modifies the once prevalent contention that only relations and integration with the Soviet Bloc could offer truly advantageous and equitable exchanges; and it allows for a more objective analysis of the West's role in fostering development.

The first book to offer the new interpretation of the international division of labor frankly admitted that the "perfect" system of Soviet-Third World exchanges was not an operative but only a hypothetical situation. As for the present, technological progress had created a world market that in turn dictated the adjustment of national development to integration. Having made his innovative suggestion, the author did not theorize but concentrated on discussing the advantages of specific measures designed to bring maximum returns from adjusting production to international trade.[20]

A more weighty book appeared two years later in 1976. Written by Viktor Tiagunenko, a doyen of postwar experts on the Third World and Corresponding Member of the Academy of Sciences, it was edited for publication, after Tiagunenko's untimely death, by the prestigious economist, Viktor Rymalov. It provided a theoretical justification for the contemporary operation of the world economy and the place of developing countries in the international division of labor. Tiagunenko held that it was impossible to study the "preconditions, nature and consequences . . . of concrete social and economic changes" without taking into account "world-wide forces with which these processes are closely connected and intertwined."[21]

The book was hailed as a synthesis of the workings of the world economy that enabled Soviet scholarship to advance to a new stage. Indeed, it gave the imprimatur to research on Third World problems with reference to the global economic forces operating independently of any political system.

The need of developing countries to intertwine with the world market (which, after all, is dominated by the capitalist economies) is by now accepted by all scholars. Although this has considerably moderated the traditional hostility to the Western presence in the LDCs, there is certainly no unanimity on the consequences. Controversy persists on where the benefits of interdependence end and the costs of dependence begin. The conservatives still regard the interaction of developing countries with the West as a necessary evil that should be eliminated as fast as possible. Representatives of the rearguard keep reiterating that exploitation remains the root economic problem of the Third World, and it can be eradicated only by "rupture with the capitalist way of production and exchange."[22]

Specialists of midrange persuasion pay obeissance to the exploitation theme but devote the bulk of their work to providing masses of factual data that speak for themselves and amply demonstrate the economic advantages resulting from the internationalization of production. But there also are outspoken proponents of the international division of labor who address the subject much less gingerly. In the words of one economist, "foreign capitalist enterprise . . . is also one of the forms of 'penetration' of modern production methods into backward countries, one of the forms of economic ties linking them up with the world capitalist economy."[23]

The intransigent complexity of the Third World's social and economic structures has long bedeviled Soviet experts. Until the early 1970s, the Marxist theory of economic formations (slightly amended in 1960 with the formula of noncapitalist development that slowed down the strict revolutionary timetable) dictated an interpretation of difficulties in terms of a slow zig-zag movement toward protosocialist institutions and solutions. Currently, the concept of the multistructural nature (*mnogoukladnost'*) of society and economy in the Third World is being increasingly used to cope with the inescapable condition of diversity. But again, although a new theory has gained acceptance, it is subject to different interpretations, and sharp disagreements rage on the bounds of the new concept.[24]

The traditionalists interpret *mnogoukladnost'* as in no way deflecting the course of general historical development from one economic order dominated by a single class and mode of production to another, that is, as "an organic part of the evolution within the system of formations." They see the simultaneous existence of various modes of production as resembling the situation that Lenin saw in Soviet Russia in the early 1920s when he talked about the concurrent operation of patriarchal, small-commodity, capitalist, state-capitalist, and socialist *uklady*. But they insist that research and analysis should be directed at locating the leading economic structure that determines the evolution of the country toward the capitalist or socialist formation.[25]

Aleksei Levkovsky, a prominent specialist on India, is a leading exponent of the open-ended interpretation of *mnogoukladnost'*. He argues that economic diversity is so pervasive and so complex that at present it is counterproductive to try to figure out which of the Marxist formations the LDCs are moving toward. Developing countries are passing through a separate "interformation" period of extremely long duration. While the conservatives object that Levkovsky's theories deviate from historical materialism, other scholars welcome them as new analytical tools that have "rescued" the field from "oversimplifications which tried to fit the whole historical development of the Afro-Asian world into strictly deterministic cells of a linear construction obligatory for all." They deny the traditionalists' contention that Lenin interpreted multiplicity as mere variations on the theme — all being part of the predetermined scheme of "from here to there." They maintain that, on the contrary, he recognized multiplicity as an objective factor. In support they cite Lenin's words: "The future revolutions in the immensely populated and socially variegated countries of the East will, without doubt, bring up . . . much more originality than did the Russian revolution."[26]

The concept of *mnogoukladnost'* is doggedly pursued by the research staff of the Institute of Oriental Studies. As well as having critics among the conservatives, they face the opposition of the Institute of World Economics and International Relations. The specialists of IMEMO, given their global and somewhat technocratic outlook, express little interest, understanding, or patience for a theory that focuses on local peculiarities and deviations from the general pattern. Thus IMEMO treats capitalist relations in the Third World as a reflection of worldwide processes, while the Institute of Oriental Studies interprets them as a phenomenon that is different from the classic West European model and shows at present many elements sui generis.

DEVELOPMENT ISSUES IN A NEW LIGHT

Now that economic heterogeneity among the developing countries, the global division of labor, and local diversity are accepted terms of discourse, many specialists are reassessing development issues in the light of these new perceptions.

First of all, economic development is often analyzed in terms of ensuring *political and social stability*. As already mentioned, ever since the dramatic and serial collapses of radical regimes, beginning with Ben Bella's in 1965, Soviet scholars have been wary of economic "extremism." However, their postmortems on these regimes remained scattered in separate articles and chapters, never examined in a systematic and sustained manner. Finally, in 1975, Nodari Simoniya published a book pinpointing the reason for the failure of numerous national liberation movements in Africa and Asia — namely, the economic preconditions for success were insufficiently established. Simoniya cogently began with one of Lenin's quotations from Marx: "our teaching is not a dogma." A correct reading of the Marxist-Leninist classics, he argued, demonstrated that stable and lasting political change derives from a properly matured economic basis. Marx saw economic and political development as firmly sequential: socialism had to be the product of a developed and advanced economic system. Should revolution occur in a "weak link," as it had in Russia, then the situation demanded special attention to economic policies to bring industrial production, managerial skills, and labor discipline up to par with the requirements of the advanced political systems. More specifically, Simoniya argued, such a regime had to rely on and develop the economic institutions left by the predecessor in order to create a firm foundation for its own survival. It could not abolish them forthwith and replace them with socialist production relations until capitalist production relations had developed sufficiently to make this possible.

Simoniya's study offered so many unorthodox and fresh interpretations that a special review session was called to assess their merit. Most of the participants, however, talked not about the book's "mistakes" but endorsed its contention that before genuine socialist revolutions or changes could take place in the East, an intermediate preparatory period of economic buildup and reconstruction was essential.[27]

Of course, on one level Simoniya's book dealt with topical political issues — it was an argument against Chinese and other leftist development theories — and that fact spared it from excessive criticism. As a scholar, however, Simoniya was concerned about something less transitory: to get away from the prevalent ad hoc political evaluations of economic policies and to define the place of economics in assuring genuine and lasting progress. In pursuing this line of interest in more recent publications, he has contrasted the relative failures of the radical economic policies that characterized the first decade of independence (1955-65) with the success of the more moderate, "more rational" programs of the succeeding decade. He has argued that it is methodologically correct to analyze the present phase of economic development not in terms of dependence but as an "essential transitional stage of accumulating elements for the future independent economic structure."[28]

With backwardness recognized as a global problem in 1980, the theme of sequential development and stability has acquired a different aspect. Whereas previously it was seen as slowing down the proper revolutionary timetable, recent publications on global issues interpret the growing impoverishment of many LDCs and the increasing gap between the former colonies and the metropoles as an inflammable situation endangering world peace. Underdevelopment is not a progressive factor in international politics offering prospects for a socialist revolution, for the disaffected millions on the verge of starvation have no "defined social orientation" and are motivated by a "hatred for material and technical culture." The contemporary implications of underdevelopment transform it into a dangerous element "of deeply reactionary" character that threatens world civilization.[29]

The concern for slower — that is, stable and balanced — economic progress has in turn prompted the recognition of less rigid and more varied development *models*. The articulation of what the Soviet example is has changed considerably, and other alternate models are discussed with greater objectivity.

At the start of the current phase, the attitude that Soviet experience in the NEP years offered the best solution still prevailed. Lev Reisner's study of economic growth is the most detailed discussion of specific NEP policies that could be useful for developing countries today. The book examines such topics as: considering agriculture the basis for capital formation; promoting light industry to provide employment and income for the peasantry; undertaking measures to end agrarian overpopulation; building up labor-intensive industries; balancing consumption with accumulation; creating a domestic industrial complex; and engaging in extensive economic and technical cooperation with the advanced states. More than that, Reisner ascribed the success of Western development theories in gaining acceptance among the LDCs to the fact that this valuable early Soviet experience has been "overshadowed" by the subsequent policy, which posited "forced industrialization as the only basis, method and strategy for overcoming backwardness."[30]

The validity of these policies is still upheld, but they are offered with a slightly different inflection. The emphasis is no longer so exclusively on the practicality of this or that measure but more on the principle of flexibility itself. It is highly interesting to read that, when addressing a foreign audience, members of the Central Committee now mention that the NEP was introduced into a "multi-sectoral economy" and therefore necessitated "different forms of running the economy — state, state-capitalist, cooperative and private."[31] In other words, broader, more fundamental aspects of NEP than merely a series of successful domestic measures are being examined. Significantly, in this connection, some scholars have also stressed that the NEP pushed the Soviet Union into participation in the world economy.

The reverse side to the reconsideration of the traditional Soviet model is a marked lessening of hostility toward Western theories. Thus the Brandt Commission report has received favorable and extensive reviews that summarized its recommendations fully and objectively (that is, they were singularly lacking in the customary derogatory remarks on "bourgeois" learning).[32] Of course, one could argue that Brandt, as one of the architects of détente and someone well-regarded by Brezhnev, was bound to get a fair hearing in the Soviet Union. However, there are enough other signs to indicate that sympathetic attention to the commission's recommendations — linking development with disarmament and a more active implementation of the green revolution, domestic reforms, stabilization of world prices, and effective control of foreign investment — does not make this an isolated instance. For example, there also were positive responses to Tinbergen's proposals in *Towards a Better International Economic Order* that the LDCs adjust their development plans to the needs of world economy. Guernier's 1980 report to the Club of Rome, *Tiers Monde: Trois Quarts du Monde*, was also commended for its consideration of backwardness from a global viewpoint.[33]

A further indication of the growing tolerance and opening up is the suggestion that untried solutions may offer workable alternatives. As one economist has written, what is needed is a "new model for development that history has not yet known and could not have known, to . . . bring about a technical-economic and subsequently a socio-economic transformation." No single comprehensive study of the subject has as yet appeared, although its elements are often touched upon in books and articles. Reisner, for example, has blamed the failures and malfunctioning of India's first three five-year plans on the direct transfer of advanced economic patterns to an underdeveloped society. Others have written more extensively on how the modern sector tends to form an isolated enclave that does not invigorate the rest of the economy but nevertheless produces such undesirable side effects as urban overpopulation, unemployment, and a lumpenproletariat.[34]

But despite the heightened concern for social stability, Soviet scholars, thus far, have not favored solving "basic human needs" through redistribution – a "utopian" solution that ignores the overall development needs. They propose building up other forms of production (such as small-scale industry, large-scale public works, or the processing of agricultural products) that have more of a "trickle down" effect than heavy industry has.[35]

At first, in the post-1974 period, agriculture received the most attention as the basis for an alternative model, carrying on a trend of the preceding decade. To be sure, many researchers continued to treat the agrarian problem in terms of radical reforms that would dispossess the propertied classes, revolutionize the countryside, and organize large-scale production on state farms or cooperatives. But others began to study the peasant-oriented ideologies of the Third World, although these, for obvious ideological reasons, have not received explicit endorsement. For others, land ownership and tenure became secondary to such top-priority issues as food sufficiency, rural employment, and capital accumulation.[36]

But with the changed Soviet view on the operations and needs of world economy, emphasis shifted by the early 1980s to another development model. Many experts began to credit the exploitation of natural resources as creating the most effective stimuli for all-around growth. The production of raw materials is no longer interpreted as locking a country into an inferior position, but as giving it an opportunity to "internationalize" its economy and to accumulate the funds and the technology for modernization. With this outlook, even the position of the least developed states does not look so hopeless, since many of them, especially those in Black Africa, have large deposits of bauxite, uranium, titanium, iron, copper, and nickel.[37]

There are new perceptions on the role of *science* in development. When the term "scientific-technological progress" or "revolution" first became current, it was snapped up by many scholars as signaling a breakthrough for development theory. Minimizing the traditional views on what generated progress, they saw science as the motive force for change, or at least as a crucial factor in economic development.

The first substantial publication on the role of science in the Third World appeared in 1970, and a theoretical conference that convened in 1971 marked a considerable step forward by posing new questions.[38] These early publications, however, were excessively concerned with Western methods of transferring technology in a manner intended to perpetuate dependence. Since then, much of the subject has become remarkably free of ideological overtones. Little or no distinction is drawn between "socialist" and "capitalist" science, for it is seen as a genuinely international phenomenon that operates over and above the existing political systems. Science, which is developing and changing faster than any other sphere of human activity, determines the character of our times. Some writers go as far as to argue that economic history proceeds through the primitive, the industrial, and the scientific-technological stages. It is scientific advances that generate and shape the whole process of change that the Third World is undergoing in the 1970s. Even a new definition of the crux of underdevelopment has been suggested:

> On the world scale the economies [of the LDCs] have already begun to be transformed into a subordinate link of the new scientific-technological production forces, while at the same time, within their own framework, they face the problem of moving from the pre-industrial to the industrial modes of production.[39]

Most authors who discussed science, however, confined themselves to the more mundane question of technology transfer. The work of Georgii Skorov represents the optimistic strain that predominated at the start. His first publications argued that because the developing countries did not have to start *ab ovo* they could skip the preliminary stages and start modernizing their economies with the help of the latest advances of world science. This initial enthusiasm was tempered somewhat in a book published in 1975, which investigated why the potentials offered by modern technology had been to a very large extent unrealized despite the unprecedented availability of new means for speeding up economic development. The work of Rachik Avakov, representing the more pessimistic strain, concentrates on analyzing the obstacles to absorbing modern, advanced technology presented by archaic societies and backward economies. In sum, Avakov holds that technology cannot be simply grafted onto backwardness; he questions the wisdom of supplying the ambitious and affluent developing countries with the most advanced hardware and favors greater attention to intermediate technology.[40]

The growing pessimism evident in the most recent writings of a small, but by no means insignificant, minority goes far beyond the problem of a suitable technology. Some experts question whether the peoples of the LDCs can master the technological expertise essential for economic development. Do they actually want to, given their cultural traditions? One now comes across references to the work habits and mentality in the developing countries as creating serious obstacles to Eurocentric prescriptions. Some specialists wonder whether the autonomy or distinctiveness of Eastern cultures tends to be underestimated. Others are more explicit, calling attention to the fact that Eastern societies have passed through a historical development that is different from that of Europe and have formed entirely different attitudes toward individual initiative, the work ethic, and the criteria of success.[41]

While official pronouncements keep denouncing Western activities in the Third World, many scholars are probing the extent and in what ways the operations of *neocolonialism* have changed. The more conservative or cautious still marshal their arguments according to the formula that although the economic appearance of many developing countries has changed noticeably, their position in the world capitalist economy has not undergone any fundamental transformation. Others concede some advance, proceeding from the premise that "the great historic changes in the world . . . have imposed certain limits on the pursuit of imperialist policy toward the periphery." Since underdevelopment acts as a brake on the expansion and profits of monopolies, they have been forced to transfer some industries (mainly labor-intensive and environmentally harmful ones) to the Third World. These authors acknowledge that the LDCs have progressed from being mere raw material suppliers to a semi-industrial, though still dependent, status.[42]

Still others look beyond these newer, more efficient methods of exploitation to examine the positive contribution of Western business and capital. (This approach, it should be noted, in no way contravenes Marx, who recognized the progressive role of the colonial powers in introducing advanced production methods to their overseas possessions.) These specialists argue that one cannot limit the study of Third World development to stressing the baneful, negative influence of the West. Rather, the positive aspects — such as the erosion of ossified social relations, the initiation of faster growth in some sectors of the economy, and inclusion in the world market — equally deserve study as part of the process. Accordingly, books now investigate the contributions of foreign capital to local development plans, to capital formation, and to the implementation of social programs.[43]

Moreover, these specialists do not treat developing countries as the perpetual helpless victims of the imperialist cabal. Some stress that the following factors have contributed to the "collapse of . . . dependent and exploitative relations": nationalization of foreign property, increased local control over natural resources, changes in capital flows and in the world price structure, and the building of national industries. Others maintain that many LDCs have even attained a partnership status in international exchanges; as such, they both invite foreign capital and invest abroad themselves.[44]

At first, the proponents of *mnogoukladnost'* offered a cogent theoretical argument for dispelling the bogey of foreign and domestic capital — the basic problem to be surmounted if development is to escape being examined exclusively in terms of systemic recipes. Their description of the Third World economies as consisting of numerous indeterminate, ever-changing, transitional *uklady* that defy traditional classification makes the point that both foreign and local capital is diffused throughout the various components and interacts on many levels and accordingly defies easy or exact identification and hence eradication. Rather than concentrate on foreign domination or the expansion of domestic capital, they find it more rewarding to investigate the changes resulting from the multidimensional diffusion and interaction. It is on this very point that they have been most severely criticized by the conservatives, who object that this interpretation of *mnogoukladnost'* removes the guilty party from the scene.[45]

But more recently two prominent specialists have advanced theories to accommodate these insights into the changing position of developing countries in the world economy. Karen Brutents, the Central Committee specialist on the Third World, has differentiated between "national" and "dependent" capitalism. While the latter type of capitalist relations nurtures and strengthens the classic neocolonial relationship, "national" capitalism in the LDCs makes genuine contributions to economic development, undermining the exploitation that formerly prevailed. Academician Evgenii Primakov, Director of the Oriental Studies Institute, has advanced the proposition that there are two types of dependence. In addition to the classic "assymetric" dependency with its exploitation and inequalities, there now exists an ordinary dependency affecting all countries — the most developed as well as the least — because of the global nature of economic relations.[46]

Since opinions differ about the nature of neocolonialism, inevitably there are disagreements about the *multinationals*. Some authors concentrate on denouncing the multinationals as instruments of capitalist or neocolonialist exploitation. Without bothering to go into any details about their evolution or operations, they simply keep citing total figures on Western overseas investment and profits and consider their case conclusively demonstrated. Others, less obscurantist in their censure, admit that the multinationals have instituted a new international division of labor, allocating some of the processes in the production cycle to the developing countries. Still, on balance, the change is no more than a new form of exploitation. However, not all the negative views are mere political argumentation. A. A. Kovalevsky, for example, has dispassionately analyzed the operations of the multinationals in terms of Raymond Vernon's "product cycle" theory and concludes that the LDCs play too passive and limited a role in this process.[47]

There is a further sizable body of opinion that regards the multinationals as an inevitable aspect of the growing extent of the internationalization of production. Included in this group are those economists who appreciate the skill of these companies in devising new management methods to maximize efficiency and profit. Their analysis concentrates on the practical lessons that can be learned from the operations of the conglomerates and pays little attention to how these operations affect the developing countries and regions.[48]

Finally there are those who either imply or openly acknowledge the large contribution of the multinationals to economic development. Evgenii Primakov has written that over the past ten years these companies have relinquished complete control over local firms and increasingly cooperate with both the state and the private sector. Another attempt at a less Manichean view of the multinationals is that of N. Volkova, who points out that the Third World is by no means the main theater of their operations; but to the extent to which the transnationals are active in these parts, they help to integrate them into the world economy. For Ivan Ivanov they are the source of capital and technology, which provide the means for overcoming backwardness: "It would be wrong to deny, while taking a realistic view, that the multinationals are in principle incapable of making a contribution to development."[49]

It goes without saying that all Soviet authors favor, in some degree or another, national control over the operations of the transnationals. While the conservatives advocate stringent curbs, the moderates envisage a reasonable dialogue leading to mutually acceptable regulations that serve the interests of both parties.

The *role of the state* in generating development and bringing about the transition to socialism has undergone further review and modification in recent years. The functions of public ownership have been looked at with greater sophistication, and the blanket endorsement of state controls as equivalent to socialist production relations has been subjected to more vigorous scrutiny.

The factual assessment of operating policies has proceeded essentially along the lines that emerged during the post-1964 rethinking, when costs and benefits were weighed more carefully. But reservations, expressed first in scattered articles, have burgeoned into full-length books. For example, Elena Bragina's volume on industrial policy focuses on the stumbling blocks facing state management in the Third World, such as the shortages of administrative talent, expert knowledge, and experience. She shifts the emphasis from scale to efficiency. Economic feasibility demonstrates that a "striving for excessive statism, unrelated to economic conditions, can lead to serious disruptions of economic life, a fall in production, and the growth of unemployment. . . . The process of state ownership in the LDCs has its objective limits." Anatolii Elianov's book on economic growth and the market is the first Soviet work to analyze the interaction between state planning and market processes. It accepts private enterprise as a necessary and useful part of a national economy, recommends the peaceful coexistence of the public and private sectors, and regards market forces as an essential indicator of the general efficiency of supply and demand.[50]

Generalizations about the systemic role of the public sector fall into two categories. The more traditionally minded specialists still tend to argue that the size of the public sector, the degree of control over private and foreign capital, and the comprehensiveness of planning pave the way for a politically more progressive and economically more advanced system. But instead of saying that the entire Third World is more or less inevitably moving in that direction, they now differentiate between the public sectors in the socialist- and the capitalist-oriented countries. Only in the former can public ownership and controls serve the cause of political and economic progress.[51]

A small group treats the state sector not as one among several components of the developing countries' economic structure but as comprising the entire set of production relations. Prominent among the scholars in this group is Aleksei Levkovsky, who maintains that the state's prominence in LDC economies is due to necessity, which has little or nothing to do with the dawning of socialism. At present and for a long time to come, the public sector fulfills general national tasks that serve the interests of the various social groupings. It is the emanation of the amorphous multisectoral economy and society. Other scholars concentrate on the totality of the state's role. To categorize that situation, they have coined the phrase "étatism" (*etakratiya*) or use the term "state sector" (*gosudarstvennyi uklad*), as designating the entire set of production relations; in other words, as being a historic formation.[52] In some respects these views are related to the theory of the Asian mode of production, not so much in detail as in the general approach that sees the East as having institutions that differ wholly from those of the West. Consequently, the East cannot repeat Western patterns.

The arguments of the latter specialists are extremely convoluted and not easy to summarize. In reference to economic development, they signify an attempt to create new theoretical constructs to permit a fresh analysis of the role of the state in the Third World — an analysis more in keeping with the realities of the modern world than with the old political theories. On the international level, the relations between the industrial West and the developing East are said to be not those of exploitation, but rather between two contending monopolists, that is, the Western multinationals on one side and the étatist monopolies of the LDCs on the other. On the domestic level, the issue of exploitation also becomes irrelevant, since both the managers and labor are state employees. Similarly, state policies have to be analyzed in a different light since they are neither purely capitalist nor purely socialist.

SOCIALIST ORIENTATION AND ECONOMIC PROGRESS

What are the practical implications of the current Soviet interest in depoliticizing development issues and urging sound economic policies on the LDCs in a global rather than a systemic setting? Is it a deeper change affecting long-range strategy or merely a temporary adjustment in tactics? No conclusive answer to so large a question is possible. But an answer inclining toward substantial changes affecting long-range policy is justifiable on two counts. First, the serious, deep-seated problems that have brought about the lumbering readjustments in theory and practice — namely, the globalization of international economic issues and Moscow's difficulties with its own economy — will not soon disappear. Second, and more tangible, is the evidence of the evolution of Soviet theories about states of "socialist orientation." Politically, this is a highly sensitive issue, for the states of socialist orientation are often cited as proof positive of Moscow's contention that socialism has become the leading force in world history.

The Soviet agenda for promoting socialism in the Third World keeps stumbling and bumping into economic obstacles. This is not always recognized in the West, where some experts argue that states like Angola or Ethiopia have gone through "the final, Soviet type revolution" and are about to be incorporated into CMEA or an enlarged Socialist Bloc.[53] However, both Soviet leaders and economists insist that these radical countries are merely on the verge of socialist transformations and, like the other LDCs, should remain and function in the capitalist world market. No one proposes that they make a speedy transition to a socialist economic system or establish a close and exclusive economic association with the Communist Bloc.

The concept of "socialist orientation" gained currency in the late 1960s to denote states whose chosen course of development betokened a "socialist perspective." It was meant to amplify and replace the formula of the "noncapitalist path," which had been devised at the Moscow meeting of Communist and Workers' parties in 1960 to signify the period of transition toward socialism in the newly independent countries. The new term was coined under pressure from the Third World radicals who felt that the earlier phrasing belittled their efforts and political goals by its ambiguity and the absence of any Marxist affirmation. So, to salve hurt sensibilities, the transitional period was renamed with the talismanic word "socialist" in the more positive-sounding formulation. In keeping with the political style of the post-Khrushchev era, the change occurred without any official announcement; one cannot point to any conference or declaration that proclaimed the concept of socialist orientation. It simply came into use right alongisde the older term; both are employed more or less interchangeably, with no indication of what, if anything, differentiates them.

At first, until about 1976, socialist orientation was discussed almost exclusively in political terms. Political institutions — especially a properly organized revolutionary-democratic or vanguard party — were deemed essential for devising, implementing, and sustaining a program of progressive change. The question of appropriate economic policies was in effect ignored, but that accorded with the persisting belief in the primacy of politics over economics. As summed up at a scholarly conference: "A characteristic feature of every type of noncapitalist development is that socialist transition starts with the superstructure. . . . The political superstructure subsequently creates conditions for restructuring the socio-economic base."[54]

The reformulation of the tasks and prospects of socialist orientation that took place around 1976 was only partially connected with the growing sophistication in the Soviet outlook on international economics. Equally pressing for reassessment were the formation of large, self-proclaimed Marxist states in Africa after the collapse of the Portuguese Empire and the pro-Western shift in Egypt's domestic and foreign policies. The appearance of new, extremely underdeveloped and needy allies coupled with the loss of an economically viable and relatively advanced partner occurred at a time when the Soviet Union had far fewer resources to spare for international socialist solidarity.

The way Brezhnev addressed the issue of socialist orientation at the 25th and 26th Party Congresses, when seen in conjunction with the evolving academic commentary, throws light on how political desiderata were modified in the face of economic realities. In February 1976 Brezhnev still characterized socialist orientation as a new, positive development that had "enriched the political content" of Soviet ties with the Third World. The way he discussed the "complicated process of the class differentiation" in the liberated countries conveyed a conviction, as well as satisfaction, that socialist orientation was gaining ground. Five years later, as already noted, the First Secretary seemed much less certain. He did not claim primacy for any one political course in the Third World but noted that while some states followed the "revolutionary democratic path," in others "capitalist relations had taken root." As for states that had chosen the "progressive road," he underscored not their increasing number but the difficulties they faced. Among the prerequisites for their success, the "gradual elimination of the positions of imperialist monopolies, of the local big bourgeoisie and the feudal elements, and restriction of foreign capital" came first.[55] Strengthening the role of the revolutionary parties came last on the list. In other words, gradualist economic policies assumed precedence over politics.

After 1976 many specialists started describing socialist orientation not as a final systemic choice but as being a process that could be reversed. At the same time a clear-cut distinction was drawn between such states as Cuba or Vietnam, which were full-fledged socialist members of the Socialist Commonwealth as well as of CMEA (where the process was irreversible), and such states as Angola or Ethiopia, which are not members of the Soviet Bloc and are granted only the status of observer in CMEA.[56]

Among the most frequent reasons given for insisting on the distance that separates the radical states from both socialism and the Socialist Bloc is their backwardness. By now there are enough hints in the specialized literature that the countries choosing socialist orientation are also among the least developed. What is openly discussed, however, is that backwardness thwarts the speedy transition to, and establishment of, socialism, which the radical parties promise in their programs. According to Anatolii Gromyko, Director of the African Institute, the low level of economic development is the most significant domestic factor impeding the revolutionary process:

> The overriding objectively inhibiting factor is backwardness, which has persisted for centuries and cannot, of course, provide foundations for building socialist society, which requires the creation of certain essential material prerequisites.[57]

Backwardness, in turn, dictates certain domestic and international economic policies that have little to do either with socialist institutions or with Soviet aid. Concerning domestic policies, there are specialists who argue that there can be no question of an

> absolute and sudden termination of capitalist development and even more of the disappearance of all its elements and manifestations. . . . Capitalism, as one of the component sectors [*uklady*] of the national economy, continues to exist and in some spheres it even grows stronger.[58]

It is worth noting that when approaching the controversial and difficult issue of capitalist relations in socialist-oriented states, Soviet writers (whether it is Boris Ponomarev, Alternate Member of the Politbureau and the Central Committee's secretary in charge of relations with foreign Communists, or Evgenii Primakov, Director of the Oriental Studies Institute) now resort to the theory of the multilevel nature of the developing countries' economies. This once-disputed concept permits them to argue that tolerating private business in a situation, where it operates alongside the state and cooperative sectors, deprives it of the power to shape the character of the entire economy. Instead of coming to dominate the economic institutions and paving the way for the establishment of capitalism, private enterprise operating in a multisectoral economy acts only as a catalyst and contributes to the general maturation of conditions for the eventual advent of socialism. It is a very long-range and gradualist perspective indeed.

As for the place of the radical states in world economics, it is now accepted that they neither can nor should isolate themselves from the capitalist market. In fact, it is pretty much taken for granted, though not too vociferously argued in the open, that the states of socialist orientation remain part of the capitalist world economy (despite their choice of a political system that denies its validity and durability). *Kommunist* made the following pronouncement:

> As a result of a number of circumstances, [these] countries cannot end dependence on world capitalism since their economies, as in the colonial period, have a dependent and peripheral character. Despite strengthened economic ties with the Socialist Bloc and the utilization of these ties in transforming relations with the capitalist world, the socialist-oriented states are at present strongly connected with the

world capitalist market and in a number of cases (those of mono-culture) are inseparable from it.[59]

No Soviet political leader (or specialist) these days will offer unlimited Soviet or socialist support and aid (as was done under Khrushchev) or refer to the socialist international division of labor (as was customary in the early 1970s) as the way to speed up the economic liberation of the radical states. It is considered best for them to continue in their former economic placement and try to make that position more equitable and advantageous. Indeed, some academic experts now hold that what differentiates the contemporary theory of socialist orientation from the earlier concept of noncapitalist development is the fact that it is no longer necessary for the states that propose to build socialism to rely on close economic alliance with the Soviet Union.[60]

The more cautious writers have tended not to dwell overmuch on the handicaps of backwardness but claim that proper political leadership could in the long run surmount the economic obstacles. A significant segment of expert opinion, however, is much less sanguine on this issue. As Aleksei Kiva dryly noted in 1978 in a scholarly monograph on socialist orientation, political goals and economic necessity worked at cross-purposes:

> The political goals demand the speediest possible subordination of the economic basis to the revolutionary democratic superstructure through the all-around development of the state sector, elimination of foreign and local private enterprise from the national economy. But the economic circumstances dictate a different political line — attracting foreign and local capital for the development of the national economy.[61]

By 1981 many specialists closer to the sources of power saw the dilemma as serious. Thus Evgenii Primakov, in commenting on the difficulties facing the socialist-oriented states, pointed out two issues: the need to preserve and encourage the private sector; and the position of the radical developing countries, closely allied to the Socialist Bloc, in the world capitalist market.[62] Coming as an elaboration on Brezhnev's comments at the 26th Party Congress about the socialist orientation, his article underscored the growing doubts and worries about the immediate and long-range prospects of radicalism in the Third World.

With all the rethinking about the dictates of the economic situation, what do Soviet scholars (and political leaders) now accept as a workable system for the radical states? The answer inescapably points to a mixed economy open to participation in an international division of labor to which each state contributes and maximizes its gains by developing its natural resources. The term "mixed economy" is not widely used in the general discussion of development policies; most authors refer to it indirectly by arguing that capitalism has not yet exhausted its potential for generating growth. Surprisingly, though, it is quite frequently mentioned in discussing the appropriate policy for the socialist-oriented countries. It is what the Soviets now propose, to spare these states the costly and counter-productive excesses of premature socialist measures.

Significantly, no specific set of economic policies is now designated as being essential for a socialist orientation, other than the somewhat vague theory about the state being the controlling agent. This is as much a "socialist" doctrine as it is an acceptance of what actually prevails in the Third World anyway. The more orthodox specialists like to dwell on what the state power in these countries can accomplish:

> A mixed economy in the countries of socialist orientation . . . permits the utilization of capitalist elements [uklady] for the development of the production forces under state control in ways that prevent the transformation of these elements into the ruling capitalist system but create the preconditions for the victory of the state and cooperative sectors.[63]

Those specialists who concentrate more on economic performance than on political labels envision the operations of a mixed economy in less manipulative terms. Recognizing the weakness of the state apparatus, they speak about the "coexistence" of state and private sectors and quote from Engels that the state can successfully manage economic development only when it does not act as the sole agent but relies on the private sector.[64]

As for foreign capital, again realities are recognized. It is admitted that the West provides as much as 70 percent of the aid and credit to many radical regimes, and no one urges the doctrinaire nationalization or exclusion of Western investment. On the contrary, even the more conservative specialists argue that the socialist-oriented state should attract foreign capital and work out "such a system of regulation . . . that will guarantee the interests of the radical regimes and grant sufficient advantages to foreign investors to attract them."[65]

The evolution of Soviet perceptions has opened a gap between Moscow and Third World radical leaders. The radicals' views very much resemble the one-sided, confident arguments the Russians propounded some 25 years earlier. To quote the General Secretary of the Yemeni Socialist Party:

> Of tremendous importance in class and ideological terms is the fact that our efforts to build up the material and technical basis of the revolutionary transition period have gone hand in hand with the struggle to be completely rid of the control by international capitalism of our national market, and with the further development of our economic cooperation with the socialist world system. . . . After the victory of the Great October Socialist Revolution, Lenin repeatedly emphasized that the stage of capitalist development is not at all inevitable for all countries dominated by feudal and semi-feudal relations. Fraternal assistance from states in which the working class has taken over would help these countries to move faster to socialism. Now, more than 60 years after the October Revolution, with the Soviet state a mighty and steadily growing power . . . the transition to socialism, bypassing the stage of capitalist development, has undoubtedly become easier and has broader prospects before it.[66]

There have been no open disagreements and disputes, but the divergence is deep and unmistakable. Tension has arisen because the current Soviet understanding of the development timetable, of appropriate economic policies, and the role of Socialist Bloc assistance in this process has little in common with the outlook of its political allies and protégés. It is another bind in Soviet-Third World economic relations.

NOTES

1. *XXII S'ezd Kommunisticheskoi Partii Sovetskogo Soyuza. Stenograficheskii otchet* 3 (Moscow: Gospolitizdat, 1962), pp. 262-63.

2. Conference proceedings, *Sovetskoe vostokovedenie* (July-August 1958): 213-25.

3. *Planovoe khoziaistvo* (February 1962): 91-95.

4. Compare the more moderate *Problemy industrializatsii suverennykh slaborazvitykh stran Azii* (Moscow: Akademiya Nauk SSSR, 1960) with R. A. Ulianovsky, "O osobennostiakh razvitiya i kharaktere gosudarstvennogo kapitalizma v Indii," *Problemy vostokovedeniya* (May-June 1960): 28-29.

5. V. Rymalov, "Soviet Assistance to Underdeveloped Countries," *International Affairs* (September 1959): 25.

6. V. M. Kollontai, *Puti preodoleniya ekonomicheskoi otstalosti* (Moscow: Mezhdunarodnye otnosheniya, 1967), p. 206.

7. M. A. Andreev, "Trudnosti razvitiya gosudarstvennogo sektora Indonezii," *Narody Azii i Afriki* (September-October 1963): 34-41. Compare with V. Shelepin, "Africa: Why the Instability," *New Times* no. 52 (December 30, 1968): 21-24.

8. Compare E. A. Utkin, *Problemy planirovaniya v razvivayushchikhsia stranakh* (Moscow: Ekonomika, 1965) with V. Kollontai, "Voprosy planirovaniya v tret'em mire," *MEMO* (July 1969): 91-100, and the discussion in the journal's following three issues of the problems Kollontai raised.

9. N. P. Shmelev, "Razvivayushchiesia strany: formirovanie khoziaistvennogo mekhanizma," *MEMO* (August 1968): 52-62; R. Andreasian and A. Elianov, "Razvivayushchiesia strany: ekonomicheskaya diversifikatsiya i strategiya industrial'nogo razvitiya," ibid. (January 1968): 29-40.

10. R. Ulianovsky, "Nauchnyi sotsializm i osvobodivshiesia strany," *Kommunist* no. 4 (March 1968): 104. Compare with his views expressed at a conference on socialism and capitalism in the developing countries, *MEMO* (April 1964): 119.

11. *New Times* no. 29 (July 1967): 13-14.

12. Kollontai, *Puti preodoleniya*, pp. 184-95.

13. *MEMO* (April 1967): 106-27 and (May 1967): 93-108.

14. *Pravda*, June 25, 1967, p. 1.

15. For the best early analysis of the NEP model, see N. A. Simoniya, *Strany Vostoka: puti razvitiya* (Moscow: Nauka, 1975).

16. *Pravda*, February 24, 1981, p. 9.

17. *Razvivayushchiesia strany: zakonomernosti, tendentsii, perspektivy* (Moscow: Mysl', 1974), p. 133. The collective work by the Institute of Oriental Studies, *Zarubezhnyi Vostok i sovremennost'* 2 vols. (Moscow: Nauka, 1974), also called for detailed statistical studies of different regions and separate countries to introduce greater precision.

18. *Tipologiya nesotsialisticheskikh stran (opyt mnogomernogo statisticheskogo analiza narodnykh khoziaistv)* (Moscow: Nauka, 1976).

19. The concept of semi-developed capitalism was outlined by V. Sheinis, "Strany srednego kapitalizma," *MEMO* (September 1977): 105-24. It was subject to public discussion and criticism at an academic conference reported in *Latinskaya Amerika* (January-February 1979): 53-100. For "subimperialist centers" see E. Primakov, "Zakon neravnomernosti razvitiya i istoricheskie sud'by osvobodivshikhsia stran," *MEMO* (December 1980); 28-47; idem, *Vostok posle krakha kolonial'noi sistemy* (Moscow: Nauka, 1982).

20. E. Obminsky, *Razvivayushchiesia strany i mezhdunarodnoe razdelenie*

truda (Moscow: Mezhdunarodnye otnosheniya, 1974).

21. V. Tiagunenko, *Mezhdunorodnoe razdelenie truda i razvivayushchiesia strany* (Moscow: Nauka, 1976), pp. 9-10.

22. R. Ulianovsky, *Sovremennye problemy Azii i Afriki* (Moscow: Nauka, 1978), p. 230.

23. A. Levkovsky, ed. *Inostrannyi kapital i inostrannoe predprinimatel'stvo v strankakh Azii i Severnoi Afriki* (Moscow: Nauka, 1977), p. 17. Tiagunenko's last work observes the more cautious line, as does V. Rymalov's *Strukturnye izmeneniya v mirovom kapitalisticheskom khoziaistve* (Moscow: Mysl', 1978).

24. The expression is a composite of two words, *mnogo* (many) and *uklady* (structures). The English translation of *uklad* (singular of *uklady*) presents problems. Being part of Marxist theory, its meaning cannot be adequately rendered by one word. To put it simply, *uklady* are the various types of production relations that make up a country's economy. In a fully mature society, they coalesce into a formation — feudal, capitalist, or socialist. But until that is achieved, they constitute separate, interacting, and ever-evolving, structures or components.

25. S. Tiul'panov, "Obshchestvo perekhodnogo tipa," *MEMO* (January 1979): 144-46.

26. See V. Maksimenko's untitled review of A. Levkovsky's *Sotsial'naya struktura razvivayushchikhsia stran* (Moscow: Mysl', 1978) in *Narody Azii i Afriki* (January-February 1979): 208-14. A. U. Roslavlev's "Eshche raz o teorii 'mnogoukladnosti' v strankakh 'tret'ego mira,'" *Rabochii klass i sovremennyi mir* (January-February 1977): 136-45 is an excellent expression of conservative opinion.

27. Simoniya, *Strany Vostoka*. See also "Obsuzhdenie knigi N. Simoniya," *Narody Azii i Afriki* (May-June 1977): 54-65.

28. "Metodologicheskie problemy analiza ekonomicheskogo razvitiya v osvobodivshikhsia strankakh," in *Ekonomika razvivayushchikhsia stran. Teorii i metody issledovaniya*, ed. L. I. Reisner (Moscow: Nauka, 1979), pp. 186-210.

29. V. V. Zagladin and I. T. Frolov, *Global'nye problemy sovremennosti: nauchnyi i sotsial'nyi aspekty* (Moscow: Mezhdunarodnye otnosheniya, 1981), p. 76.

30. L. I. Reisner, *Razvivayushchiesia strany: ocherk teorii ekonomicheskogo rosta* (Moscow: Nauka, 1976), pp. 51-72, 321.

31. Boris Ponomarev at the international conference in Berlin, October 1980. See *Working Class and National-Liberation Movements: Joint Struggle against Imperialism, for Social Progress* (Moscow: Novosti, 1981), pp. 50-51.

32. See P. Khvoinik in *MEMO* (October 1980): 44-57 and L. Zevin in *Voprosy ekonomiki* (April 1982): 129-37.

33. *Strany SEV v mirokhoziaistvennykh sviaziakh* (Moscow: Nauka, 1978), pp. 115-17; N. N. Inozemtsev, ed., *Global'nye problemy sovremennosti* (Moscow, Mysl', 1981), p. 80.

34. A. I. Dinkevich, ed., *Razvivayushchiesia strany: nakoplenie i ekonomicheskii rost* (Moscow: Nauka, 1977), p. 23; L. I. Reisner, *Razvivayushchiesia strany: ocherk teorii ekonomicheskogo rosta* (Moscow: Nauka, 1976), p. 321; T. Pokataeva, *Razvivayushchiesia strany: problema urbanizatsii* (Moscow: Mysl', 1977).

35. M. Volkov, "Kontseptsiya osnovnykh potrebnostei," *Voprosy ekonomiki* (July 1981): 133-42 offers an orthodox, conservative response. For a greater range of views, see report on a round table conference on egalitarianism in the developing countries: *Narody Azii i Afriki* (November-December 1978): 3-19.

36. V. G. Khoros, "Udzhamaa: opyt nekapitalisticheskogo razvitiya," *Narody Azii i Afriki* (September-October 1977): 199-210; I. A. Svanidze, *Sel'skoe khoziaistvo i agrarnyi stroi Tropicheskoi Afriki* (Moscow: Nauka, 1977).

37. For an early expression of this position, see G. Rubinstein, "Problemy i trudnosti naibolee otstalykh stran," *MEMO* (August 1977): 128-33. For a later interpretation, see I. D. Ivanov, "Perestroika mezhdunarodnykh otnoshenii," in *Global'nye problemy sovremennosti*, ed. N. N. Inozemtsev (Moscow: Mysl', 1981), p. 253.

38. A. Yu. Shpirt, *Nauchno-tekhnicheskaya revoliutsiya i razvivayushchiesia strany* (Moscow: Nauka, 1970). The conference was reported in the June, July, and August issues of *MEMO* and led to the publication of '*Tret'ii mir' i nauchno-tekhnicheskii progress* (Moscow: Nauka, 1974).

39. V. Krylov, "Osobennosti razvitiya proizvoditel'nykh sil i vosproiz-vodstvennogo protesessa v razvivayushchikhsia stranakh," in *Ekonomika razvivayushchikhsia stran. Teorii i metody issledovaniya*, ed. L. I. Reisner (Moscow: Nauka, 1979), p. 183. See also M. A. Cheshkov's contribution on the state sector to the same volume, pp. 324-51.

40. G. E. Skorov, *Razvivayushiesia strany: obrazovanie, zaniatost', ekonomi-cheskii rost* (Moscow: Nauka, 1971); idem, ed., *Razvivayushchiesia strany: nauka, tekhnika, ekonomicheskii rost* (Moscow: Mysl', 1975); R. M. Avakov, *Razvivayushchiesia strany: nauchno-tekhnologicheskaya revoliutsiya i problema nezavisimosti* (Moscow: Mysl', 1976).

41. V. Sheinis, "O spetsifike sotsial'nykh protsessov v razvivayushchikhsia stranakh," *Aziya i Afrika segodnia* (November 1981): 27; O. Ul'rikh, "Preodolenie otstalosti v razvivayushchikhsia stranakh," *MEMO* (September 1981): 55.

42. B. G. Gafurov's *Aktual'nye problemy sovremennogo natsional'no-osvoboditel'nogo dvizheniya* (Moscow: Nauka, 1976) is a good example of conservative opinion. The discussion, "Neo-Colonialism – A New System of Dependence and Enslavement?," *International Affairs* (November 1978): 65-93, from which this quote is taken (p. 66), is a good example of the latter type of analysis.

43. L. V. Gavrilov's *Eksport kapitala v razvivayushchiesia strany Afriki* (Moscow: Nauka, 1976) was among the first works to be written in this spirit.

44. A. I. Medovoi and V. A. Yashkin, "Krizis kapitalisticheskoi formatsii," in *Razvivayushchiesia strany: problemy ekonomicheskogo razvitiya*, ed. A. I. Dinkevich (Moscow: Nauka, 1978), p. 28; A. S. Kodachenko, *Vneshneekonomi-cheskaya polityka imperializma i razvivayushchiesia strany* (Moscow: Nauka, 1977), pp. 26-51.

45. This view is specifically defined and defended by Levkovsky in the introduction to the volume he edited in 1977, *Inostrannyi kapital*. A. U. Roslavlev, "Eshche raz o teorii 'monogoukladnosti,'" pp. 144-45, attacks such opinions.

46. K. Brutents, *Osvobodivshiesia strany v 70-e gody* (Moscow: Politi-cheskaya literatura, 1979); E. Primakov, "Nekotorye problemy razvivayush-chikhsia stran," *Kommunist* no. 11 (July 1978): 81-91.

47. A. A. Kovalevsky, "Vozhmozhnosti tekhnologicheskogo transferta v eksportnye otrasli razvivayushchikhsia stran," in *Ekonomika razvivayushchikhsia stran. Teorii i metody issledovaniya*, ed. L. I. Reisner (Moscow: Nauka, 1979), pp. 7-21.

48. M. Maksimova, *SSSR i mezhdunarodnoe ekonomicheskoe sotrudni-chestvo* (Moscow: Mysl', 1977), pp. 35ff.

49. E. Primakov, "Nekotorye problemy," pp. 81-91; N. Volkova, "Nekotorye aspekty deyatel'nosti mnogonatsional'nykh korporatsii v razvivayushchikhsia stranakh," in *Inostrannyi kapital i inostrannoe predprinimatel'stvo v stranakh Azii i Severnoi Afriki*, ed. A. I. Levkovsky (Moscow: Nauka, 19,77), pp. 52-65; I. Ivanov, "Multinationals: What Kind of 'New World'?" 21 *World Marxist Review* (July 1978): 124.

50. E. Bragina, *Razvivayushchiesia strany: gosudarstvennaya polityka i promyshlennost'* (Moscow: Mysl', 1977); A. Elianov, *Razvivayushchiesia strany: problemy ekonomicheskogo razvitiya i rynok* (Moscow: Mysl', 1976).

51. V. P. Kolesov, *Gosudarstvennyi sektor ekonomiki razvivayushchikhsia stran* (Moscow: Moskovskii Universitet, 1977).

52. A. I. Levkovsky, *Sotsial'naya struktura razvivayushchikhsia stran* (Moscow: Mysl', 1979), pp. 148-73; M. A. Cheskov, "Metodologicheskie problemy analiza gosuklada," *Ekonomika razvivayushchikhsia stran. Teorii i metody issledovaniya*, ed. L. I. Reisner (Moscow: Nauka, 1979), pp. 324-51; V. Yashkin, "Gosudarstvennyi uklad v mnogoukladnoi ekonomike," *Aziya i Afrika segodnia* (March 1979): 40-44.

53. Peter Wiles, ed., *The New Communist Third World* (New York: St. Martin's Press, 1982).

54. "The Theory and Practice of the Non-Capitalist Way of Development," *International Affairs* (November 1970): 13. For a later work with a similar bend, see *Afrika: problemy sotsialisticheskoi orientatsii* (Moscow: Nauka, 1976).

55. *Pravda*, February 25, 1976, p. 2; ibid., February 24, 1981, p. 2.

56. R. Ulianovsky, "O stranakh sotsialisticheskoi orientatsii," *Kommunist* no. 11 (July 1979): 118; idem, "Dvadtsatyi vek i natsional'no-osvoboditel'noe dvizhenie," *Narody Azii i Afriki* (March-April 1980): 6-7.

57. "Socialist Orientation in Africa," *International Affairs* (September 1979): 103.

58. E. Primakov, "Strany sotsialisticheskoi orientatsii: trudnyi no real'nyi put' perekhoda k sotsializmu," *MEMO* (July 1981): 8, 16.

59. Ulianovsky, "O stranakh sotsialisticheskoi orientatsii," p. 117.

60. Primakov, "Strany sotsialisticheskoi orientatsi," pp. 4-7.

61. A. Kiva, *Strany sotsialisticheskoi orientatsii. Osnovnye tendentsii razvitiya* (Moscow: Nauka, 1979), p. 28.

62. Primakov, "Strany sotsialisticheskoi orientatsii," p. 16.

63. G. B. Starushenko, *Sotsialisticheskaya orientatsiya v razvivayushchikhsia stranakh* (Moscow: Politicheskaya literatura, 1977), pp. 51-52.

64. Yashkin, "Gosudarstvennyi uklad," p. 41.

65. Starushenko, *Sotsialisticheskaya orientatsiya*, p. 51.

66. Abdel Fattah Ismail, "A New Vanguard Party," *World Marxist Review* 22 (January 1979): 24, 28.

4

THE NEW INTERNATIONAL ECONOMIC ORDER: THE PARTING OF THE WAYS

From the outset Moscow's response to the New International Economic Order (NIEO) has been marked by anti-imperialist rhetoric and the assertion of common Soviet-Third World interests. This stance has led many observers to conclude that Moscow's main objective is to utilize the NIEO negotiations to exacerbate the confrontation between the industrialized North and the developing South. Although that disruptive aim cannot be discounted, it is evident that at present the persistence of the traditional anti-Western arguments also serves to camouflage difficulties arising from the incompatibility of political and economic aims: the pursuit of an anti-imperialist diplomacy does not always square with the Soviet Bloc's growing involvement in the world market where the interests of the Soviet Union and the developing countries do not necessarily coincide.

For the first 20 years, the Soviet penetration of the Third World was facilitated by a congruence between political and economic policies. Regardless of whether Moscow granted huge sums for demonstration-effect projects or began to seek tangible benefits from its aid-trade programs, the assumption was that the international economic interests of the Soviet Union and the Third World coincided. But the appearance of the developing countries' own program of demands vis-à-vis the industrialized North, coming as it did in the mid-1970s when the Soviet Union became engrossed in internationalizing its own economy, has undercut the former harmony.

There has been no open break between the USSR and the Third World on international economic matters. But a parting of the ways is occurring. Conflicting aims, unresolved policies, and some serious fissures can be detected from several sources.

First, there is a definite evolution in the Soviet response to the NIEO program. The growing integration of the Soviet economy with an acknowledged single world market made Moscow lose zest for a radical restructuring of international economic relations for the benefit of the developing countries. A separate Soviet program is emerging in the formal presentations at the United Nations. Its basis is worldwide economic coexistence, a perception that is more evident in specialist writings than in official statements, where it tends to be muted so as not to contradict Moscow's diplomatic line of a common anti-imperialist front with the LDCs.

Second, there are the needs and views of Eastern Europe, where economic imperatives have already qualified dogma. In Moscow it is still an unresolved issue to what extent, and in what manner, to integrate in the world economy, but the problem is much more clear-cut for Eastern Europe. These countries are trade dependent and because of the recent Soviet decision to restrict their fuel supplies, trade has become a question of solvency. As a result, the East Europeans have been pressing for economic policies far more clearly divorced from political dogma than is the case in the USSR. Hence, Hungarian or Polish discussions of the NIEO shed light on an alternate policy the Soviet Union could follow should it choose to separate economic from political behavior to a greater degree than it does at present.

Finally, there are the developing countries themselves, which are no longer the passive objects of world politics. As independent actors on the global scene, their economic views and their requirements have visibly diverged from what Moscow professes or can offer. On the ideological level, many Third World economists espouse various versions of the dependency theory, which departs from and supplants Marxism. In matters of trade, the current needs of the more advanced countries have outstripped the technological capacity of the Soviet Union to supply them. The poorest countries, on the other hand, tend to espouse Marxism and press in its name for international and domestic policies more radical than the ones the USSR cares to pursue. The increased assertiveness on the part of the LDCs creates ideological challenges and practical problems for the Soviet Union, which are all the more difficult to meet because of the diversification in the Third World.

THE FOURTH AND FIFTH UNCTAD SESSIONS AND BEYOND

At first Moscow welcomed the concerted economic claims the Third World began to press against the West in the early 1970s. In Soviet eyes, the demands of the Group of 77 had resulted, in part, from the exemplary economic relations ("self-less" and "equivalent") that the USSR had instituted in its dealings with the former colonial areas. By exposing Western exploitation, Bloc aid and trade programs, the Soviets believed, served as the model for the just economic order the developing countries were seeking. Any concessions they managed to wrest from the West, it was further assumed, would automatically bring political and economic gains for the Soviet Union.

Given this interpretation, when the grievances and demands of the developing countries coalesced in the Declaration of the New International Economic Order, adopted at the sixth special session of the U.N. General Assembly in 1974, the Soviet Union endorsed it. In the words of Andrei Gromyko, the Soviet representative at that session, "it was a progressive code of rules by which states should be guided in their economic relations."[1]

The optimistic appraisal of the NIEO demands was apparent on many levels. To begin at the obvious propagandistic level, May Day and October Revolution slogans began to express support for the "transformation of international economic relations on a just and democratic basis" in the customary appeals to the newly independent peoples to struggle for the consolidation of their independence and for a progressive road of development.[2] Similarly, the June 1976 Berlin Conference of Communist and Workers' Parties mentioned the common struggle of the Socialist countries, the nonaligned movement, and the LDCs for the "establishment of new international . . . economic relations on the basis of justice and equality."[3]

Among scholars specializing on Soviet-Third World economic relations, the same upbeat note prevailed with many references to the "common struggle" for creating a NIEO based on justice, sovereign equality, and the right of developing countries to manage their own resources. On the eve of the fourth UNCTAD for example, one specialist gave a sanguine appraisal of the LDCs' growing role in world affairs. It rested on three aspects of "the attack against the positions of imperialism, colonialism and neocolonialism," mounted by the Third World. First, the initial inchoate movement for partial concessions had developed into a united front and into a comprehensive program for the reconstruction of international economic relations that would undermine the very basis of the world capitalist economy. Second, these demands carried real weight since the newly independent states controlled the world's supplies of natural resources. Third, some concessions (regarding the removal of trade discrimination, price stabilization, compensatory financing, and so on) already granted to developing countries had not only started to redistribute resources in favor of the LDCs but also weakened their dependence on international capital.[4]

Optimism about the thrust of the Third World's demands for the reconstruction of global economic relations, the leverage the developing countries could exert, and the ability of the Soviet Union to shape the new forces suffused the joint statement presented by the Soviet Bloc to the fourth UNCTAD at Nairobi in May 1976. In effect, it was an attempt to weave the demands of the Soviet Union and the LDCs into a separate program, standing as an alternative to the existing world order dominated by the capitalist powers. It welcomed various "progressive resolutions" proposed by the developing countries at the U.N. forums as "important milestones" toward a "radical restructuring of the capitalist international division of labor." It enumerated the baneful consequences the LDCs had suffered in their interaction with the capitalist states, and argued that "there exist in the world . . . two fundamentally different bases for the conduct of commercial and economic relations with the developing countries." Delineating the diametrically opposed ways of dealing with the developing countries offered by the socialist and the capitalist systems, the joint statement went on to offer the practice that had evolved in Soviet Bloc-Third World arrangements as a "new kind of economic relations" and a model for the implementation of the NIEO. After stating all this in 4 pages of preamble, the following 20 pages outlined the existing or a slightly expanded and improved pattern of

Soviet Bloc-Third World exchanges. Specifically, it proposed specialization in industrial production, coordination in national planning, and pooling of resources for the development of entire regions as the basis for a new international division of labor. In general, the principles of planning, long-term intergovernmental agreements, production cooperation, and compensation agreements between states to establish fair prices and limit the effects of market forces and of the multinationals were set forth as measures that would improve both the functioning of international trade and the position of the LDCs.

The technical aspects of the Soviet Bloc's proposal are not central to the subject of this book, beyond the fact that they were predicated, as already stated, on existing practices. What is pertinent are the political and other assumptions about the nature of Soviet-Third World relations the proposal was based on. The statement held that the "essence of mutual interest of the socialist and the developing countries" derived from the fact that both sides were "firmly on the side of progress" and for the "creation of a favorable climate for the breaking-up . . . of the outmoded system of inequitable economic relations within the world capitalist system." Furthermore, there were references to the "increased capacity" of CMEA members to "undertake large-scale projects in the developing countries" and to "enrich the concrete forms of mutual economic relations." In other words, there were common anticapitalist interests, which could be sustained by the economic strength of the Bloc.[5]

Press commentary on the Nairobi meeting echoed the same spirit. It was argued that the developing countries' struggle for the NIEO involved "issues that go to the heart of the capitalist system." Furthermore, the development of "diverse and firm links between the young national and the socialist states" would have "a strong impact on the relations between the developing and the advanced capitalist states," and the nature of contacts between the Soviet Bloc and the LDCs would help the future reconstruction.[6]

However, signs of strain that belied this sanguine scenario were evident on a more important level. On October 4, 1976, the Soviet Union submitted to the thirty-first session of the U.N. General Assembly the Declaration on the Restructuring of International Economic Relations in which Moscow for the first time articulated objections to some items in the LDC program. The declaration listed three shortcomings of the NIEO program, as presented by the developing countries: namely, it held the socialist and the capitalist countries equally responsible for the plight of the LDCs; it ignored the connection between disarmament and increased aid; and it did not address the whole gamut of discrimination in international trade.[7]

The growing distance between the Soviet and the Third World approaches to international economics was being marked in other ways. Beginning in 1978 the anniversary slogans stopped including the NIEO demands among the anti-imperialist and anticapitalist issues that merited the praise and support of the CPSU. In addition, specialized works on international economic problems began to distinguish between three different programs for the new world order. According to one study, the developed capitalist countries strove to overcome various crises that afflicted them by proposing a world order that would firmly integrate the LDCs into the capitalist system; the LDCs wanted to attain an equivalent position through the redistribution of world resources to their own benefit; and the Socialist Bloc sought to utilize the international division of labor to further disarmament and détente, to aid the LDCs, and to create more favorable conditions for socialist construction.[8]

Not surprisingly then, the Soviet Union presented a proposal based on a different set of assumptions to the fifth UNCTAD session held in Manila in May 1979. To be sure, it contained many arguments that were familiar by then, reiterating that the industrialized West was responsible for the developing countries' plight, that Soviet-Third World relations were qualitatively different from those between the West and the South, and that a close affinity obtained between the Socialist and the LDC aims to change world economic relations.

But what was unfamiliar, indeed novel, was the articulation of five points that retreated from previous positions. Foremost, the Soviet Bloc's statement conceded that the developing countries were being more and more closely "bound to capitalism's main industrial centers" (point 8). Second, it acknowledged that because of the closer association between the South and the West, it was becoming difficult for the Socialist countries to "increase their participation in the world-wide division of labor and to develop . . . new forms of long-term, large-scale economic, scientific and technical cooperation" (point 13). Third, there was an implicit distancing from the developing countries' demands, in the sense that the restructuring of international economic relations was treated as a separate issue that was *not* equivalent to the "efforts to ensure normal conditions for the development of the young states" (point 4). Fourth, the idea (only tangentially mentioned at the fourth UNCTAD) that what was required was a "comprehensive restructuring in all areas of world trade" (that is, including East-West exchanges) was much more explicitly expressed (point 21). Finally the statement held that it was possible to "democratize" international economic relations and to "ensure the equitable and mutually profitable participation in such relations of all groups of countries and systems of property ownership" even before the "inherent defects of capitalism" had been eliminated from the operations of the world economy (point 22).[9]

These new points, scattered throughout ten pages filled with the old slogans, clearly showed the rudiments of a new Soviet approach. It went far beyond the previous demands to include disarmament issues and objections to having the Socialist countries counted with the affluent North.

The Communist Bloc's statement to the fifth UNCTAD reflected the evolving Soviet views on the nature of the international economy, namely, its globally interdependent character, which in turn dictates a more universalistic approach based on economic coexistence, not on confrontation. For the overarching aim of restructuring the world economic order, it posited the principle of nondiscrimination (economically a more neutral term) whose introduction would benefit more nations than the elimination of exploitation (politically a normative notion).

Another novel point was the admission of the Soviet Bloc's difficulties in expanding its economic activities in the Third World. It was a statement of fact that did not touch on ideology. And undoubtedly it was that hard fact that stirred the Bloc's interest for codifying the general rules of the game.

This more moderate global vision certainly diverged from the developing countries' outlook, which still embodied many assumptions of the traditional Soviet demonology. Yet, despite the striking contrast with old ways of thinking, the Bloc's statement to the fifth UNCTAD was not meant to herald or justify a break with the Third World program. It advanced the argument that only .by a closer adherence on the part of the developing countries to Soviet desiderata could they be assured of a truly equitable place in the international economy. To quote one ingenious line of reasoning that tried to prove the unity of Soviet and Third World interests from the global vantage point:

> There is no alternative to joint action by the socialist and the developing countries because, in view of the degree of economic rapprochement between countries, it would be illusory to believe that the pattern and standards of international trade can be reconstructed for one group of countries alone while restrictions and discrimination are maintained for another. . . . The developing and socialist countries alike are harmed . . . by protectionism. (point 21)

Since the fifth UNCTAD marked changes have occurred in the Soviet handling of the Bloc's agenda in the context of the NIEO debates. At first the Socialist countries tried what might be termed a policy of "sitting on both stools." This course was followed at the third UNIDO conference in February 1980. The Soviet Bloc voted for the New Delhi Declaration and Plan of Action, which were duly vetoed by the Western states. But at the same time, the Bloc also tabled an additional statement disavowing this vote:

> The vote . . . in favor of the Declaration and Plan of Action is not to be regarded as implying their automatic support for those decisions . . . in the formulation of which [the socialist states] did not participate or regarding which, at the time of their adoption, they expressed reservations.[10]

In short, the Bloc voted for the resolutions and then shelved them. (The Socialist states had principally objected to the call for the establishment of a Global Fund to which all the richer countries, regardless of differences in their social systems, should contribute.)

By the fall of 1982, a much clearer line was evident. The Soviet statement to the twenty-fifth session of the UNCTAD Trade and Development Board — held in preparation for the sixth UNCTAD meeting in June 1983 — omitted any references to imperialism, to the disadvantaged position of the LDCs, or to common Socialist Bloc-Third World interests. Phrased in legal terms, it objected to manipulating trade for political purposes: "Trade restrictions that are introduced for other than economic reasons cannot be justified from the point of view of international trade law and violate the fundamental principles of the operations of the international trade system."[11]

Put briefly, the Soviet Union now claims that trade subordinated to political goals "conflicts with the objective trends in the development of world economic activity." Furthermore, it considers this "depoliticized" approach appropriate for an international meeting convened to redress the injustices the developing countries claim they incur in world trade. Although the Soviet statement fully reflects the course of recent reassessment by specialists, it remains to be seen whether the USSR will choose to pursue such an unideological line in its official proposals to the sixth UNCTAD.

REASSESSMENT AMONG SOVIET SPECIALISTS

At international meetings Moscow has shown a stubbornly contrary, even if not always consistent, profile. But at home, there is much discussion and reassessment among the specialists. This active interest in the NIEO testifies to the perceived need to undertake new initiatives to break out of the ideological and practical impasse.

Basically, two approaches are evident in the community of specialists. One group has a more ideological and essentially "optimistic" outlook; the other displays a more economic concern and in that sense tends to be realistic or even "pessimistic." (But one must constantly keep in mind all the qualifications one should have at hand when discussing group interests or positions in Moscow, as well as the relevance of Western labels to Soviet situations.)

The so-called optimists tend to take ideology as the starting point and proceed from the position of strength. Thus they emphasize that the achievements and policies of the Soviet Bloc have already changed the nature of international economic relations and will heavily influence future transformations. Further, they tend to argue that it is the capitalist countries that are beset by various crises and need the restructuring, while the Socialist Bloc has already solved the problems of production and exchange within its own area and in its relations with the developing countries. In fact, they contend that current Bloc practices in long-term cooperation and exchange provide ready models for reforming the world economic order. The latter group, on the other hand, proceeding from a global viewpoint, acknowledges much more explicitly the suprasystemic nature of world problems. Since interdependence is so patent for this group, it is more open-minded about reform and not insistent that Soviet-type solutions provide the best model.[12]

Hence, the responses of the two groups to the demands of developing countries differ. With an eye to the diplomatic aspects, the optimists prefer to argue that the Soviet and the LDC programs coincide "in the main," that Moscow supports the Group of 77 "in principle" (because of its generally democratic and anti-imperialist nature), and that the developing countries rely on and cherish this support. The realists have tended to be more forthright about the conflict of interests and admit that there are "substantial differences" in the Soviet and the Third World conceptions of NIEO issues.[13] Nevertheless, despite these different inflections, the fact remains that Soviet experts currently share a common point of departure and "do not idealize the NIEO movement."[14] Although the first, so-called optimistic, group repeats some of the familiar arguments from official statements, when it comes to specific issues it is as hardnosed and realistic as the second. Regardless of their starting points, Soviet experts, in their discussions, increasingly express reservations and objections to the Third World program and in the process are hammering out the conceptual framework for a Soviet response. The theoretical clarity and factual specificity that has been lacking in official statements to the United Nations is much more present in the exchanges at home.

Objections to the developing countries' version of the NIEO extend far beyond its grouping the Soviet Union with the rich North and burdening the Socialist states with the same responsibilities (or bill) as the other industrial powers. Ideological and economic axioms are spun out for the programmatic rejection of the premises and specifics in the proposals the Group of 77 advances.

On the theoretical level, objections to three fundamental shortcomings in the developing countries' version of the NIEO have been spelled out: the departures from universalistic principles, indifference to domestic reforms, and divergence from Marxism. The first two objections are voiced quite openly at home and abroad. The last is still restricted to domestic discussions since it concerns infighting between the ideologues and the pragmatists on the very sensitive issue of the degree to which the economic aspects of Soviet relations with the Third World can be depoliticized.

It is a well-articulated Soviet position that to be effective any restructuring of international economic relations must include all states (capitalist, socialist, and developing). In other words, it cannot be narrowly interpreted as an aggregate of measures in the interest of the LDCs alone or only concerning North-South relations. Specialists write extensively that the NIEO program, as it now stands, is much too limited in scope, being directed primarily at rectifying the malfunctionings in the system of exchanges with the former metropoles. Some use political arguments, claiming that the universal application of the principles of equality, justice, and nondiscrimination is what makes the Soviet Bloc's proposals "democratic" and "progressive." This is pretty much the line the Soviets proclaim at international meetings. Thus the Bloc's statement at the fifth UNCTAD maintained that only the policy of the Socialist states is "aimed from the very outset at the restructuring of international economic relations on an equitable and democratic basis." (point 18)

But technical, economic arguments in support of universalism are advanced in domestic discussion. Here, specialists argue that given the internationalization and interdependence of the world economy and the intensifying global problems, genuine solutions must be based on the needs and capacities of the entire international economic community. Even so staid an organ as the Party's theoretical journal, *Kommunist*, posits the following in introducing a discussion on restructuring the economic order:

> The internationalization of various spheres of economic activity is an inseparable, important part of contemporary international life. Scientific technological progress has opened up unforeseen prospects for increasing the scale of economic exchange and raising the effectiveness of foreign economic relations. . . . However, the current state of world economic relations with all certainty bears witness to the fact that the enormous opportunities of international exchange are being as yet utilized to an insignificant degree.[15]

Such a view of the world economy removes foreign capital's pernicious control of the developing countries from stage center. Discrimination is seen as universal and not just affecting the LDCs alone. Alongside the well-known inequities suffered by the former colonies, there is mention of the difficulties experienced by the advanced capitalist countries — that is, the trade, financial and payment crises that contribute to mass unemployment. Not only that, but the Soviets are more explicit about the losses sustained by the Socialist countries because of the prevailing inequalities:

> In their relations with the non-socialist world, [they] lose tens and at times hundreds of millions of dollars from the unfavorable relationship of export and import prices, devaluation of capitalist currencies, discriminatory trade and credit policies, the bankruptcy and nonpayment of [their] capitalist partners, restrictions on the acquisition of latest technology.[16]

The developing countries' version of the NIEO is also found wanting in its indifference to domestic reform. A redistribution of wealth among states is pressed, while social equality at home is ignored. This criticism is reiterated at international meetings and in Soviet scholarly publications:

> Some theoreticians and political leaders of the Third World detach the problem of transforming external economic ties from domestic transformation. . . . It is fully evident that if the reconstruction of international economic relations will take place without radical domestic socio-economic transformation . . . the increase in the inflow of external resources can result in enriching the ruling elites and the further growth of social inequality in a number of states.[17]

And concerning Soviet support, it is now stated that:

> the Socialist countries, while cooperating with the LDCs for the reconstruction of international economic relations, advance from the position that the success of that movement can be assured under conditions of combining democratic changes in the old system of the international division of labor and trade with progressive social transformations in the developing countries themselves.[18]

At international forums the Soviets are as critical of the Third World elites who seek to appropriate the riches to be derived from NIEO as they are in their domestic publications; they insist on linking the restructuring of international economic relations with progressive domestic changes in the developing countries. This requirement was stressed in the Bloc's statement at the fifth UNCTAD meeting (points 8 and 12), whereas it was conspicuously absent in the Bloc's statement at the fourth conference. Moreover, this view is expressed by Soviet speakers at international seminars held under the auspices of the United Nations. Thus, at the UNITAR seminar in Moscow, Vladimir Yashkin stipulated that economic and social justice is an integral part of NIEO:

> No reform of the international economic relations, even the most progressive one, can yield desirable results unless it is reinforced by progressive changes in the internal structure of the developing countries, i.e., by the establishment of a new social order which would meet the fundamental interests of the majority of the working people.[19]

Finally, some specialists question the propriety of Soviet support for the Third World program on Marxist grounds. The issue was first broached in general articles explicating the Marxist view of the determinants of change in international economic relations. Change results not from the developing countries' claims against the capitalist states but from the growth of the Socialist community's economic power, the configuration of class forces in the developed capitalist countries, and the class nature of the LDC regimes. Later, upon conceding the diversity of the LDCs and their varying roles in the capitalist world market, it became possible (and logical) to argue that the NIEO program was not aimed at undermining capitalism as a world system. To quote one opinion: "Despite the anti-imperialist and anti-monopoly direction [of NIEO], it remains in the framework of capitalism and does not question the basic principles on which the world capitalist economy is based."[20]

Other specialists take the class argument further and in the context of NIEO discussions draw attention to the fact that some developing countries have become "sub-imperialist centers" with a "tendency toward economic expansion into less developed regions and increased participation in the struggle for spheres of influence." Or they focus on the class composition of many Third World regimes — rich oil bourgeoisie, bureaucratic bourgeoisie, military dictatorships — and question whether the NIEO concept promoted by such governments can truly be anti-imperialist and coincide with the interests of the genuine revolutionary forces.[21]

THE INTERNATIONAL DIVISION OF LABOR AT PRESENT

What is the substance of the new democratic world order proposed by Soviet specialists? They favor the expansion of international trade as largely conditioned by an appropriate specialization among all countries. This production and export-oriented plan is touted as an improvement over the "utopian" distribution-oriented program of the developing countries. Soviet economists deny that the goals of the NIEO can be reached merely through redistribution measures or by a more equitable apportioning of the world's income:

> The decisive condition for a full achievement of the purposes of the new international economic order is all-out growth of productive capacity, to be achieved through the optimum combination of domestic resources and the potential of international cooperation.[22]

Within that context, then, existing domestic and international situations suggest that Third World countries concentrate on developing their natural resources. Fuel and raw materials are generally located in the Third World, and the more advanced countries need them. Therefore, there is a natural complementarity between what most of the LDCs have in abundance and what the rest of an interdependent world requires. This commodity-based development strategy should not be taken as the crass relegation of the developing countries to their traditional role as suppliers of raw materials. Instead, it is seen as the optimal and most feasible solution to get the LDCs started on the road to development and eventual industrialization by making maximum use of their own resources rather than relying on foreign aid handouts. In an ideal, equivalent, and balanced international division of labor, the developing countries will specialize in the production of what is already at their disposal, acquiring the necessary surpluses and skills in the process in order to advance toward a diversification of their economies. They will proceed first to labor-intensive food and processing industries with their intermediate technologies and eventually advance to a heavy industry buildup utilizing the latest know-how.[23]

This Soviet version of the new economic order dovetails with the economic needs and plans of the CPEs. By the late 1970s, Moscow began showing genuine concern about the availability of fuel and raw materials for both itself and its European allies. Although the huge reserves in the USSR are usually cited as assuring the Bloc against serious shortages, it is increasingly argued by Soviet economists that the inhospitable location of many natural resources makes their extraction exceedingly costly. As noted in Chapter 1, the comparative advantage of importing raw materials from the developing countries in return for Soviet machinery exports has to a large extent guided Soviet aid-trade operations since the late 1960s. Expansion of this economic policy has become crucial because of more recent development – the rise in fuel prices, the resulting payment difficulties and shortages in Eastern Europe, plus the Soviet decision of 1980 to start tapering off its fuel exports to the European CMEA members.

The CMEA plans call for increased trade and cooperation with the LDCs, and the East European economists write that their countries will increasingly rely on imports from the Third World for their raw material supplies. (Imports of foodstuffs and shifting some labor-intensive industries to the Third World are also discussed, but with less urgency.) Because ready cash is lacking, the Soviet Bloc specialists propose a concerted effort to expand a regularized division of labor based on compensation-type credits to develop natural resources, repayable in products resulting from that cooperation:

> These credits represent, in essence, a real alternative to domestic investment by CMEA countries and assure an economic gain, help find effective solutions by way of optimal combination of domestic and foreign factors in the solution of the fuel-raw material problems in the CMEA countries.[24]

Against this background, the optimal international economic strategy the Soviets offer as a socialist variant for the NIEO looks like a panacea for the Bloc's problems.

In addition to solving domestic supply problems, this international division of labor also enhances the role the Soviet Union would like to see itself play on the world market. Experts tend to treat Soviet-Third World relations as complementing East-West exchanges, that is, as fitting into a global three-way relationship in which the USSR occupies the middle ground. To simplify the schema to its barest elements, what they would like to see occur in Soviet relations with the Third World is a mirror image of their idealized version of the complementary nature of East-West relations, as reflected in the following passage:

> An important element of the Soviet Union's long-term and large-scale economic cooperation with Western countries takes the form of compensation transactions of mutual interest to both sides. The Soviet Union is interested in buying from the industrially developed countries machines and equipment on a credit basis . . . to develop its natural resources and to create more capacity for manufacturing new products for domestic consumption and for export. In their turn, its Western partners are interested in large-scale Soviet purchases as well as in reliable and stable supplies of primary materials and other goods in repayment of the credits granted.[25]

The ideal scenario of global cooperation, where some sort of "invisible hand" would guide the multilevel flow of goods and services among the three groups, would look something like this: while the most advanced countries would find it profitable to invest in the development of Soviet raw materials and industry, the Socialist Bloc with its less advanced technology would in turn find it advantageous to deal with the LDCs. The role of the Third World would be to produce the natural resources to fuel the economies of all the industrialized states, benefiting in turn from their assistance and accumulating funds and know-how for building up processing industries. This harmonious interaction would emerge not only from bilateral but also through various multilateral arrangements. These include joint Soviet/CMEA and Western projects in the developing countries or joint ventures of the Soviet Union and the more advanced LDCs in third countres. In the first type of arrangement, the West would provide the advanced technology; the USSR or the Bloc, much of the middle-level technology; and the LDCs chiefly their labor and raw materials, at least in the early stages and where it would be appropriate. In the case of joint USSR-Third World ventures in other developing countries, the Soviet Union would be the technologically advanced partner.[26]

To repeat, although, this triangular vision of how the world economy should operate has not been spelled out, it underlies arguments such as this:

The similarity between the developing countries' economic structures and assortment of export goods, as well as their inability at present to deal with the more complex production and scientific-technical problems, induce them to cooperate with the developed countries, including those with different social systems. Among the most worthwhile spheres of cooperation one can list the following: joint participation of organizations from socialist and capitalist countries in the construction of major hydropower stations or thermal and nuclear stations; metallurgical complexes; prospecting for and producing minerals.[27]

Unlikely as such schemes may seem, they comport with the newly found significance, for the Soviets, of the single world economy and global interdependence. Moreover, disenchantment with the developing countries' version of the NIEO stimulated Soviet efforts, both officially and in the academic community, to somehow bridge the gap in the treatment of East-South and East-West economic relations. As already indicated, until the NIEO issue became pressing, relations with the West and with the LDCs were kept strictly separate. The advantages of expanding trade with the West were presented in a fairly matter-of-fact manner; the benefits of interdependence were patent and unencumbered by political rationalization. But the pursuit of economic advantage in the Third World was not presented with equal candor, being obfuscated by normative assumptions and claims. Two different sets of economic laws seemed to obtain.

It was a remarkable departure for the Soviets to argue in their statement to the fifth UNCTAD in May 1979 not merely that East-West relations must be included in the process of restructuring international economic relations but further that East-West trade "constituted an integral part of the UNCTAD global mandate" (point 21). Since then the Soviet Union has consistently pressed that UNCTAD act as a universal organization and concern itself with all the flows of international trade.[28]

While Soviet pronouncements at the United Nations press for the equal treatment of all systems, discussion among specialists sometimes goes well beyond systemic bounds. For instance, there is the recent argument that East-West relations serve as exemplars for wider application; in other words, that the same economic laws and legal norms should apply to all Soviet economic exchanges whether they are with the West or the South. In such proposals, the former distinction between purely and not-so-purely economic laws and modes of action tends to disappear. Thus in no less a place than the pages of the Party's theoretical journal, it has been argued that the principles outlined in Basket II of the Helsinki agreements (and the East-West exchanges that ensue) offer pertinent lessons and good prospects for relations with the South.[29]

The seriousness of the Soviet intention to have the developing countries participate in international cooperation on the basis of ordinary economic principles — as now understood in the USSR — is underscored by the criticisms made of Third World plans for regional cooperation and self-reliance (discussed below). As Soviet interest and advocacy of global interdependence grows, so does the aversion to any hints of economic isolationism on the part of the LDCs. Two recent books on global problems both censured it. The Zagladin-Frolov volume approved of regionalism only to the extent that it fended off the multinationals (in other words, as self-defense), but it frowned on regionalism as a basic component for development strategy. The IMEMO study took a more outspokenly negative line on regionalism and self-reliance as creating serious hindrances to the operations of the world economy. It was natural for the developing countries to seek ways to overcome their asymmetric dependence. But in its extreme manifestations, the book argued, such a policy became one of economic separatism, "communicating with the rest of the world in the language of raw material anti-cartels. . . . Of course, this extreme variant does not offer genuine solutions to global problems, not to mention that from a technical-economic viewpoint it is deliberately utopian."[30]

These reservations on regionalism betray a sense of uneasiness about the compatibility between the Soviet and Third World programs for the new economic order. Other possible obstacles are not discussed in detail in the printed materials; analysis centers predominantly on the advantages to be gained from the arrangements the Soviets propose. This skirting of the difficulties indicates that how to respond to the NIEO remains an unresolved issue. An internal debate is going on, which turns on two related questions: To what extent and in what manner should the Soviet economy be internationalized? To what extent should economic desiderata be subordinated to political and diplomatic interests? The lack of consensus on these two questions prevents a clear-cut response to the NIEO.

EAST EUROPEAN VIEWS

Since Soviet internal debates are obfuscated by ideology and indecision, it is instructive to see what other Socialist Bloc members have to say about the CPEs' interest in Third World trade and about the obstacles to devising an appropriate NIEO policy. Basically, they are urging a positive, pragmatic, and hence depoliticized response in order not to lose out on the world market.

Reflecting the greater trade dependence of their countries, East European studies of NIEO issues are much more candid in addressing needs, prospects, and problems. Hungarian, Bulgarian, or Polish economists can be more forthright for other reasons as well. Since the Soviet Union preempts the leadership of the Socialist camp and proclaims the principles of socialist international behavior, the East Europeans do not have to shoulder that diplomatic and political burden. Moreover, the tradition of much less politicized scholarship permits them to address issues as they are without having to find justification in the classics of Marxism-Leninism or Brezhnev's latest pronouncements as their Soviet colleagues must. In short, East-South economic relations are discussed much more openly and dispassionately in Budapest, Warsaw, or Sophia than in Moscow.

There is further reason to look into East European studies: they are becoming an integral part of the Soviet reassessment. Following Brezhnev's 1977 meeting with representatives of the Bloc's Academies of Sciences, at which he called on scholars to contribute to the modernization effort, experts from other CPEs have become active in the joint meetings of the Academies and specialized commissions on various international problems. Some collaborative publications that have resulted from this cooperation show the marks of fresh thinking. Moreover, Russian specialists have been increasingly citing the pertinence of the East European experience for new Soviet departures.[31]

The Bloc's dependence on the Third World's natural resources is candidly noted by the East Europeans. Two Hungarian economists have calculated that the

European CMEA countries [annual] import demand *vis-à-vis* the developing countries may by 1990 attain 80 to 100 million tons of petroleum, 30-40 thousand million cu.m. of natural gas, 30-40 million tons of iron ore, 13-15 million tons of rock phosphate, bauxite and alumina equivalent to 1 to 1.5 million tons of primary aluminum, and 100,000 tons of copper.

They attributed the increasing dependence to the growing domestic demand, the inadequacy of domestic resources, the high costs of extraction, and the diminishing imports from other Socialist countries.[32]

Regarded as a highly restricted information on national security, the dependence on outside resources is hardly ever mentioned in Soviet publications. (An unusual exception was Maksimova's argument that the increased internationalization of the Soviet economy would not weaken USSR's defense capacity.)[33] Even so, some East European analyses of the problem have been published in Russian translation. Among the first was a Bulgarian study of CMEA and the Third World, which did not follow the usual Soviet practice of presenting the joint exploitation of natural resources as a saving on alternate investment but referred to the domestic shortages that necessitated such projects. Only recently has a similar viewpoint appeared in Soviet publications. Now that the existence of global problems is acknowledged (which includes the world supply of fuels and other resources), Soviet economists have broached the question of shortages and hint that the USSR should increase raw material imports from developing countries for reasons other than comparative advantage.[34]

Profit is the second reason for East European interest in expanding trade with the Third World. For quite a few years, Hungarians and others have frankly discussed the practice of importing textiles from developing countries to manufacture specialty clothing for reexport as well as the practice of focusing on sales of equipment and services to the oil-rich states of the Near East and Africa. Likewise, they suggest expanding such activities as inviting petrodollar investment in Eastern Europe, equity investment by Bloc countries in the oil-producing states, utilizing the cheap labor resources of the Third World, and using surplus earnings from trade with the developing countries to finance deficits with the West.[35]

Because trade is so vital for Eastern Europe, the Bloc's statement to the fifth UNCTAD acknowledged that some Socialist countries "derive a significant part of their national income from foreign trade." But matters are not that simple for the Soviets. To use the word "profit" is still ideologically embarrassing at home and continues to be regarded as politically damaging abroad. Denying that the profit motive enters into its calculations, the Soviet Union can claim in its pronouncements at the United Nations and other international forums that by

> reason of its contents, principles and goals, the economic and trade cooperation of the USSR with developing countries represents a new type of international economic relations, opposed to the system of exploitation of the natural and human resources of Asian, African and Latin American countries imposed by imperialism.[36]

The operative euphemism abroad is "mutual benefit." Yet at home, Soviet specialists have started to discuss the notion less gingerly, and the word "profit" crops up. Some justify profit on political grounds, arguing that since the developing countries are part of the capitalist world, Soviet economic relations with them should not amount to handouts. These exchanges have to be "remunerative," for otherwise the Socialist Bloc would be contributing its resources to the development of capitalist states. Others argue in more objective terms, namely, that profit is the most convenient measure of efficiency.[37]

Significantly, in proposing new steps to turn economic relations with the Third World to advantage, Soviet economists invariably cite East European practices. Three types of activity perfected and successfully pursued by the East Europeans attract the attention of Soviet specialists. They advocate joint production ventures with developing countries for export to nonsocialist states and not merely to the Soviet Bloc or its aid recipients, as had been the practice. They are interested in founding mixed companies in fields other than trade, services and fishing, especially joint equity ventures for the extraction of raw materials. Third, they advocate supplanting the prevalent form of aid credits with outright commercial loans.[38] But there is a feeling among specialists that as long as the Soviet Union seeks to make political capital out of the NIEO debates, it is debarred from making these new forms of economic cooperation into a predominant form of its economic policy in the Third World.

East Europeans are also less patient with the ideological binds. While supporting in principle the developing countries' efforts to alter their disadvantaged position in the world economy through the NIEO, they nevertheless point out the practical problems thereby created for the Socialist Bloc. In the words of a Hungarian economist:

> The exclusion of exploitation and dependence would suggest, for example, a ban for Hungary to export investment capital to developing countries in the form of long-lasting and cumulatively growing productive assets for the purpose of gaining profit thereby.
>
> Similarly, the respect for national sovereignty over natural resources and the recognition that one-sided specialization in primary production is harmful to the developing countries do not answer the question of how Hungary, a country poor in mineral resources, could satisfy her growing need for raw materials by imports from the developing countries without strengthening thereby their one-sided specialization.
>
> And the principle of supporting industrialization does not specify the possible and mutually advantageous spheres of industrial cooperation, nor the way in which the transfer of technology should be carried out.[39]

No printed Soviet commentary on NIEO issues contains such an open admission of the conflict between the ideological and the economic determinants in policies. Specialists do admit that investigating international economic policies is complicated by the fact that "the production relations of the world economy are under the influence of both objective economic factors and non-economic factors." Moreover, the recent spate of writing on global problems, by emphasizing the dictates of interdependence, is certainly, in part, intended to help depoliticize Soviet discussion of international economic relations. Still, when discussing exchanges between the USSR and developing countries in a broader context, Soviet scholars will not argue, as a Bulgarian economist did, that although there is a link between economics and politics, on the whole, "economy determines politics."[40]

The unequivocal acknowledgment of the mounting competition between the Socialist and the developing countries on Western markets is another indication of the practical East European concerns. This analysis rests on the contention that both groups of states are investment-hungry and seek capital resources from the West, consider export receipts as a source of import financing, and strive to sell manufactures on Western markets. While Soviet specialized publications contain only scattered references to the emergence of "sub-imperialist" centers in the Third World, brief statements without comment that countries like India have turned to investing abroad, and allusions to the "possibility" of the developing countries becoming competitors of the Bloc in the export of light industrial products, the full implications of these developments are discussed only in East European publications.

According to one Polish economist, the future of trade between the Soviet Bloc and the Third World does not look promising:

> The pattern of trade relations between the socialist and developing countries is based upon the exchange of industrial products for primary commodities. . . . The rule is to treat the developing countries . . . almost exclusively as suppliers of commodities that are to be paid off by exports of industrial goods, especially capital goods. . . . There is no justification for basing the long-run program . . . on the old model of international specialization. . . . The change in the economic structure of the developing countries and the nature of their international specialization [indicates a change] from a complementary to a competitive [trade pattern]. . . . The dominant tendency will be to increase trade in industrial goods within a competitive model of international specialization, especially since our principal partners in the Third World are countries where intensive industrialization is already under way."[41]

The Hungarians have published detailed analyses of how Third World competition has already become a factor impeding the expansion of East-West trade. They cite rather alarming figures to substantiate the point: Some LDCs had managed to modernize and upgrade their exports to the degree that "while in 1970 the total machinery export of the developing countries to developed industrial countries lagged somewhat behind those of CMEA countries . . . by 1977 the former already exceeded the latter more than fourfold."[42]

Because East European economists do not believe in the natural complementarity of the Soviet Bloc and Third World economies, they are seeking ways to overcome the drawbacks. They have urged the coordination of Bloc activities and extensive reforms in the domestic institutions of the CPEs to meet the challenge of the changing trade pattern. The first public call came at the November 1976 conference of Africanists in Budapest, where it was decided to propose "to the governmental organizations responsible for international economic relations and also to the CMEA Secretariat that economic relations with the developing countries and the drawing up of joint agreements should be coordinated more precisely."[43] While some Western observers interpreted this appeal as yet another scheme for increased economic penetration of the Third World, the East European specialists see the proposal in an entirely different light — as a step dictated by weakness and vulnerability. They advocate overall planning and coordinated actions to give the Bloc the strength it lacks and to reverse the trend toward slackening trade activity that has surfaced in the 1970s.

Among the boldest practical proposals for common action was one advanced by a Polish economist: the Socialist Bloc should form its own multinationals in order to approximate the power of Western transnational corporations and become an effective competitor. Operations on that level would enable the CPEs to "develop large-scale market strategies." Arguments for coordinated action have also appeared in Soviet publications, but they merely propose the pooling of resources through the existing CMEA channels: "Common action by the Socialist states is . . . essential because the financial and material capacities of separate countries are often insufficient for the realization of projects requiring large financial outlays."[44]

As for reforming domestic institutions in order to perform better on the world market, the East Europeans are also very frank, if not always in print, at least in the more or less off-the-record meetings. Thus at the spring 1979 gathering of the Bloc's Academies of Sciences, one Polish expert maintained that the chief factor impeding a well-articulated and active Bloc participation in the NIEO debates was the absence of a "global" (i.e., universalistic) vision of the problems of world economy, as well as the discrepancy between international aspirations and the arbitrary, uneconomic performance of domestic institutions. The equivocal response, he stated was:

conditioned to a large extent by the lack of the necessary degree of cohesion of the domestic economic policy in the socialist countries with their international economic policy and also by the imperfection of their multilateral economic policy. It weakens our status in the multilateral debate on the NIEO and — as a natural consequence — leaves the field for dialogue with the "Third World" to the developed capitalist countries.[45]

However vague his words, their import was quite clear in the context.

Basically, what the East Europeans advocate to stimulate a more active and more remunerative foreign trade is multilateralization and a greater opening up to the world economy. Multilateralization has been one of the Third World demands consistently directed at the Soviet Bloc. It has figured in various statements since the Manila Declaration (February 1972) alongside the insistence on preferential treatment based on nonreciprocity. Unlike the latter demand, multilateralization has not been rejected by the CPEs. Their statement to the fourth UNCTAD addressed the following issues: "reinforcing the multilateral aspects of trade and economic relations" through "multilateral accounting on the basis of the transferable ruble"; "multilateral cooperation of CMEA with individual LDCs and their organizations"; as well as tripartite schemes involving East, West, and South.[46] That goal has not been disavowed in later statements, but there has been no visible progress. Here, too, there are large differences between East European and Soviet views.

The East Europeans tend to favor far-reaching decentralization of domestic controls and management.[47] But there is no agreement among Soviet economists about the reforms necessary to carry out to best advantage a greater participation in the international economy and to manage the increasingly complex network of economic relations. The more conservative experts believe that the advantages the Soviet Union seeks from the international division of labor will best accrue from the more efficient operations of existing institutions, improved quality of production, better planning, a more flexible structure of exports, plus more efficient and more aggressive sales promotion abroad. Specialists associated with the Ministry of Foreign Trade and with various research institutes attached to it take the state monopoly of foreign trade as their starting point. They presume that the greatest gains will accrue from perfecting the centralized foreign trade decision-making apparatus and operations. This will enable the Soviet Union to find the optimal opportunities in foreign markets, without exposing the country to the fluctuations and other undesirable effects of the capitalist-dominated world economy.[48]

The less tradition-bound economists, associated chiefly with the research Institutes of the Academy of Sciences argue for a more open and flexible intertwining with the world economy. Rather than relying on strengthening the state monopoly of foreign trade, they discuss certain structural changes as essential to giving Soviet operations abroad a greater comparative advantage. They do not believe that the USSR and its Bloc hold a sufficiently impregnable position to benefit most from insulation and extensive protectionism. They foresee that a greater opening up and decentralization of the economy will permit the Soviet Union to derive the most advantage from the dynamic effects of foreign trade operations.

Four reforms are most frequently mentioned. First, there has been discussion of the desirability of instituting the true convertibility of socialist currencies to replace the current multilateral arrangements within CMEA for unloading trade surpluses. Second, there is the need for a more rational and unified system of pricing — one closely related to the world market — to allow the Soviet Union to judge accurately the effectiveness of foreign trade transactions. Third, there has been talk about extending the rights of individual enterprises to stimulate their interest and participation in foreign trade by providing them with such powers as the authority to bid, buy, and sell abroad and to retain a share of the resulting hard currency earnings. Finally, proposals to introduce greater flexibility into planning have been put forth. The more cautious suggest that the five-year plans should be replaced with longer-range plans to encourage more thoroughgoing innovations and adjustments. Others refer wistfully to the period of the New Economic Policy in the early 1920s, when the state monopoly of trade did not give the central organs authority over all operations but empowered them only to plan general targets for production and trade.[49]

Although by 1982 Brezhnev and Soviet scholars were increasingly talking about the need to learn from the East European experience in order to improve the working of the Soviet economy, there was no indication that the USSR was about to embark upon extensive reforms to open up to a greater participation on the world market. Before Brezhnev's death, Soviet experts doubted the possibility of serious change. Many agreed with the East Europeans that it was the Socialist Bloc's institutions that prevented it from participating meaningfully in world trade and in the NIEO debates. But they conceded that for the present, bilateralism would prevail in international economic relations, with elements of multilateralism playing only a secondary role.

THE THIRD WORLD LOOKS AT SOVIET THEORY

The equivocal Soviet line on the NIEO, aimed at preserving the semblance of an anti-Western unity with the Third World, has spawned ideological disagreements with developing countries. Until the early 1970s, the normative assumptions of Soviet views on international economics and development theory coincided in many respects with the equally normative outlook of the Third World. The polemics of anti-imperialism betokened a perhaps specious unity in the assertions from both quarters. Certainly, Moscow propagated at home and abroad the idea of common Marxist-LDC aims.

However, the recent rise of economic pragmatism in the Soviet Union and the attempts to probe political abstractions to resolve various international economic problems without creating chaos collide with the independent Third World outlook. The decision of the Group of 77 at the fifth UNCTAD in 1976 to impose the same demands for economic assistance and trade concessions on capitalist and socialist states alike, derived from the dependency theory. The theory was formulated by Raul Prebisch in the 1960s and since then has been elaborated by leftist Latin American and African economists. It presents a coherent Third World explanation of exploitation on the global scale that substitutes for Marxian class conflict the dichotomy between the rich, industrial centers and the poor periphery supplying primary products.

The Soviets have been worried by the widespread adoption of this explanation for inequality. Of course, to maintain the façade of the common, progressive Socialist-Third World front, the criticism of theorists from the developing countries is infrequent and circumspect. What is written tends to center on Samir Amin, the influential director of the Economic Commission for Africa's Institute of Economic Development and Planning in Dakar. In the USSR, he personifies the theoretical extremism of the Third World establishment.

The Soviets object to more than his claims to be a socialist. (It is pointed out that Amin ignores class analysis and does not regard the Soviet Union as the source of theory and practice.) He is also criticized for flouting the very principles of economics. Soviet scholars take issue with his proposal for a substantial upward revision in raw material prices to benefit the producing LDCs, which, Amin claims, is a simple matter of political will. "Price formation," the Soviet scholars argue, "is part of the international economic mechanism and subject to its objective laws." Although they concede that prices can be used as a political weapon, as has been the case with oil, they point out that this policy brought a steep rise in world prices for manufactured goods from which all the developing countries have suffered, and foremost the poorest among them. As a result, the relative price of oil increased less significantly than the absolute price.[50]

(In Eastern Europe, criticism of Third World economic thought is more sweeping; it is regarded as "irrational." Thus in a report on the First Congress of Third World Economists, held in Algeria in February 1976, a Polish economist took exception to the ideas propounded by both Celso Furtado, the chief speaker at the congress, and Samir Amin, its deputy chairman. He was disturbed that universal technical principles were being jettisoned in favor of political solutions; the objective achievements of economic science were being ignored while economic obscurantism prevailed.)[51]

Amin's opinion that it is impossible to realize the aims of the NIEO within the framework of the existing order is likewise rejected. Soviet specialists maintain that the "reconstruction of economic relations should proceed . . . not by way of abolition, as S. Amin urges, but by going over to a noncapitalist and eventually a socialist path of development."[52] Should the reader be puzzled by this verbiage, the official Soviet statement at the fifth UNCTAD puts it somewhat more clearly, saying that it was possible to democratize international economic relations even before the "inherent defects of capitalism" had been eliminated. In other words, the Soviets are willing to work within the existing system. Theirs is a reformist, not a revolutionary, position.

The third set of objections concerns self-reliance. The concept has been subject to extensive criticism in the Soviet professional literature. While careful to acknowledge the need for economic and political cooperation among the LDCs to weaken dependence on the imperialist powers and to speed up development, Soviet specialists are worried that, pushed to an extreme, the collective approach leads to a "utopian" faith in the viability of autarky. The intensity of Soviet fears of Third World isolationism is well illustrated by lectures to LDC audiences in defense of an open system. For example, one Soviet economist, speaking at a UNITAR seminar in Moscow, stressed the shortsightedness of "collective self-reliance":

> One should not forget, however, that this integration pattern as such has also negative sides because the centers of scientific and technical progress and those of the international division of labor are at present beyond the reach of the developing countries, and the system of exchange [among the LDCs] for all its importance is nevertheless of minor significance. Therefore, every attempt on the part of the LDCs to shut themselves up within the framework of such groupings would actually mean their deliberate renouncement to share the world scientific and technical progress. And on the contrary, if such pattern of cooperation is to produce a maximum effect, it will have to . . . promote cooperation among all nations irrespective of their socio-economic systems.

Another Soviet speaker at the same seminar waxed lyrical about the benefits to be derived from participation in the world economy. He called the "expansion of world-wide system of business relations between states" a "global democratic school" from which each participant would derive great benefits. And, carried away in linguistic flight, he equated exclusion from that "ever durable boon-school" with "emasculation."[53]

Disagreements on the basic principles for reconstructing the international economy also plague Moscow's relations with its close political allies, the leaders of radical states and revolutionary and Communist parties. An international conference convened in October 1980 in Berlin, for instance, displayed the clash between an uncompromising ideological line and practical economic interests. In addition, the Socialist Bloc's position was confused and muddled.

Boris Ponomarev's political commentary on the operations of the world economy denounced the transnationals for their exploitation of the developing countries. He freely offered the Soviet Bloc's support for radically restructuring international economic relations through the elimination of all discrimination, *diktats*, and exploitation. But speakers from other Bloc countries were more circumspect, talking about improving the international climate and institutions and coming to terms with the transnationals. Whereas Ponomarev extolled existing Bloc-Third World exchanges as paradigmatic, they cited East-West economic cooperation as a good example of effective economic relations. Joint production deals removed the incubus of foreign capital by turning direct investment into a form of loan-capital repayable from the revenues of the enterprises under construction.[54]

By contrast, no such divergence between economic moderation and radical political posturing showed among the Third World delegates. Their speeches were an unrelieved denunciation of capitalist relations on the international and domestic levels alike. Creating a new, more equitable order on either level required the eradication of capitalism. Unlike this maximalist position, with its rabid hostility to capitalist institutions, the speeches from the Soviet Bloc sounded equivocal. (In fact, even Ponomarev at one point mentioned the "useful role" private enterprise could play.)[55] Printed materials on the Berlin conference laconically report contrasting opinions, but verbal accounts of this and other international meetings describe heated clashes: Third World radicals scorn Soviet moderation and charge ideological slippage in Moscow's complaisant view of capitalism's role.

The uncompromising ideological attitude among the Third World radicals extends beyond theory (i.e., the role of capitalism) and tactics (i.e., the speed and degree of transformation); it creates friction over aid as well. Their socialist élan prompts the radicals to claim greater Soviet assistance in the name of proletarian internationalism. As Marxist-Leninists they feel entitled to demand that the Soviet Union make good its professed support of national liberation movements and provide generous aid to help "eliminate the impact of the capitalist market" on the "new economic structures" in their countries.[56] To quote the delegation from Mozambique at the Berlin conference:

> The existence of developed socialist nations is equally important for us also from the economic point of view. After winning independence, the new states that take the road of socialist construction draw upon the economic, scientific, and technological achievements

of these nations. This is of fundamental significance, for it allows lessening and neutralising dependence on the capitalist world system and, on the basis of the resultant alternative, restructuring our economy and speeding up development.[57]

Soviet counterarguments — that increased aid should come from savings gained through disarmament, that the Bloc is ever ready to expand economic relations on a mutually advantageous basis, that the existing channels of economic exchange must be improved not eliminated, and that the developing countries should better utilize their own domestic resources — are an ineffective rejoinder to appeals based on faith in the solidarity of the international revolutionary movement. The counterarguments only underscore the distance that separates the Soviet position from that of the Third World leftist politicians. An extreme expression of that separation at the Berlin conference was voiced by the Communist Party of Réunion:

The new economic order is inseparable from a new social order. . . . Eurocentrism, or any other narrow vision, must be transcended; we should set the example ourselves of a new international economic order for which we strive and which requires a new internationalism standing at a level hitherto never attained, an internationalism that would unite the revolutionary forces of socialism and the international working class more closely with the national liberation movement.[58]

Imputations of a Eurocentric position on the NIEO present a serious challenge to Moscow, for they bring the arguments of the Third World radicals close to Peking's version of what is wrong with international economics. Ever since the Sino-Soviet break in the early 1960s, the Chinese have been propagating the concept and the cause of the exploited world "countryside" against the exploiting world "urban centers" — and the USSR is one of the hegemonist, imperialist powers. Although China cannot compete with the Soviet Union in economic assistance, it outmatches Moscow in identifying with the normative assumptions and maximalist demands of the Third World. It can also supplement its revolutionary anti-imperialist and anticapitalist line with ethnic anti-Western arguments. Ethnic appeals are a potent political weapon these days and one that Moscow cannot use. Hence the charges of "Eurocentrism" leveled at the Soviet NIEO proposals touch a vulnerable spot.

Whatever the ups and downs in Sino-Soviet relations, the Chinese challenge to Soviet interests in the Third World (including the NIEO issues) has remained constant. During and following the fifth UNCTAD, the Chinese endorsed the line of collective self-reliance and argued that the USSR was no "true ally" of the world "country-side." Moscow, they charged, opposed the program of the Group of 77, refused to earmark a percentage of its GNP for preferential aid, and was mainly interested in finding ways to "wring huge profits out of its trade with third world countries."[59]

The Soviet reaction to these charges is nervously defensive. That is why the 1980 Berlin conference was devoted in part to reaffirming the unity on the NIEO among the three sources of revolutionary change — the Socialist countries, the working-class movement in the West, and the national liberation struggle. After the conclusion of the meeting, Soviet media felt it necessary to claim that the conference had fully recognized the benefits of Soviet support for the creation of equitable economic relations and had successfully dealt with attempts "to besmirch [the policy of] the socialist states . . . in the struggle surrounding the problems of a new international economic order."[60]

THIRD WORLD AND SOVIET BLOC AIMS

The likelihood of the Third World seizing the practical advantages of the international division of labor favored by the Soviet Union is also problematical. Before going into detail about the current views of the developing countries on Soviet economic performance and potential, their perceptions at the outset of Moscow's activism should be noted. In some respects, the impasse at present is the consequence of the initial Soviet success.

Regardless of whether political or economic factors predominated in Soviet aid and trade, the benefits derived by the developing countries were considerable. As pointed out in Chapter 1, Soviet assistance was nowhere as large as Western aid in overall amounts, but its nature and terms were advantageous to the LDCs. Thus the plaudits it earned from the LDCs were disproportionate to its size. Looked at objectively or from the Third World viewpoint, there is no denying that the impact, both direct and indirect, of Soviet economic activity was large. Directly, Soviet assistance helped build up local economic potential; indirectly, it changed the prevailing terms in Western aid and business practices.

For the first 20 years or so, Soviet readiness to help the developing countries eliminate backwardness and to create modern industrialized economies was no empty political platitude. There was a genuine economic sense and content to Soviet policy. There was a good match between the type of machinery the USSR had available for export and the equipment required by the LDCs for their industrialization programs. Relatively simple, basic sets of heavy machinery that Moscow had in excess corresponded to the developing countries' needs and capacities at the start of their long climb to economic independence and higher development levels.[61] Structural changes in the world economy during the course of the 1970s have eroded the complementarity between Soviet capacities and the needs of many LDCs. Some countries have become oil rich; others now produce a wide assortment of capital goods and are implementing plans for even more sophisticated levels of industrialization. Both groups know that there is practically nothing the East can provide that the West does not do better. The more advanced states need a different mix of imports, especially high-level technology, to increase their capital goods exports. And this at a time when the Soviet Union has shown its own technological lag by embarking on an ambitious modernization program with Western assistance yet hopes to turn exchanges with the Third World into profitable operations.

Recent developments in Soviet-Indian relations demonstrate how the improved financial position and advancing development level of a Third World partner introduce elements of competition and reveal Soviet inadequacy. In 1970 machinery constituted 64.9 percent of Soviet exports to India, but by 1977 it made up only 15.5 percent. The decline can be attributed to two factors. First, over the years India has become increasingly self-sufficient in basic industrial hardware. Second, to keep competitive on the world market, India found it best to have recourse to advanced Western know-how. The chronic deficit operations of many public sector projects built with Soviet aid have been blamed in part on their simple and outdated technology. Hence the Indian government has increasingly turned to Western sources to improve the operations of these plants. For example, during the second stage of expansion of the Bokaro steel plant (the second steel plant built with Soviet aid), India used U.S. technology for part of the mill since the Soviet Union was itself using sophisticated technology from the West. Similarly, the government-owned Bharat electrical plant, which has been making heavy-duty transformers with Soviet help, has also turned to the United States and West Germany for sophisticated tooling equipment not available from the Soviet Union.[62]

As a result, by the late 1970s, trade negotiations between the two countries centered on how to restore the "original dynamism," how to find products that India could import now that it had become an industrial power in its own right. The agreements concluded in 1979/80 partially settled the problem by providing both ordinary commercial credits and concessional aid for imports of Soviet machinery to help develop India's raw material resources. These agreements answered the needs of the moment. On the one hand, they gave the Soviet Union an opportunity to increase machinery exports and eventually perhaps to reduce fuel shipments to India; on the other, they dovetailed with India's plans to solve its fuel supply problem. But they do not bode well for the type of exchanges the USSR would like to see grow. Moscow's pet project for increasing machinery exports is that the two partners engage in joint ventures in third countries. Though repeatedly proposed over recent years, the plan has not gotten off the ground. The Indians do not fancy inviting the USSR into areas where they stand a good chance of getting a large part of the market anyway. As for the old, traditional method for promoting machinery exports − production cooperation on a compensation basis − the Indians fear that building plants to Soviet specifications is not an optimal solution. Such arrangements would create "captive units" whose production could not be exported anywhere else but to the Socialist Bloc and could give the Soviet Union the possibility of dictating terms. In addition, the Indians no longer consider machinery exports a one-way street. They press Moscow for increased imports of their own capital goods production, but the Soviet Union has been unwilling and/or unable to absorb enough of Indian output to satisfy New Delhi.[63]

Similar difficulties beset much of Soviet-Third World trade and hinder the growth of the lasting, dynamic exchanges that the USSR and the other CPEs would like. The Socialist Bloc's version of the international division of labor, based on a planned and specialized cooperation in production and trade, hardly conforms either with reality or with the Third World vision of a new order. This is made amply clear by Deepak Nayyar, an Indian economist who in the past wrote approvingly about the pattern of Soviet-Third World economic relations. He now points out that experts from the Socialist countries mistakenly equate the help rendered by the CPEs in setting up planning machinery in the LDCs with the process of planning itself and thus overestimate the prospects for planned joint action. Second, they assume, also without foundation, that during 1980-90 the CMEA countries will increase their trade with the developing countries faster than their total trade. Finally, the composition of that trade is unacceptable, for capital goods and manufactures are supposed to account for an even larger proportion of the Bloc's exports (about 80 percent), while diversification of Third World exports to the Bloc would basically amount to substituting minerals and fuels for agricultural commodities. In addition to being unrealistic, Bloc proposals of this nature are "clearly not the basis for a new international division of labor."[64]

NOTES

1. *Pravda*, April 12, 1974, p. 4.

2. The slogans first appeared in *Pravda* on October 16, 1976.

3. *World Marxist Review* 19 (August 1976): 16.

4. G. Skorov, "Vozrastanie roli osvobodivshikhsia gosudarstv v mirovom razvitii," *MEMO* (April 1976): 37-50.

5. "Joint Statement by the Socialist Countries . . . at the fourth session of the United Nations Conference on Trade and Development," *Foreign Trade* (September 1976): 1-24 (Supplement).

6. E. Obminsky, "Problems of Restructuring Economic Relations," *International Affairs* (January 1977): 67.

7. *Foreign Trade* (December 1976): 2-5.

8. N. P. Shmelev, *Sotsializm i mezhdunarodnye ekonomicheskie otnosheniya* (Moscow: Mezhdunarodnye otnosheniya, 1979), pp. 219-20.

9. "Evaluation of the world trade and economic situation and consideration of issues, policies and appropriate measures to facilitate structural changes in the international economy," UNCTAD, TD/249 (April 19, 1979).

10. "Statement and Position Paper by Group D," ID/Conf. 4/22 (April 11, 1980), Annex II, p. 131.

11. "Obstacles to the Development of Contemporary International Trade and Economic Relations," TD/B/924 (September 3, 1982); text in *Foreign Trade* (October 1982): 2-3.

12. Compare O. T. Bogomolov, *Strany sotsializma i mezhdunarodnoe razdelenie truda* (Moscow: Nauka, 1980), with N. N. Inozemtsev, ed., *Global'nye problemy sovremennosti* (Moscow: Mysl', 1981).

13. Compare O. T. Bogomolov, ed., *Sotsializm i perestroika mezhdunarodnykh ekonomicheskikh otnoshenii* (Moscow: Mezhdunarodnye otnosheniya, 1981), Introduction, with E. Primakov, "Strany Vostoka v sovremennom mire," *Pravda*, August 11, 1982, pp. 4-5.

14. *Kommunist* no. 11 (July 1979): 126.

15. A. Chekhutov, "Perestroika mezhdunarodnykh ekonomicheskikh otnoshenii – trebovanie zhizni," ibid., no. 16 (November 1981): 88.

16. Bogomolov, ed., *Sotsializm i perestroika*, p. 9.

17. G. Georgiev, "Razvivayushchiesia strany v bor'be za ekonomicheskoe ravnopravie," *MEMO* (May 1977): 21.

18. *Sotrudnichestvo sotsialisticheskikh i razvivayushchikhsia stran: novyi tip mezhdunarodnykh otnoshenii* (Moscow: Nauka, 1980), p. 106.

19. "Prospects for the Establishment of the New International Economic Order and Development Strategy for the 80s," *Joint UNITAR/Foreign Trade Academy Seminar* (Moscow, April 1980), mimeographed, p. 21.

20. Shmelev, *Sotsializm i mezhdunarodnye*, p. 237. This argument was first and best formulated by Georgiev in "Razvivayushchiesia strany v bor'be."

21. Primakov, "Strany Vostoka"; K. Maidanik and G. Mirsky, "Natsional'no-osvoboditel'naya bor'ba: sovremennyi etap," *MEMO* (June 1981): 17-29.

22. L. Zevin, "The New International Economic Order and Reorientation of the Economic Development Policy of the Developing Countries," *International Social Science Journal* 32 (1980): 776-77.

23. For the best description of this scenario, see *Strany SEV v mirokhoziaistvennykh sviaziakh* (Moscow: Nauka, 1978), pp. 99-139.

24. Bogomolov, ed., *Sotsializm i perestroika*, p. 285.

25. V. Akhimov, "Bank's Participation in Soviet Union's Foreign Trade," *Foreign Trade* (June 1978): 13.

26. For one of the earliest descriptions of such a world, see N. P. Shmelev, "Sotsializm i vsemirnoe khoziaistvo," *MEMO* (October 1976): 3-18.

27. L. Zevin, "Concepts of Economic Development of the Developing Nations and Problems of Tripartite Cooperation," in *East-West-South. Economic Interaction between Three Worlds*, ed. Christopher T. Saunders (New York: St. Martin's Press, 1981), pp. 299-300.

28. G. Krasnov, "Yunktad i problemy torgovlii stran s razlichnymi sotsial'no-ekonomicheskimi sistemami," *Vneshniaya torgovlia* (August 1981): 49-53.

29. Chekhutov, "Perestroika mezhdunarodnykh," pp. 98-99.

30. V. V. Zagladin and I. T. Frolov, *Global'nye problemy sovremennosti: nauchnyi i sotsial'nyi aspekty* (Moscow: Mezhdunarodnye otnosheniya, 1981), pp. 84-85; Inozemtsev, ed., *Global'nye problemy*, pp. 268-69.

31. Two books of interest have resulted from joint consultations by the Academies: *Sotrudnichestvo sotsialisticheskikh i razvivayushchikhsia stran: novyi tip mezhdunarodnykh otnoshenii* (Moscow: Nauka, 1980); and *Sotsializm i perestroika mezhdunarodnykh ekonomicheskikh otnoshenii* (Moscow: Mezhdunarodnye otnosheniya, 1982). N. A. Ushakova's *Strany SEV i*

razvivayushchiesia gosudarstva sotsialisticheskoi orientatsii: ekonomicheskoe sotrudnichestvo (Moscow: Nauka, 1980) relies heavily on East European practice in her suggestions for more remunerative exchanges.

32. I. Dobozi and A. Inotai, "Prospects of Economic Cooperation between CMEA Countries and Developing Countries," in *East-West-South. Economic Interaction between Three Worlds*, ed. Christopher T. Saunders (New York: St. Martin's Press, 1981), p. 54.

33. *SSSR i mezhdunarodnoe ekonomicheskoe sotrudnichestvo* (Moscow: Nauka, 1977), p. 61.

34. I. Ganev, *SEV i 'Tret'ii Mir': problemy sotrudnichestva i razdeleniya truda* (Moscow: Ekonomika, 1976), p. 150; Inozemtsev, ed., *Global'nye problemy*, p. 156.

35. A. Inotai, "Hungary's Economic Relations with Developing Countries," *Marketing in Hungary* no. 2 (1978): 21-26.

36. Letter of the USSR Delegation to the President of the Economic and Social Council, E/1982/86 (July 12, 1982).

37. A Chekhutov, "Razvitie finansovo-ekonomicheskogo sotrudnichestva sotsialisticheskikh i osvobodivshikhsia stran," *MEMO* (April 1981): 50-62; R. N. Andreasian, "Sotsialisticheskoe sodruzhestvo i razvivayushchiesia strany: ekonomicheskoe sotrudnichestva, *Narody Azii i Afriki* (March-April 1981): 3-13.

38. For the best discussion, see T. V. Teodorovich and V. V. Efanov, *Sotrudnichestvo pri sooruzhenii ob'ektov za rubezhom. Iz opyta sovetskikh organizatsii* (Moscow: Mezhdunarodnye otnosheniya, 1979). See also A. B. Kupriyanov, *Razvivayushchiesia strany i mezhdunarodnoe sotrudnichestvo. Regional'nyi aspekt* (Moscow: Nauka, 1980).

39. I. Dobozi, ed., *Economic Cooperation between Socialist and Developing Countries.* (Budapest: Hungarian Scientific Council for World Economy, 1978), p. 144.

40. *Global'nye problemy mirovogo rynka* (Riga: Gosudarstvennyi Latviiskii Universitet, 1980), p. 58; Proceedings of the Sixth International Seminar on the Problems of the Developing Countries, Varna, *Mezhdunarodni otnosheniya* (1980): 183.

41. M. Paszynski, "Developing Countries in the International Division of Labor," *Oeconomica Polona* 6, no. 4 (1979): 524-25.

42. E. Palocz-Nemeth, "Exports of Manufactures of CMEA and Developing Countries to Developed Industrial Countries," *Acta Oeconomica* 26, no. 1-2 (1981): 101.

43. *Kulpolitika* 4, no. 1 (1977): 132.

44. L. Zurawicki, *Multinational Enterprises in West and East* (Alphen aan den Rijn, Netherlands: Sijthoff and Noordhoff, 1979), p. 98; *Sotrudnichestvo sotsialisticheskikh*, p. 139.

45. M. Paszynski, "Socialist Countries and the Concept of the New International Economic Order," Problem Commission of the Multilateral Scientific Cooperation of the Academies of Sciences of the Socialist Countries: Economy and Politics of the Developing Countries (Warsaw, May 1979) mimeographed, pp. 26-27.

46. "Joint Statement by the Socialist Countries," p. 21.

47. For a good discussion, see A. Inotai's review of A. Koves's book on the challenges presented by the need to open up in *Acta Oeconomica* 26, no. 1-2 (1981): 201-5.

48. Y. Krasnov, "Sixty Years of Trade Monopoly," *New Times* no. 17 (April 1978): 18-19; N. Tretiukhin, "Novye napravleniya vo vneshneekonomicheskikh sviaziakh SSSR," *Vneshniaya torgovlia* (January 1977): 7-14.

49. These reforms were first cogently and thoroughly discussed in N. P. Shmelev, ed., *Ekonomicheskie sviazi Vostok-Zapad: problemy i vozmozhnosti* (Moscow: Mysl', 1976).

50. *Zarubezhnye kontseptsii ekonomicheskogo razvitiya stran Afriki* (Moscow: Nauka, 1980), p. 153.

51. Jerzy Kleer, "Rozterki Trzeciego Swiata," *Polityka* (February 21, 1976): 13.

52. *Zarubezhnye kontseptsii*, p. 155.

53. See V. Yashkin, "Prospects for the Establishment of the New International Economic Order," pp. 17-18 and E. Pletnev, "Major Problems in International Economic Relations," p. 26 in *Joint UNITAR/Foreign Trade Academy Seminar* (Moscow, April 1980), mimeographed.

54. *Working-Class and National-Liberation Movements: Joint Struggle against Imperialism, for Social Progress* (Moscow: Novosti, 1981), p. 43; *World Marxist Review* 24 (March 1981): 36-40.

55. *Working-Class and National-Liberation Movements*, p. 50.

56. *World Marxist Review* 22 (March 1979): 81.

57. *Working-Class and National-Liberation Movements*, pp. 58-59.

58. *World Marxist Review* 24 (March 1981): 40.

59. "5th UNCTAD. Destroying the Old and Establishing the New," *Beijing Review* no. 24 (June 15, 1979): 18-19.

60. K. Brutents, "A Great Force of Modern Times," *International Affairs* (March 1981): 84.

61. For the best single treatment of the advantages derived and acknowledged, see Deepak Nayyar, ed., *Economic Relations between Socialist Countries and the Third World* (London: Macmillan, 1977). See also Padma Desai, *The Bokaro Steel Plant: a study of Soviet economic assistance* (Cambridge: MIT Press, 1971).

62. Kustari Rangan, "India Is Showered with Soviet Largesse," *New York Times*, December 14, 1980.

63. K. V. Subrahmanyan, "The Soviet Technology. The Cost of Collaboration," *Economic Times*, April 9, 1979; Jaya Shekar, "Economic Links," *Seminar* (September 1981): 21-26.

64. See Deepak Nayyar's comments on paper by I. Dobozi and A. Inotai, "Prospects of Economic Cooperation between CMEA Countries and Developing Countries," presented at the Vienna Institute for Comparative Economic Studies workshop on economic interaction between three worlds, in Christopher T. Saunders, ed., *East-West-South. Interaction between Three Worlds* (New York: St. Martin's Press, 1981), pp. 80-84.

5

IN CONCLUSION

What does one learn from an examination of Soviet economic relations with the developing countries over the past 30 years? Granted, economic relations comprise but one of Moscow's instrumentalities in the Third World. Moreover, the extent to which economic rather than geostrategic interests determine foreign policy is a moot point. Nevertheless, one can learn a good deal about Moscow's Third World policies from studying the gamut of economic relations, from the actual course of aid and trade to the changing perceptions of what comprises a just international economic order.

An understanding of the evolving practice and ideology enables one to go beyond the simple static assertion that Moscow seeks to expand its influence in the Third World and to add a more dynamic element, that is, how Moscow sees its ability to pursue this goal. The means the Soviet Union has at its disposal and the conception it has of their efficacy qualify the way Moscow proceeds in promoting its interests. Here, over the years it has become evident that Soviet economic capabilities do not match Soviet political aspirations. Hence the book's subtitle, "an economic bind," the dimensions of which the four chapters explore as it affects practice and ideology.

Rather than recapitulate the various binds created by the marked discrepancy between political goals and the available economic means, or draw out their consequences in possible scenarios of the future conduct of Soviet policy, I find it more productive to consider the three schools of thought on how to deal with the Third World. All three schools actively contend for their viewpoint, but each corresponds to and reflects the type of policies the Soviet Union was able to pursue in the several stages of its economic relations with the Third World over the past quarter century. In short, economic realities have a way of inducing reexamination and change.

The oldest school, obviously, comprises the ideologues. They held sway during the Khrushchev period and exemplified its aggressive confidence. They are not just starry-eyed Marxists carrying on the communist tradition of the common interests and shared destiny of socialism and the oppressed colonial peoples. On the policy level, they hold that Soviet rivalry with the United States is well served by manipulating Third World resentments against the West. These specialists are by now regarded by many others as old-fashioned conservatives, who are so out of touch with present realities that at midnight they will maintain the sun is shining (to quote one exasperated comment I heard in Moscow).

The skeptical realists came to prominence during the middle Brezhnev years. They argue, in effect, that developing countries behave like the proverbial clever calves that suck two cows. Accordingly, they hold that too close an identification of Soviet interests with those of the Third World is counterproductive and far too expensive. The realists seek to puncture the doctrinaire claims of the conservative ideologues. They point out that the colonial stage of imperialism is over: instead of being the helpless victims of exploitation that automatically gravitate toward the Socialist Bloc, the LDCs have become independent (and often ungrateful) actors in international relations and on the world market. The policy implication is that the Soviet Union had better conduct a policy based on a careful cost-benefit analysis rather than on outdated ideology, for the Third World will take care of its own interests in ways that will not necessarily redound to Moscow's advantage.

The emergence of the globalists in the past two or three years has coincided with the more visible fissures in the Soviet-Third World anti-imperialist front. These experts do not regard the problems of the developing countries as a useful lever for tilting the balance of forces in favor of the Soviet Union, but as threatening international equilibrium and peace. They argue that the growing gap between the developing countries and the industrial states has created a sense of alienation, which has transformed the nationalism directed against the West into a Third World chauvinism, hostile to all advanced nations, whether socialist or capitalist.

Furthermore, the specialists with a global outlook express concern that the increasing poverty of the developing countries is creating political and social pressures, which in turn lead to domestic and interstate strife that could bring on great-power involvement and worldwide conflagration. They have not explicitly proposed an international code of conduct to reduce the likelihood of Soviet-U.S. confrontation on Third World-related issues. But they concede that the Socialist Bloc does not have all the answers. They urge the broad, constructive cooperation of all the advanced countries in solving the problems that create unrest in the LDCs — overpopulation, food shortages, and backwardness. Moreover, they consider access to raw materials another destabilizing factor and advocate global regulations to assure the legitimate interests not only of the producing Third World countries but also of all the consuming industrial states, socialist and capitalist alike.

What can one make of these three schools? I do not mean to suggest that because the global-minded viewpoint has emerged last, it is bound to prevail and guide Soviet policies in the future. Obviously, any combination of political and economic factors, both domestic and international, can dictate either a more aggressive or even a more isolationist policy. There is nothing inevitable about the USSR coming to adopt policies that would dilute or moderate competition in the Third World with some degree of cooperation, based on the awareness of interdependence.

Nevertheless, the appearance of new currents of analysis in the USSR should not be either overlooked or discounted. The fact that new interpretations appear most prominently in academic publications does not mean that these opinions do not inform or reflect the policy-making process. Key academic experts supply information and recommendations to people directly responsible for the formulation and implementation of foreign policy. As this book shows, the evolution of Soviet aid-trade practices, as well as Moscow's changing response to the NIEO issues, have followed the course recommended by the academic specialists.

What is more significant is that the discussion, now so clearly articulated, gives evidence of flexibility and adaptation to the changing world. The debates and disagreements outlined in this book belie the contention that the Soviets, because of the straightjacket of Marxism-Leninism, are incapable of adaptation, change, or moderation.

Finally, these two themes of my book do have policy implications for the American side. We should be aware that some circles in the USSR are coming to grips with the demonstrable fact that there are limits to Soviet power in the Third World, as well as to the advantages to be derived from close identification with the post-colonial grievances. Some even hold that support of Third World causes is disruptive to Soviet-American relations and threatens world peace. Should this "globalist" view come to shape concrete Soviet proposals, Washington should be ready to respond and not miss the chance to seek mutual restraint or a cooperative relationship.

APPENDIX

LIST OF TABLES AND FIGURES   Page

Tables

A.1 Soviet Economic Aid Agreements with Major
     Third World Partners   153
A.2 Communist Countries: Economic Aid to Non-Communist
     Developing Countries   154
A.3 Communist Countries: Military Aid to Non-Communist
     Developing Countries   155
A.4 Soviet-aided Projects, Completed and Under Construc-
     tion, in Developing Countries   157
A.5 Geographic Distribution of Soviet-aided Projects   158
A.6 Share of USSR Trade Turnover with Developed and
     Developing Countries   159
A.7 Trade between the Developing Countries and European
     CMEA Countries, 1978, and Forecast Share for 1990   160

Figures

A.1 Sectoral Distribution of Soviet Aid, 1954-79   156
A.2 Share of National Economy Sectors in the Total Volume
     of USSR Economic and Technical Assistance   156

TABLE A.1 Soviet Economic Aid Agreements with Major Third World Partners

(in million U.S. $)

	1955-64	1965-74	1975-79	Total
Total	3,805	6,255	8,120	18,190
Middle East	1,450	2,520	3,895	7,870
Egypt	1,000	440	0	1,440
Iran	65	725	375	1,165
Iraq	185	370	150	705
Syria	100	360	310	770
Other	100	625	3,060	3,790
North Africa	250	300	2,365	2,920
Algeria	230	195	290	715
Morocco	0	100	2,000	2,100
Other	20	5	75	105
South Asia	1,440	2,355	1,185	4,980
Afghanistan	530	300	450	1,290
India	810	1,130	340	2,280
Pakistan	40	655	225	920
Other	60	270	170	490
Sub-Saharan Africa	490	380	335	1,200
Latin America	30	595	340	965
East Asia	150	110	NEGL	260

Note: Because of rounding, components may not add to the totals shown.

Source: Central Intelligence Agency, National Foreign Assessment Center, *Communist Aid Activities in Non-Communist Less Developed Countries, 1979 and 1954-79* (Washington, D.C., October 1980), p. 7.

TABLE A.2 Communist Countries: Economic Aid to Non-Communist Developing Countries (in million U.S. $)

Year	Extended				Drawn			
	Total	Soviet Union	Eastern Europe	China	Total	Soviet Union	Eastern Europe	China
Total	32,980	18,190	9,830	4,960	14,500	8,170	3,590	2,740
1954-69	10,395	6,565	2,790	1,040	4,720	3,225	910	590
1970	1,175	200	195	780	605	390	145	70
1971	2,190	1,125	485	585	795	420	190	190
1972	2,180	655	920	605	860	430	170	260
1973	1,920	715	605	600	960	500	220	240
1974	1,915	815	820	280	1,190	705	230	255
1975	2,810	1,935	510	365	940	505	250	185
1976	1,930	980	800	150	1,160	465	375	320
1977	1,030	425	405	195	1,250	545	470	235
1978	4,850	3,060	1,575	220	1,110	485	380	240
1979	2,585	1,720	730	135	910	500	255	160

Note: Because of rounding, components may not add to the totals shown.

Source: Central Intelligence Agency, National Foreign Assessment Center, *Communist Aid Activities in Non-Communist Less Developed Countries, 1979 and 1954-79* (Washington, D.C., October 1980), p. 17.

TABLE A.3 Communist Countries: Military Aid to Non-Communist Developing Countries (in million U.S. $)

Year	Agreements Concluded				Equipment Delivered			
	Total	Soviet Union	Eastern Europe	China	Total	Soviet Union	Eastern Europe	China
Total	52,770	47,340	4,285	1,145	39,670	35,340	3,405	920
1955-69	7,075	5,875	935	265	6,110	5,060	840	210
1970	1,265	1,150	50	65	1,095	995	75	30
1971	1,790	1,590	120	80	1,050	865	125	60
1972	1,925	1,690	155	80	1,365	1,215	75	80
1973	3,045	2,890	130	25	3,340	3,135	130	80
1974	6,460	5,735	635	90	2,460	2,225	210	25
1975	4,000	3,325	635	40	2,425	2,040	285	100
1976	6,035	5,550	345	145	3,520	3,085	330	100
1977	9,260	8,715	475	75	5,125	4,705	345	75
1978	3,155	2,465	555	135	5,965	5,400	470	95
1979	8,750	8,365	250	140	7,205	6,615	525	70

Note: Because of rounding, components may not add to the totals shown.

Source: Central Intelligence Agency, National Foreign Assessment Center, *Communist Aid Activities in Non-Communist Less Developed Countries, 1979 and 1954-79* (Washington, D.C., October 1980), p. 13.

FIGURE A.1   Sectoral Distribution of Soviet Aid, 1954-79

Source: Central Intelligence Agency, National Foreign Assessment Center, *Communist Aid Activities in Non-Communist Less Developed Countries 1979 and 1954-79* (Washington, D.C., October 1979), p. 7.

FIGURE A.2   Share of National Economy Sectors in the Total Volume of USSR Economic and Technical Assistance

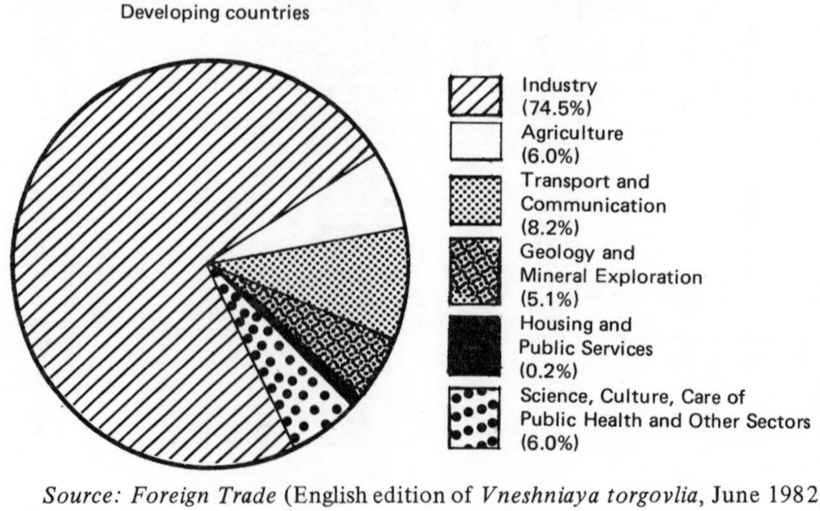

Developing countries

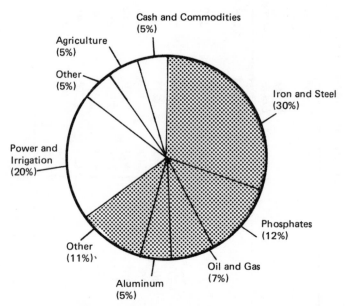

Source: Foreign Trade (English edition of *Vneshniaya torgovlia*, June 1982), p. 9.

TABLE A.4   Soviet-aided Projects, Completed and Under Construction, in Developing Countries
(by sectors)

Sector	Under Agreements		Completed	
	1976[a]	1981[b]	1976[a]	1981[b]
Total	954	1,193	507	680
Industries	426	501	208	300
Power	74	–	33	–
Ferrous and nonferrous metals	38	–	15	–
Coal, gas, and oil	37	–	18	–
Chemical, oil-processing, and petroleum industries	26	–	13	–
Engineering and metal-working industries	53	–	40	–
Construction materials	35	–	10	–
Light and food industries	149	–	67	–
Agriculture	138	152	66	73
Transport and communications	88	130	58	72
Geology and prospecting	63	89	28	44
Education, culture, and health	215	303	129	183
Other fields	–	18	–	8

[a]As of January 1, 1976.
[b]As of January 1, 1981.

Source: Vneshniaya torgovlia (June 1976): 11 and (June 1981): 5.

TABLE A.5 Geographic Distribution of Soviet-aided Projects (as of January 1, 1982)

	Total		*Industrial Enterprises*	
Country	*Under Agreements*	*Put into Operation*	*Under Agreements*	*Put into Operation*
Total	1,271	705	513	310
Asia	690	408	326	203
Afghanistan	167	78	46	19
India	92	56	65	38
Iraq	99	73	49	38
Iran	121	81	87	59
People's Democratic Republic of Yemen	33	15	11	5
Kampuchea	23	2	4	5
Pakistan	13	8	4	2
Syria	64	35	24	16
Turkey	15	8	13	8
Africa	556	295	174	106
Angola	28	11	1	—
Algeria	120	65	29	25
Egypt	107	95	47	36
Guinea	33	26	12	9
People's Republic of the Congo	20	10	5	2
Libya	15	2	6	2
Madagascar	9	1	1	—
Mali	17	13	3	1
Mozambique	33	6	7	—
Nigeria	12	2	2	—
Ethiopia	41	4	18	2

Source: Vneshniaya torgovlia (June 1982): 7.

TABLE A.6   Share of USSR Trade Turnover with Developed and Developing Countries (in percent)

Year	Developed Countries	Developing Countries
1955	15.5	4.6
1958	15.7	10.3
1960	19.0	7.8
1964	19.9	10.3
1970	21.3	13.5
1971	21.5	13.1
1972	22.6	12.9
1973	26.6	14.9
1974	31.4	14.6
1975	31.3	12.4
1976	32.9	11.5
1977	29.6	13.1
1978	28.0	12.2
1979	32.1	11.8
1980	33.5	12.7
1981	32.2	14.5
1982*	32.5	13.1

*January-June 1982 only.

Source: Vneshniaya torgovlia za . . . god (annual) and *Vneshniaya torgovlia* (monthly).

TABLE A.7 Trade between the Developing Countries and European CMEA Countries, 1978, and Forecast Share for 1990 (in billion U.S. $ and percent)

	Total	Developing Countries (in billion U.S. $)		Share of Developing Countries (percent)	
	1978	1978		1978	1990
Exports					
Bulgaria	7.4	0.71		9.5	12
Czechoslovakia	11.7	0.93		7.9	10
GDR	13.3	0.64		4.8	7-10
Hungary	6.3	0.55		8.7	12-13
Poland	13.5	1.12		8.3	12-14
Romania	8.0	1.58		20.0	25-30
Soviet Union	52.2	8.24		15.8	17-20
European CMEA	112.4	13.77		12.2	14.5-16.5
Imports					
Bulgaria	7.6	0.31		4.3	12.5
Czechoslovakia	12.6	0.58		4.6	9.5-10
GDR	14.6	0.73		5.0	8-10
Hungary	7.9	0.76		9.6	12-13
Poland	15.3	0.90		5.9	14-15
Romania	8.0	1.44		18.0	30
Soviet Union	50.5	4.04		8.0	18-20
European CMEA	116.5	8.76		7.6	15-17

Source: Christopher T. Saunders, ed., *East-West-South. Economic Interaction between Three Worlds* (New York: St. Martin's Press, 1981), p. 62. Estimates based on various issues of the U.N. *Monthly Bulletin of Statistics*, on national statistics, oral information, and consultations.

BIBLIOGRAPHY

Afrika: problemy sotsialisticheskoi orientatsii [Africa: Problems of Socialist Orientation]. Moscow: Nauka, 1976.

Andreasian, R. "Sotsialisticheskoe sodruzhestvo i razvivayushchiesia strany: ekonomicheskoe sotrudnichestvo" [The Socialist Community and the Developing Countries: Economic Cooperation]. *Narody Azii i Afriki* (March-April 1981): 3-13.

Andreasian, R., and Elianov, A. "Razvivayushchiesia strany: ekonomicheskaya diversifikatsiya i strategiya industrial'nogo razvitiya" [The Developing Countries: Economic Diversification and Strategy for Industrial Development]. *MEMO* (January 1968): 29-40.

Andreev, M. A. "Trudnosti razvitiya gosudarstvennogo sektora Indonezii" [Difficulties in the Development of the State Sector in Indonesia]. *Narody Azii i Afriki* (September-October 1963): 34-41.

Avakov, R. M. *Razvivayushchiesia strany: nauchno-tekhnologicheskaya revoliutsiya i problema nezavisimosti* [The Developing Countries: Scientific Technological Revolution and the Problem of Independence]. Moscow: Mysl', 1976.

Berton, P., and Rubinstein, A. *Soviet Works on Southeast Asia: A Biography of Non-Periodical Literature, 1946-65.* Los Angeles: University of Southern California Press, 1967.

Billerbeck, K. *Soviet Bloc Aid to the Underdeveloped Countries.* Hamburg: Hamburg Archives of World Economy, 1960.

Bogomolov, O. "The CMEA Countries and the New International Economic Order." In *East-West-South. Economic Interaction between Three Worlds*, edited by C. T. Saunders, pp. 246-56.

———. "Material'naya osnova prochnogo mira" [The Material Basis for a Stable Peace]. *Kommunist* no. 2 (January 1978): 95-106.

_____, ed. *Sotsializm i perestroika mezhdunarodnykh ekonomicheskikh otnoshenii* [Socialism and the Reconstruction of International Economic Relations]. Moscow: Mezhdunarodnye otnosheniya, 1982.

_____. *Strany sotsializma i mezhdunarodnoe razdelenie truda* [Countries of Socialism and the International Division of Labor]. Moscow: Nauka, 1980.

Bragina, E. *Razvivayushchiesia strany: gosudarstvennaya politika i promyshlennost'* [The Developing Countries: State Policy and Industry]. Moscow: Mysl', 1977.

Brutents, K. "A Great Force of Modern Times." *International Affairs* (March 1981): 74-85.

_____. "Imperializm i osvobodivshiesia strany" [Imperialism and the Liberated Countries]. *Pravda*, February 10, 1978, pp. 3-4.

_____. *Osvobodivshiesia strany v 70-e gody* [The Liberated Countries in the 1970s]. Moscow: Politicheskaya literatura, 1979.

Central Intelligence Agency, National Foreign Assessment Center. *Communist Aid Activities in Non-Communist Less Developed Countries, 1979 and 1954-1979*. Washington, D.C.: CIA, 1980.

_____. *Soviet Commercial Operations in the West*. Washington, D.C.: CIA, 1977.

Chekhutov, A. "Perestroika mezhdunarodnykh ekonomicheskikh otnoshenii – trebovanie zhizni" [The Reconstruction of International Economic Relations – the Requisite of Life]. *Kommunist* no. 16 (November 1981): 88-99.

_____. "Razvitie finansovo-ekonomicheskogo sotrudnichestva sotsialisticheskikh i osvobodivshikhsia stran" [The Development of Financial-Economic Cooperation between the Socialist and the Developing Countries]. *MEMO* (April 1981): 50-62.

Cheshkov, M. A. "Metodologicheskie problemy analiza gosuklada" [The Methodological Problems of Analyzing the State Sector]. In *Ekonomika razvivayushchikhsia stran. Teorii i metody issledovaniya*, edited by L. I. Reisner, pp. 324-51.

Cooper, Orah, and Fogarty, Ann. "Soviet Economic and Military Aid to Less Developed Countries, 1958-78." In *Soviet Policy in Developing Countries*, edited by W. R. Duncan (Huntington, N.Y.: Robert E. Krieger, 1981), pp. 11-32.

Department of State. *Communist Economic Policy in the Less Developed Areas.* Washington, D.C.: Government Printing Office, 1960.

_____. *The Sino-Soviet Economic Offensive.* Washington, D.C.: Department of State, 1962.

Desai, Padma. *The Bokaro Steel Plant: a study in Soviet economic assistance.* Cambridge: MIT Press, 1971.

Dinkevich, A. I., ed. *Razvivayushchiesia strany: nakoplenie i ekonomicheskii rost* [The Developing Countries: Accumulation and Economic Growth]. Moscow: Nauka, 1977.

_____, ed. *Razvivayushchiesia strany: problemy ekonomicheskogo razvitiya* [The Developing Countries: Problems of Economic Development]. Moscow: Nauka, 1978.

Dobozi, I., ed. *Economic Cooperation Between Socialist and Developing Countries.* Budapest: Hungarian Scientific Council for World Economy, 1978.

Dobozi, I., and Inotai, A. "Prospects of Economic Cooperation between CMEA Countries and Developing Countries." In *East-West-South. Economic Interaction between Three Worlds,* edited by C. T. Saunders, pp. 48-65.

Elianov, A. *Razvivayushchiesia strany: problemy ekonomicheskogo razvitiya i rynok* [The Developing Countries: Economic Development and the Market]. Moscow: Mysl', 1976.

Fundamentals of Marxism-Leninism. Moscow: Foreign Languages, 1963.

Gafurov, B. G. *Aktual'nye problemy sovremennogo natsional'no-osvoboditel'nogo dvizheniya* [Topical Problems of the Contemporary National Liberation Movement]. Moscow: Nauka, 1976.

Ganev, I. *SEV i 'Tret'ii Mir': problemy sotrudnichestva i razdeleniya truda* [CMEA and the 'Third World': Problems of Cooperation and Division of Labor]. Moscow: Ekonomika, 1976.

Gavrilov, L. V. *Eksport kapitala v razvivayushchiesia strany Afriki* [Export of Capital to the Developing Countries of Africa]. Moscow: Nauka, 1976.

Georgiev, G. "Razvivayushchiesia strany v bor'be za ekonomicheskoe ravno-pravie" [The Developing Countries in the Struggle for Economic Equality]. *MEMO* (May 1977): 13-22.

Glebov, S. "Problema obespecheniya chelovechestva syr'em i energei" [The Problem of Providing Mankind with Raw Materials and Energy]. *MEMO* (October 1980): 30-41.

Global'nye problemy mirovogo rynka [Global Problems of the World Market]. Riga: Gosudarstvennyi Latviiskii Universitet, 1980.

"Global'nye problemy nauchno-tekhnicheskoi revoliutsii" [Global Problems of the Scientific Technological Revolution]. *MEMO* (November 1981): 133-37.

Goldman, Marshall. *Soviet Foreign Aid*. New York: Praeger, 1967.

Gromyko, A. "Socialist Orientation in Africa." *International Affairs* (September 1979): 95-104.

Gutman, Patrick. "Tripartite Industrial Cooperation and Third Countries." In *East-West-South. Economic Interaction between Three Worlds*. edited by C. T. Saunders, pp. 337-64.

Hannigan, J. B., and McMillan, C. H. "CMEA Trade and Cooperation with the Third World in the Energy Sector." Paper prepared for the 1981 NATO Colloquium on *CMEA: Energy 1980-1990*, Brussels, April 8-10, 1981.

———. "The Soviet Energy Stake in Afghanistan and Iran: Rationale and Risk of Natural Gas Imports." Carleton University, Institute of Soviet and East European Studies, *East-West Commercial Relations Series* (August 1981).

Illyn, Yu. "African Studies in the USSR: the 1960s and the 1970s." *Social Science* no. 4 (1979): 64-69.

Inotai, A. "Hungary's Economic Relations with Developing Countries." *Marketing in Hungary* no. 2 (1978): 21-26.

Inozemtsev, N. N., ed. *Global'nye problemy sovremennosti* [Contemporary Global Problems]. Moscow: Mysl', 1981.

Ivanov, I. "Multinationals: What Kind of 'New World'?" 21 *World Marxist Review* (July 1978): 117-26.

Ivanov, I. D. "Perestroika mezhdunarodnykh otnoshenii — vazhnoe uslovie resheniya global'nykh problem" [Reconstruction of International Relations — An Important Condition for Resolving Global Problems]. In *Global'nye problemy sovremennosti*, edited by N. N. Inozemtsev, pp. 251-79.

"Joint Statement by the Socialist Countries . . . at the fourth session of the United Nations Conference on Trade and Development." *Foreign Trade* (September 1976): 1-24 (Supplement).

"Kak otsenivat' osobennosti i uroven' razvitiya kapitalizma v Latinskoi Amerike" [How to Evaluate the Traits and Level of Capitalist Development in Latin America]. *Latinskaya Amerika* (January-February 1979): 53-100.

Kalecki, M. *Essays in Developing Economies*. Hassock, England: Harvester, 1976.

Khoros, V. G. "Udzhamaa: opyt nekapitalisticheskogo razvitiya" [Ujamaa: An Experiment in Noncapitalist Development]. *Narody Azii i Afriki* (September-October 1977): 199-210.

Khvoinik, P. "Mirovoi kapitalizm i razvivayushchiesia strany" [World Capitalism and the Developing Countries]. *MEMO* (October 1980): 44-57.

Kim, G. F. *Ot natsional'nogo osvobozhdeniya k sotsial'nomy* [From the National to the Social Liberation]. Moscow: Nauka, 1982.

Kiva, A. *Strany sotsialisticheskoi orientatsii. Osnovnye tendentsii razvitiya* [Countries of Socialist Orientation. Basic Tendencies in Development]. Moscow: Nauka, 1979.

"Klassovaya bor'ba i kontseptsiya egalitarizma v razvivayushchikhsia stranakh" [Class Struggle and Egalitarian Concepts in the Developing Countries]. *Narody Azii i Afriki* (November-December 1978): 3-19.

Klassy i klassovaya bor'ba v razvivayushchikhsia stranakh [Classes and Class Struggle in the Developing Countries]. 3 vols. Moscow: Mysl', 1967-68.

Kleer, J. "Rozterki Trzeciego Swiata" [The Third World at a Loss]. *Polityka* (February 21, 1976): 13.

_____. *Vsemirnoe khoziaistvo. Zakonomernosti razvitiya* [World Economy. Regularities of Development]. Moscow: Mysl', 1979.

Kodachenko, A. S. *Vneshneekonomicheskaya polityka imperializma i razviv-ayushchiesia strany* [Foreign Policy of Imperialism and the Developing Countries]. Moscow: Nauka, 1977.

Kolesov, V. P. *Gosudarstvennyi sektor ekonomiki razvivayushchikhsia stran* [State Sector in the Economies of the Developing Countries]. Moscow: Moskovskii Universitet, 1977.

Kollontai, V. M., ed. *Global'nye problemy i mezhdunarodnye ekonomicheskie otnosheniya* [Global Problems and International Economic Relations]. Moscow: Institut sistemnykh issledovanii, 1981.

_____. *Puti preodoleniya ekonomicheskoi otstalosti* [Ways of Overcoming Economic Backwardness]. Moscow: Mezhdunarodnye otnosheniya, 1967.

_____. "Voprosy planirovaniya v tret'em mire" [Planning Problems in the Third World.] *MEMO* (July 1969): 91-100.

Kovalevsky, A. A. "Vozmozhnosti tekhnologicheskogo transferta v eksportnye otrasli razvivayushchikhsia stran" [Opportunities for Technology Transfer to the Export Branches in the Developing Countries]. In *Ekonomika razvivayushchikhsia stran. Teorii i metody issledovaniya*, edited by L. I. Reisner, pp. 7-21.

Krasnov, G. "Yunktad i problemy torgovlii stran s razlichnymi sotsial'no-ekonomicheskimi sistemami" [UNCTAD and Problems of Trade among Countries with Different Social Systems]. *Vneshniaya torgovlia* (August 1981): 49-53.

Krylov, V. "Osobennosti razvitiya proizvoditel'nykh sil i vosproizvodstvennogo protsessa v razvivayushchikhsia stranakh" [Specifics of the Development of Production Forces and Processes in the Developing Countries]. In *Ekonomika razvivayushchikhsia stran. Teorii i metody issledovaniya*, edited by L. I. Reisner, pp. 152-85.

Kupriyanov, A. B. *Razvivayushchiesia strany i mezhdunarodnoe sotrudnichestvo. Regional'nyi aspekt* [The Developing Countries and International Cooperation. The Regional Aspect]. Moscow: Nauka, 1980.

Kuznetsova, N. A., and Kalugina, L. M. *Iz istorii sovetskogo vostokovedeniya, 1917-1967* [From the History of Soviet Oriental Studies]. Moscow: Nauka, 1970.

Levkovsky, A., ed. *Inostrannyi kapital i inostrannoe predprinimatel'stvo v stranakh Azii i Severnoi Afriki* [Foreign Capital and Foreign Enterprise in Asian and in North African Countries]. Moscow: Nauka, 1977.

_____. *Sotsial'naya struktura razvivayushchikhsia stran* [Social Structure of the Developing Countries]. Moscow: Mysl', 1979.

Lowenthal, R. "Soviet 'Counterimperialism.'" *Problems of Communism* 25 (November-December 1976): 52-63.

Maidanik, K., and Mirsky, G. "Natsional'no-osvoboditel'naya bor'ba: sovremennyi etap" [The National Liberation Struggle: The Present Stage]. *MEMO* (June 1981): 17-29.

Maksimova, M. *SSSR i mezhdunarodnoe ekonomicheskoe sotrudnichestvo* [USSR and International Economic Cooperation]. Moscow: Mysl', 1977.

_____. "Vsemirnoe khoziaistvo i mezhdunarodnoe ekonomicheskoe sotrudnichestvo" [World Economy and International Economic Cooperation]. *MEMO* (April 1974): 3-16.

Mirsky, G. "Meniayushchiisia oblik 'tret'ego mira'" [The Changing Appearance of the Third World]. *Kommunist* no. 2 (January 1976): 106-15.

_____. "UAR: Home Front." *New Times* no. 50 (December 18, 1968): 8-10.

"Meropriyatiya po vypolneniyu resheniya XXV S'ezda KPSS v oblasti ekonomicheskoi nauki" [Measures for the Fulfillment of the Decisions of the 25th CPSU Congress in the Field of Economics]. *Voprosy ekonomiki* (March 1977): 4-6.

McLane, Charles. *Soviet-Third World Relations*. 3 vols. London: Central Asian Research Center, 1973-74.

McMillan, Carl H. "Growth of External Investment by the COMECON Countries." *The World Economy* 2 (September 1979): 363-86.

McMillan, Carl H., and Hannigan, J. B. "The Soviet-Iranian Relationship." Carleton University, Institute of Soviet and East European Studies. *Studies in the Soviet Union's International Energy Arrangements* (November 1979).

Natsional'no-osvoboditel'noe dvizhenie v Azii i Afrike [The National Liberation Movement in Asia and Africa]. 3 vols. Moscow: Nauka, 1967-68.

"Natsional'no-osvoboditel'noe dvizhenie: nekotorye voprosy differentsiatsii" [The National Liberation Movement: Some Problems of Differentiation]. *Aziya i Afrika segodnia* (June 1978): 28-35.

Nayyar, Deepak. *Economic Relations Between Socialist Countries and the Third World*. London: Macmillan, 1977.

"Neo-Colonialism — New System of Dependence and Enslavement?" *International Affairs* (November 1978): 65-93.

Obminsky, E. "Problems of Restructuring Economic Relations." *International Affairs* (January 1977): 59-67.

———. *Razvivayushchiesia strany i mezhdunarodnoe razdelenie truda* [The Developing Countries and the International Division of Labor]. Moscow: Mezhdunarodnye otnosheniya, 1974.

Osnovy Marksizma-Leninizma [Fundamentals of Marxism-Leninism]. Moscow: Gospolitizdat, 1959.

Osnovy nauchnogo kommunizma [Fundamentals of Scientific Communism]. Moscow: Politicheskaya literatura, 1966.

Palocz-Nemeth, E. "Exports of Manufactures of CMEA and Developing Countries to Developed Industrial Countries." *Acta Oeconomica* 26, no. 1-2 (1981): 93-101.

Paszynski, M. "Developing Countries in the International Division of Labor." *Oeconomica Polona* 6, no. 4 (1979): 499-526.

———. "Economic Relations between Socialist and Developing Countries in the Changing World." In *Economic Cooperation between Socialist and Developing Countries*, edited by I. Dobozi, pp. 55-68.

———. "Socialist Countries and the Concept of the New International Economic Order." Problem Commission of the Multilateral Scientific Cooperation of the Academies of Sciences of the Socialist Countries: Economy and Politics of the Developing Countries. Warsaw, May 1979. Mimeographed.

Patolichev, N. S. "Razvitie vneshnei torgovlii SSSR i perspektivy rasshireniya sovetsko-indiiskikh torgovykh otnoshenii" [The Development of USSR's Foreign Trade and the Prospects for the Broadening of Soviet-Indian Trade Relations]. *Vneshniaya torgovlia* (October 1981): 2-4.

Pletnev, E. "Major Problems in International Economic Relations." *Joint UNITAR/Foreign Trade Academy Seminar.* Moscow, April 1980. Mimeographed.

Pokataeva, T. *Razvivayushchiesia strany: problema urbanizatsii* [The Developing Countries: Urbanization Problems]. Moscow: Mysl', 1977.

Primakov, Evgenii. "Nekotorye problemy razvivayushchikhsia stran" [Some Problems of the Developing Countries]. *Kommunist* no. 11 (July 1978): 81-91.

____. "Strany sotsialisticheskoi orientatsii: trudnyi no real'nyi put' perekhoda k sotsializmu" [Countries of Socialist Orientation: The Difficult but Real Possibility of the Transition to Socialism]. *MEMO* (July 1981): 3-16.

____. "Strany Vostoka v sovremennom mire" [Countries of the East in the Contemporary World]. *Pravda*, August 11, 1982, pp. 4-5.

____. *Vostok posle krakha kolonial'noi sistemy* [The East after the Collapse of the Colonial System]. Moscow: Nauka, 1982.

____. "Zakon neravnomernosti razvitiia i istoricheskie sud'by osvobodivshikhsia stran" [The Law of Unequal Development and the Historical Fate of the Liberated States]. *MEMO* (December 1980): 28-47.

Prokhorov, G. M. *Problemy sotrudnichestva sotsialisticheskikh i razvivayush-chikhsia stran* [Problems of Cooperation between the Socialist and the Developing Countries]. Moscow: Nauka, 1966.

Ra'anan, Uri. "Moscow and the Third World." *Problems of Communism* 14 (January-February 1965): 22-31.

Radu, M., ed. *Eastern Europe and the Third World: East vs. South.* New York: Praeger, 1981.

Razvivayushchiesia strany: zakonomernosti, tendentsii, perspektivy [The Developing Countries: Regularities, Tendencies, Prospects]. Moscow: Mysl', 1974.

Reisner, L. I., ed. *Ekonomika razvivayushchikhsia stran. Teorii i metody issledovaniya* [The Economy of the Developing Countries. Theories and Research Methodologies]. Moscow: Nauka, 1979.

_____ . *Razvivayushchiesia strany: ocherk teorii ekonomicheskogo rosta* [The Developing Countries: Essay on the Theory of Economic Growth]. Moscow: Nauka, 1976.

Roslavlev, A. U. "Eshche raz a teorii 'mnogoukladnosti' v stranakh 'tret'ego mira'" [Once Again about the Multisectoral Theory in the Countries of the Third World]. *Rabochii klass i sovremennyi mir* (January-February 1977): 136-45.

Rubinstein, G. "Problemy i trudnosti naibolee otstalykh stran" [Problems and Difficulties of the Least Developed Countries]. *MEMO* (August 1977): 128-33.

Rymalov, V. "Ekonomicheskoe sorevnovanie dvukh sistem i problema pomoshchi slaborazvitym stranam" [The Economic Competition of the Two Systems and Assistance to the Underdeveloped Countries]. *MEMO* (February 1960): 30-42.

_____ . "Soviet Assistance to Underdeveloped Countries." *International Affairs* (September 1959): 23-31.

_____ . *Strukturnye izmeneniya v mirovom kapitalisticheskom khoziaistve* [Structural Changes in the World Capitalist Economy]. Moscow: Mysl', 1978.

Saunders, Christopher T., ed. *East-West-South. Economic Interaction between Three Worlds.* New York: St. Martin's Press, 1981.

Sheinis, V. "O spetsifike sotsial'nykh protsessov v razvivayushchikhsia stranakh" [On the Specifics of the Social Processes in the Developing Countries]. *Aziya i Afrika segodnia* (November 1981): 26-29.

_____ . "Razvivayushchiesia strany: osobennosti ekonomicheskogo rosta" [The Developing Countries: Peculiarities of Economic Growth]. *MEMO* (December 1981): 54-61.

_____ . "Strany srednego kapitalizma" [Countries of Middle-level Capitalist Development]. *MEMO* (September 1977): 105-24.

Shekar, Jaya. "Economic Links." *Seminar* (September 1981): 21-26.

Shmelev, N. P., ed. *Ekonomicheskie sviazi Vostok-Zapad: problemy i vozmozhnosti* [East-West Economic Relations: Problems and Opportunities]. Moscow: Mysl', 1976.

_____. "Razvivayushchiesia strany: formirovanie khoziaistvennogo mekhanizma" [The Developing Countries: Formation of the Economic Mechanism]. *MEMO* (August 1968): 52-62.

_____. *Sotsializm i mezhdunarodnye ekonomicheskie otnosheniya* [Socialism and International Economic Relations]. Moscow: Mezhdunarodnye otnosheniya, 1979.

Shpirt, A. Yu. *Nauchno-tekhnicheskaya revoliutsiya i razvivayushchiesia strany* [The Scientific-Technological Revolution and the Developing Countries]. Moscow: Nauka, 1970.

Simoniya, N. A. "Metodologicheskie problemy analiza ekonomicheskogo razvitiya v osvobodivshikhsia stranakh" [Methodological Problems of Analyzing Economic Development in the Liberated Countries]. In *Ekonomika razvivayushchikhsia stran. Teorii i metody issledovaniya*, edited by L. I. Reisner, pp. 186-210.

_____. *Strany Vostoka: puti razvitiya* [Countries of the East: Paths of Development]. Moscow: Nauka, 1975.

Skachkov, S. A. "Ekonomicheskoe sotrudnichestvo Sovetskogo Soyuza s zarubezhnymi stranami" [Economic Cooperation between the USSR and Foreign Countries]. *Vneshniaya torgovlia* (March 1981): 3-10.

Skorov, G. E., ed. *Razvivayushchiesia strany: nauka, tekhnika, ekonomicheskii rost* [The Developing Countries: Science, Technology, Economic Growth]. Moscow: Mysl', 1975.

_____. *Razvivayushchiesia strany: obrazovanie, zaniatost', ekonomicheskii rost* [The Developing Countries: Education, Employment, Economic Growth]. Moscow: Nauka, 1971.

_____. "Vozrastanie roli osvobodivshikhsia stran v mirovom razvitii" [Growth of the Liberated Countries' Role in World Development]. *MEMO* (April 1976): 37-50.

Slavnyi, B. I. "Nekotorye voprosy formirovaniya obshchei kontseptsii slaborazvitosti v burzhuaznoi nauke" [Some Problems in Forming General Concepts of Underdevelopment in Bourgeois Scholarship]. *Narody Azii i Afriki* (July-August 1979): 183-201.

_____. "Problemy izucheniya razvivayushchikhsia stran v burzhuaznoi nauke" [Problems of Studying the Developing Countries in Bourgeois Scholarship]. *Narody Azii i Afriki* (July-August 1976): 136-45.

Sotrudnichestvo sotsialisticheskikh i razvivayushchikhsia stran: novyi tip mezhdunarodnykh otnoshenii [Cooperation between the Socialist and the Developing Countries: A New Type of International Relations]. Moscow: Nauka, 1980.

SSSR i mezhdunarodnoe ekonomicheskoe sotrudnichestvo [The USSR and International Economic Cooperation]. Moscow: Nauka, 1977.

Stalin, J. V. *Economic Problems of Socialism.* New York: International Publishers, 1952.

Starushenko, G. B. *Sotsialisticheskaya orientatsiya v razvivayushchikhsia stranakh* [Socialist Orientation in the Developing Countries]. Moscow: Politicheskaya literatura, 1977.

Strany SEV v mirokhoziaistvennykh sviaziakh [The CMEA Countries in International Economic Relations]. Moscow: Nauka, 1978.

Subbotin, A. K. *Mirovye ekonomicheskie problemy: perspektivy resheniya* [The World Economic Problems: The Prospects for a Solution]. Moscow: Mezhdunarodnye otnosheniya, 1980.

Svanidze, I. A. *Sel'skoe khoziaistvo i agrarnyi stroi Tropicheskoi Afriki* [Agriculture and the Agrarian System in Tropical Africa]. Moscow: Nauka, 1977.

Szentes, T. "The Development of Economic, Technical and Scientific Relations between Hungary and the Developing Countries." In *Economic Cooperation between Socialist and Developing Countries,* edited by I. Dobozi, pp. 139-60.

———. *'Tret'ii Mir': problemy razvitiya* [The Third World: Development Problems]. Moscow: Progress, 1974.

Teodorovich, T. V., and Efanov, V. V. *Sotrudnichestvo pri sooruzhenii ob'ektov za rubezhom. Iz opyta sovetskikh organizatsii* [Cooperation in the Construction of Project Abroad: From the Experience of Soviet Organizations]. Moscow: Mezhdunarodnye otnosheniya, 1979.

"The Theory and Practice of Non-Capitalist Development" *International Affairs* (November 1970): 11-25.

Tiagunenko, V. L. *Mezhdunarodnoe razdelenie truda i razvivayushchiesia strany* [The International Division of Labor and the Developing Countries]. Moscow: Nauka, 1976.

_____. *Problemy sovremennykh natsional'no-osvoboditel'nykh revoliutsii* [Problems of the Contemporary National Liberation Revolutions]. Moscow: Nauka, 1966.

Tipologiya nesotsialisticheskikh stran (opyt mnogomernogo statisticheskogo analiza narodnykh khoziaistv) [Typology of the Non-socialist Countries (An Attempt at Multidimensional Statistical Analysis of the National Economies)]. Moscow: Nauka, 1976.

Tiul'panov, S. "Obshchestvo perekhodnogo tipa" [Transitional-type Society]. *MEMO* (January 1979): 144-46.

'Tret'ii mir' i nauchno-tekhnicheskii progress [The Third World and Scientific Technological Progress]. Moscow: Nauka, 1974.

Tretiukhin, N. "Novye napravleniya vo vneshneekonomicheskikh sviaziakh SSSR" [New Directions in Foreign Economic Relations of the USSR]. *Vneshniaya torgovlia* (January 1977): 7-14.

Tuzmukhamedov, R. *Razvivayushchiesia strany v mirovoi politike* [The Developing Countries in World Politics]. Moscow: Mezhdunarodnye otnosheniya, 1977.

Ulianovsky, R. A. "Dvadtsatyi vek i natsional'no-osvoboditel'noe dvizhenie" [Twentieth Century and the National Liberation Movement]. *Narody Azii i Afriki* (March-April 1980): 2-9.

_____. "Natsional'no-osvoboditel'noe dvizhenie v bor'be za ekonomicheskuyu nezavisimost'" [The National Liberation Movement in the Struggle for Economic Independence]. *Kommunist* no. 14 (September 1976): 112-22.

_____. "Nauchnyi sotsializm i osvobodivshiesia strany" [Scientific Socialism and the Liberated Countries]. *Kommunist* no. 4. (March 1968): 92-106.

_____. "O osobennostiakh razvitiya i kharaktere gosudarstvennogo kapitalizma v Indii" [On the Peculiarities and Character of State Capitalism in India]. *Problemy vostokovedeniya* (May-June 1960): 23-41.

_____. "O stranakh sotsialisticheskoi orientatsii" [On Countries of Socialist Orientation]. *Kommunist* no. 11 (July 1979): 114-23.

_____. *Sovremennye problemy Azii i Afriki* [Contemporary Problems of Asia and Africa]. Moscow: Nauka, 1978.

Ul'rikh, O. "Preodolenie otstalosti v razvivayushchikhsia stranakh" [Overcoming Backwardness in the Developing Countries]. *MEMO* (September 1981): 47-58.

Ushakova, N. A. *SEV i razvivayushchiesia gosudarstva sotsialisticheskoi orientatsii: ekonomicheskoe sotrudnichestvo* [CMEA and the Developing Countries of Socialist Orientation: Economic Cooperation]. Moscow: Nauka, 1980.

Utkin, E. A. *Problemy planirovaniya v razvivayushchikhsia stranakh* [Problems of Planning in the Developing Countries]. Moscow: Ekonomika, 1965.

Vaganov, B. S., ed. *Vneshniaya torgovlia sotsialisticheskikh stran: voprosy teorii* [Foreign Trade of the Socialist Countries: Problems of Theory]. Moscow: Mezhdunarodnye otnosheniya, 1966.

Valkenier, E. K. "Development Issues in Recent Soviet Scholarship." *World Politics* 32 (July 1980): 485-508.

―――. "New Trends in Soviet Economic Relations with the Third World." *World Politics* 22 (April 1970): 415-33.

―――. "Soviet Economic Relations with the Third World." In *The Soviet Union and the Developing Countries*, edited by R. Kanet. Baltimore: Johns Hopkins University Press, 1974, pp. 215-36.

―――. "The USSR, the Third World, and the Global Economy." *Problems of Communism* 28 (July-August 1979): 17-33.

Vneshniaya torgovlia SSSR za . . . god [Foreign Trade of the USSR for year . . .]. Moscow: Vneshtorg, annual.

Volkov, M. "Kontseptsiya osnovnykh potrebnostei" [The Basic Needs Concept]. *Voprosy ekonomiki* (July 1981): 133-42.

Volkova, N. "Nekotorye aspekty deyatel'nosti mnogonatsional'nykh korporatsii v razvivayushchikhsia stranakh" [Some Aspects of the Multinational Corporations' Activities in the Developing Countries]. In *Inostrannyi kapital i inostrannoe predprinimatel'stvo v stranakh Azii i Severnoe Afriki*, edited by A. I. Levkovsky, pp. 52-65.

Wiles, Peter, ed. *The New Communist Third World*. New York: St. Martin's Press, 1982.

Working-Class and National-Liberation Movements: Joint Struggle against Imperialism, for Social Progress. Documents of the International Scientific Conference, Berlin, October 20-24, 1980. Moscow: Novosti, 1981.

Yashkin, V. "Gosudarstvennyi uklad v mnogoukladnoi ekonomike" [The State Sector in the Multisectoral Economy]. *Aziya i Afrika segodnia* (March 1979): 40-44.

——. "Prospects for the Establishment of the New International Economic Order and Development Strategy of the 80s." *Joint UNITAR/Foreign Trade Academy Seminar.* Moscow, April 1980. Mimeographed.

Zagladin, V. V., and Frolov, I. T. "Global'nye problemy sovremennosti" [Contemporary Global Problems]. *Kommunist* no. 16 (November 1976): 93-104.

——. *Global'nye problemy sovremennosti: nauchnyi i stosial'nyi aspekty* [Contemporary Global Problems: Scientific and Social Aspects]. Moscow: Mezhdunarodnye otnosheniya, 1981.

Zarubezhnye kontseptsii ekonomicheskogo razvitiya stran Afriki [Foreign Conceptions of the Economic Development of African Countries]. Moscow: Nauka, 1980.

Zarubezhnyi Vostok i sovremennost' [The East Beyond Soviet Borders and Contemporary Times]. 2 vols. Moscow: Nauka, 1974. 2d ed., 3 vols., 1980.

Zevin, L. "Concepts of Economic Development of the Developing Nations and Problems of Tripartite Cooperation." In *East-West-South. Economic Interaction between Three Worlds*, edited by C. T. Saunders, pp. 295-302.

——. *Economic Cooperation of Socialist and Developing Countries: New Trends.* Moscow: Nauka, 1975.

——. "Proekt razvitiya ekonomicheskikh otnoshenii 'Sever-Yug'" [Project for the Development of North-South Economic Relations]. *Voprosy ekonomiki* (April 1982): 129-37.

——. "Voprosy povysheniya ustoichivosti i effektivnosti ekonomicheskikh sviazei SSSR s razvivayushchimisia stranami" [Problems of Raising the Stability and Effectiveness of the USSR's Economic Ties with the Developing Countries]. *Planovoe khoziaistvo* (July 1971): 17-26.

——. "Vzaimnaya vygoda ekonomicheskogo sotrudnichestva sotsialisticheskikh i razvivayushchikhsia stran" [Mutual Advantage in the Economic Cooperation between the Socialist and the Developing Countries]. *Voprosy ekonomiki* (February 1965): 72-83.

Zurawicki, L. *Multinational Enterprises in West and East*. Alphen aan den Rijn, Netherlands: Sijthoff and Noordhoff, 1979.

_____ . "Prospects for Tripartite Cooperation." *Intereconomics* 12 (July-August 1978): 184-87.

Soviet Periodicals

Aziya i Afrika segodnia (monthly)

Foreign Trade (monthly, English edition of *Vneshniaya torgovlia*)

International Affairs (monthly)

Kommunist (18 times a year)

Latinskaya Amerika (bimonthly, 1961-80; monthly 1981-   ).

MEMO [*Mirovaya ekonomika i mezhdunarodnye otnosheniya*] (monthly)

Narody Azii i Afriki (bimonthly)

New Times (weekly)

Planovoe khoziaistvo (monthly)

Problemy vostokovedeniya (bimonthly, 1959 to January-February 1961)

Vneshniaya torgovlia (monthly)

Voprosy ekonomiki (monthly)

World Marxist Review (monthly)

SUBJECT INDEX

Academic debates, USSR
development theory, 81ff
domestic reform, 54-55, 132-35
global economy, 38-39, 46-49, 53-59,
62-69, 83-85, 126-27, 148-49
neo-colonialism, 92-93
NIEO, 117-21, 127ff
relations with LDCs, 65-69, 148-50
Academic experts, USSR
on Central Committee staff, 57, 63
and policy making, 27, 38-39, 56-
58, 64-65, 81, 148-50
and policy needs, 38, 40-42, 50, 127
Academic institutes, USSR, 134
Africa, 41, 42, 99
Economy of the World Socialist
System, 12, 13, 42, 48, 59
Latin America, 41, 42
Oriental Studies, 41, 42, 50-51, 57,
71n, 75, 86, 93, 100
World Economy and International
Relations, 41-42, 47, 50-51, 67-69,
71-72n, 79-80, 82, 86, 126
see also Research, USSR
Academies of Sciences, CMEA, 58, 61,
127, 132-33
Academy of Sciences, USSR, 12, 38,
62-63; see also Academic Institutes,
USSR
Adria pipeline, 19, 31
Agriculture and development, 77, 79-
80, 88, 90
Anti-imperialist front
new Soviet view of, 59, 64-65, 67,
109-13, 121, 135
old Soviet view of, 6ff, 67, 109

Asian mode of production, 96
Aswan Dam, 4, 12
Aziya i Afrika segodnia, 42

Backwardness, see Underdevelopment
Baghdad Pact, 6
Basic human needs, 90
Bauxite, joint production of, 17
Bhilai steel mill, 8
Bokaro steel plant, 141-42

Capitalism
dependent, 83, 93-94
national, 93
semi-developed, 83
Capitalist institutions
and backwardness, 7, 73, 74-76
as spur to development, 73-74, 79,
83-86, 100ff
Capitalist-oriented states, 82, 96
Capitalist world market
and NIEO, 115ff, 136, 138-39
see also World economy; World
market
Club of Rome, 89
CMEA, See Council of Mutual Economic Assistance
Colonialism
new Soviet view on, 65, 81, 83-85,
92-93, 148
traditional Soviet view on, 43-44,
60, 74-76
see also Imperialism
Commodity production and development, 2, 7, 74, 79, 90, 122, 124,
130

Communits Parties
Berlin Conference (1980), 137-39, 140
Berlin Meeting (1976), 111
Moscow Meeting (1960), 6
Third World, 6-7
Congress of Third World Economists (1976), 136
Convertible accounts, 22
Council of Mutual Economic Assistance (CMEA),
aid, 16, 23
economic policy, 16, 22-24, 123, 127ff
foreign trade, 16, 24, 123, 143
raw materials imports from LDCs, 13-14, 23-25, 31, 123-25, 127-28
and socialist oriented states, 97-99
see also Economic policy, Eastern Europe; Foreign trade, East Europe
CPSU (Communist Party of the Soviet Union) Congresses
20th (1956), 40-41, 53
21st (1959), 5, 13
22nd (1961), 6, 11-12
23rd (1966), 13, 16
24th (1971), 16-17, 47-48
25th (1976), 49, 56, 57, 64, 65, 98
26th (1981), 54, 64-66, 81, 98, 101
CPSU Program (1961), 43-44, 47, 54, 65, 74
CPSU, and research, 38-39, 40ff, 50, 52, 53, 65-66

Declaration on New International Economic Order (1974), 111
Declaration on the Restructuring of International Economic Relations (1976), 113-14
Dependency theory, LDC
coincidence with Soviet, 11, 74, 103, 113
divergence from Soviet, 110-11, 135-40

Dependency theory, USSR
new, 52ff, 81-85, 87, 90, 92-95, 110-111, 148
traditional, 7, 43-44, 45, 47, 74-76, 81, 83, 110
Development model, Chinese, 87, 139-40
Development model, LDC sui generis, 85-86, 92; see also Asian mode of production
Development model, Soviet
commodity production, 74, 81ff, 90, 122
industrialization, 7, 11, 74, 79, 83, 88, 141
mixed economy, 79-80, 85, 88-89
Development model, Western, 86, 88, 89
Development theory, Chinese, 87, 139-40
Development theory, East European, 130
Development theory, LDC, 74, 87, 90, 103; see also, Dependency theory, LDC; Economic policy, LDC
Development theory, Soviet, 73
current debates, 81ff
pre-1964, 6-7, 11, 43-45, 74-76, 78
post-1964, 45, 49-52, 76-80
post-1975, 45, 73-74, 81ff, 122
see also Underdevelopment
Disarmament, 114
Domestic reforms, East European, and trade, 132-35
Domestic reforms, LDC, and development, 118, 120-21
Domestic reforms, USSR, 54, 132-35
and trade, 54, 133-35

East-West trade, 2, 22, 37, 40, 45, 46, 48, 115, 125-26, 128
Ecology, 38, 54, 63
Economic aid, USSR
Africa, 24, 32-33, 98

fishing companies, 20, 29, 33, 129
food production, 18
impact on Western aid, 10-11, 141
joint production schemes, 14, 17-18, 23, 24, 33, 48, 113, 129
LDCs' demand for, 22, 103, 110-11, 138-39
periodization: pre-1954, 2-3; post-1954, 3-11, 109, 140-41; post-1964, 11-22, 109, 140-41; post-1974, 22-26; post-1980, 30-33
and raw material extraction, 14, 17-18, 23-24, 29, 123, 128
repayment problems, 14, 77, 123
tables, 153, 154, 156, 157, 158
and transition to socialism, 6ff, 75-76, 80, 85, 101-103
tripartite agreements, 29-32, 33, 48, 124-25, 142
Economic coexistence, East West, 53ff, 64, 110, 115
see also Interdependence, global
Economic competition, East-West, 4ff, 10-11, 20-22, 37, 39-40, 47-48, 109, 111-15
Economic complementarity, Soviet-LDC, 8-9, 21-22
erosion of, 22ff, 28, 59, 141-43
Economic policy, East Europe, 2, 18, 19, 20, 23, 31, 110ff, 127ff
Economic policy, foreign, USSR
Chinese criticism of, 139-40
current reassessment, 26-33, 37-39, 114ff, 149
and domestic reforms, 54, 132-35
groupings in debates, 53-59, 133-35
ideological motivation of, 37-38, 47-48, 49, 53, 129-30, 147
NIEO, *see* NIEO
periodization: pre-1953, 1-2; post-1953, 3-13, 140-41; post-1964, 13-22, 76-77; post-1974, 22-26, 38, 46ff, 109
political thrust of, 1-2, 3ff, 12-13,

20-22, 26ff, 39, 74-76, 80, 109, 114, 116ff
pragmatic motivation of, 1-3, 11-20, 37, 47, 54, 76ff, 114ff, 122ff
radical LDC criticism of, 74, 103, 137-38
UNCTAD, *see* UNCTAD
Western reaction to, 3, 9-10, 21
Economic policy, LDC
coincidence with Soviet, 11, 21, 74, 103, 109-10, 113ff, 135
divergence from Soviet, 110-11, 135-40
Soviet criticism of, 77-78, 87, 90, 101, 113-14, 117-21, 125, 126-27, 135ff
Economic policy, socialist oriented states, 97ff
Economic power, Soviet, and foreign policy, 37-38, 73, 109-10, 147-50
Employment, 88, 89, 90
Energy crisis, 22, 52, 59
and Soviet Bloc-LDC exchanges, 22ff, 110, 123
Energy resources, *see* Oil; Raw materials
Five Year Plan, 10th (1976-80), 17, 25
Five Year Plan, 11th (1981-85), 24, 25, 54
Food
as global problem, 54, 90, 149
Soviet imports of, 1, 25, 123, 143
Foreign investment, East European, 20, 129, 130
Foreign investment, LDC, 58, 59, 83, 93, 121, 131
in CMEA, 19, 31, 128
Foreign investment, Soviet, 8, 19-20, 29, 48-49, 124, 129
joint with LDCs, 30, 124, 129, 142
Foreign investment, Western
in socialist-oriented states, 99, 102-

123
as spur to development, 77, 78-79, 80, 83, 85, 92-95, 119
Foreign trade, Eastern Europe, 19, 21-22, 24, 123
oil imports, 23-24, 31, 110, 128
Foreign trade, LDC
competition with USSR, 28, 130-32, 141-42
Foreign trade, USSR
competition from the LDCs, 28, 130-32, 141-42
and domestic reform, 54, 133-35
experts' analyses of, 12, 13-14, 26-30, 42, 48, 54, 59, 128
food imports, 1, 25, 123, 143
international restrictions on, 114-17, 119-20, 125
machinery exports, 1, 2, 8-9, 19, 21, 22, 23, 25, 28, 29-30, 123, 131, 141-42
manufactured goods imports, 14, 21, 29, 143
military equipment, 25-26, 155 *table*
with oil-producing states, 25, 27-28, 128
periodization: pre-1953, 1-2; post-1953, 2-3, 6, 8-10; post-1964, 13ff, 19, 21-22; post-1974, 22-26; post-1980, 30-33
prospects for, 24-25, 141-43, 160 *table*
raw material imports, 1, 13-14, 21, 25, 123-25, 127-28, 143
tables, 159, 160
with the West, 2, 22, 37, 40, 45, 46, 48, 115, 125-26
see also Economic policy, USSR; International division of labor, socialist
Fuel, *see* Oil; Raw materials
Fundamentals of Marxism-Leninism, 43, 49
Fundamentals of Scientific Commu-

nism, 49

Global economy, 26
Soviet debates on, 38-39, 46-47, 53-59, 62-69, 83-85, 126-27, 148-49
see also World market, Soviet doctrine of
Global problems, 38-39, 54, 58, 63ff
backwardness as, 38, 62-69, 73-74, 87-88, 149
and systemic competition, 38, 64, 65ff
Great Soviet Encyclopedia, 46, 48

Helsinki agreements, 126

Imperialism
alleged Third World, 58, 59, 83, 121, 131
new Soviet view on, 56-58, 64-65, 67-68, 77, 81, 92-93, 115, 116ff
traditional Soviet view on, 40, 56, 64, 74, 81, 112
Industrialization, 7, 11, 73-74, 75, 76, 77, 79-80, 83, 88
see also Colonialism; Neocolonialism
Interdependence, global, 48, 61
and development, 73-74, 81-82, 83-84
and international peace, 65, 67-68, 88, 149
Soviet debate on, 38-39, 53-56, 62-69, 83-86, 117ff, 148-49
and Soviet response to NIEO, 110, 113ff
see also World economy, Soviet doctrine of
International division of labor, 12, 13, 54
International division of labor, social-ist, 13ff, 37, 47-48
failure of, 22-26, 52
from global viewpoint, 26, 81-82, 83-85, 122-27, 137, 142-43
political thrust of, 20-22, 26, 80

and socialist-oriented states, 101-103
as Soviet NIEO proposal, 109-13
International Economic Conference (1952), 1
International Investment Bank, 16, 20
International Monetary Fund, 15, 20
International peace and underdevelopment, 65, 67-68, 88, 149

Joint equity firms
East European, 20, 129
Soviet, 8, 19-20, 29, 48-49, 124, 129

Kommunist, 56, 78, 100, 119, 126

Latinskaya Amerika, 42
LDCs, *see* Third World

Manila Declaration (1972), 133
Military aid, *tables*, 155
Military sales, USSR, 25-26, 155 *table*
Mirovaya ekonomika i mezhdunarodnye otnosheniya, 42, 51
Mixed economy
as development model, 79-80, 85, 88-89
in socialist-oriented states, 100-103
Mnogoukladnost', 82, 85-86, 88-89, 93
Modernization model, *see* Development theory
Multilateralization, proposed, 133-35
Multinationals
LDCs', 96
Socialist, 132
Western, 58, 68-69, 94-95, 96

Narody Azii i Afriki, 42, 50, 77
Nationalization, 11, 75, 76, 78, 93
Natural gas
joint production of , 17-18, 19, 30
transshipment to West, 30-31

Neocolonialism, 28, 57, 112
Soviet debate on, 92-93
New Delhi Declaration (1980), 116
New Economic Policy (NEP), 79-80, 85, 88-89, 134
NIEO (New International Economic Order), 111
Chinese response to, 139-40
current Soviet debate on, 117-21, 126-27, 129-30
current Soviet scenario for, 122-25
East European response to, 110, 127-35
Soviet pre-1976 response, 109-13
Soviet post-1976 response, 110, 113-17, 125-26, 127ff, 149-50
Nonalignment, 4, 6, 59, 111
Noncapitalist path, 6-7, 77, 97-98
North-South issues, *see* NIEO (New International Economic Order)

Oil
in intra-CMEA trade, 122-23, 128
joint production of, 23-24, 122-23
Oil-producing states, 82
investment in CMEA, 19, 31, 128
trade with East Europe, 19, 23-24
trade with USSR, 25, 27-28, 128
OPEC, *see* Oil-producing states

Petrodollars, 19, 52, 58, 59; *see also* Oil-producing states
Phosphates, joint production of, 33
Planning, 134
and development, 11, 21, 75, 76, 77, 78, 95
of Soviet-LDC exchanges, 3, 9, 12, 14, 15-17, 21, 113, 142-43
Political stability
and development, 86-87
and international peace, 67-68, 149
Population
and development, 88, 89
as global problem, 38, 63, 149

Pravda, 57
Private sector
  and development, 73-74, 79, 80, 95
  in socialist-oriented states, 100-103
Problems of Leninism, 43
Public sector
  and development, 7, 75, 77-78, 79,
  95-96

Raw materials
  denial of, 3ff, 10, 21
  and development, *see* Commodity
  production and development
  East European imports, 14, 23-24,
  31, 110, 122-23, 128-28
  as global problem, 38, 54, 68-69,
  149
  joint production of, 14, 17-18, 23-
  24, 29, 33, 123, 128, 129
  LDC control of, 79, 93, 112
  Soviet imports, 1, 13-14, 21, 25,
  123-25, 127-28, 143
Regionalism and development, 126
Research, Eastern Europe, 2, 59-61,
  127ff
  Bulgaria, 128, 130
  Hungary, 24, 60-61, 127-28, 131
  Poland, 60-61, 131, 132-33
Research, USSR
  current trends in, *see* Academic
  debates, USSR
  on development, *see* Development
  theory, Soviet
  and East European research, 2, 58,
  59-61, 127ff
  and foreign policy, *see* Academic
  experts, USSR, and policy needs
  and Party direction of, 38-39, 40ff,
  50, 52, 53, 65-66, 127
  on trade, 12, 13-14, 26-30, 42, 48,
  54, 59, 128
  and Western scholarship, 45, 50, 59-
  60, 63, 82, 88, 89
  see also Academic institutes, USSR;

Academy of Sciences, USSR
Revolutionary democrats, 6-7, 44, 98,
  99

Scientific Technological Revolution,
  46, 90-92
Self-reliance and development, 49,
  126, 136-37, 140
Social reform and development, 90,
  120-21
Social stability
  and development, 86-87, 89-90
  and international peace, 67-68, 149
Socialism, transition to
  Lenin on, 79, 80-81, 85, 86, 87,
  103
  pre-1964 Soviet views, 7, 43-45, 75,
  97
  post-1964 Soviet views, 13, 47, 49,
  80
  recent Soviet views on, 64-65, 85-
  88, 97ff, 121
  and Soviet aid, 6ff, 75-76, 80, 85,
  101-103
Socialist orientation, theory of, 97-
  99, 101
Socialist-oriented states, 27, 64-65, 82,
  96
  and capitalist market, 97, 99, 100-101
  economic policy for, 97-103
  and foreign investment, 99, 102-103
  as part of CMEA, 97, 99
  and Soviet aid, 27, 32-33, 110-11
Socialist world market, 37-38, 39-40,
  46-47, 80
  see also International division of
  labor, socialist
State sector, *see* public sector
Suez Canal, 4

Technology and development, 45, 46,
  79, 88, 90-92
Third World
  chauvinism in, 67, 88, 149

common interests with Soviet Bloc, 37, 52, 56-58, 64-65

disagreements with Soviet Bloc, 74, 103, 110-11, 135-40, 148-49

diversity of, 58, 59, 60, 64-65, 81, 82

economic competition with USSR, 28, 130-32, 141-42

socioeconomic complexity of, 82, 85-86, 88-89, 93, 100

unity of, 50, 51-52, 56, 59, 61, 65, 80, 82, 83

Transferable ruble, 16, 133

Tripartite cooperation, 29-32, 33, 48, 124-25, 133, 142

UNCTAD (United Nations Conference on Trade and Development)

I (1964), 12, 15

IV (1976), 112-113, 121, 133

V (1979), 114-116, 119, 121, 125, 129, 135, 136, 140

VI (1983), 116-17

Underdevelopment

from a global perspective, 62-69, 73-74, 81ff, 149

and international peace, 65, 67-68, 88, 149

and military expenditures, 67

and private sector, 73-74, 75

and social unrest, 67-68, 86-87, 149

and transition to socialism, 81ff, 97ff

see also Development theory

UNIDO Conference (1980), 116

UNITAR seminars (1980), 121, 137

Urbanization, 89

Vanguard party, 98

World Bank, 20

World economy, Soviet doctrine of, 73

pre-1953, 37, 39-40, 46

pre-1964, 37, 39, 40-45

pre-1975, 26, 38-39, 45-52, 80

post-1976 debates, 38, 52ff, 61, 83-85, 126-27, 148-49

World market, East European views on, 2, 60-61

World market, Soviet doctrine of

bifurcated, 1-2, 20, 26, 37-38, 39-40, 46-47, 80

global, 38-39, 52-59, 61, 62-69, 83-86, 123-25

single, 37, 46-52, 81

see also World economy, Soviet doctrine of

COUNTRY INDEX

Afghanistan, 4
  gas deal, 17
  Soviet aid, 2, 6, 8
  Soviet trade, 9
Africa, 41, 82, 86, 98
  North, 82, 128
  Soviet aid to, 24, 32-33, 98
  Sub-Saharan, 82, 128
Algeria, 77, 86
  Soviet aid, 8, 23-24, 32
  Soviet trade, 25
Angola, 33, 97, 98, 99
Argentina, 2, 3
Asia, 15, 82, 86
  Khrushchev's tour, 3-4
Austria, 30, 31

Belgian Congo, 79
Brazil, 9, 19, 33, 83
Burma, 4, 9, 14, 15, 75

Chile, 19
China, Peoples Republic of
  economic aid, 154 *table*
  economic theories, 87, 139-40
  military aid, 155 *table*
  and NIEO, 139-40
Congo Brazaville, 32
Cuba, 41, 99
Czechoslovakia, 19, 31

East Germany, 18
  economic policy, 18
Egypt, 75, 77, 98
  Soviet aid, 4, 8, 12, 14-15, 18, 32
  Soviet trade, 9, 15, 19

Ethiopia, 19, 97, 98, 99

France, 5, 6, 30

Ghana, 6, 8, 9, 14, 15, 32
Greece, 83
Guinea, 76
  phosphate deal, 17
  Soviet aid, 5, 6, 18
  Soviet trade, 9

Holland, 6
Hungary, 31
  economic policy, 18
  economic research, 24, 60, 61

India, 6, 75, 76, 85, 89, 131
  joint production with USSR, 18, 142
  Soviet aid, 3, 4, 6, 8
  Soviet trade, 2, 9, 141-43
Indonesia, 75, 76, 77
  Soviet aid, 4, 6, 8, 14
  Soviet trade, 3, 9, 10
Iran
  gas deal, 18, 19, 30-31
  Soviet aid, 15
  Soviet trade, 15, 19
Iraq, 6, 8, 16, 23, 25
Italy, 32, 83

Japan, 32

Kuwait, 19

Latin America, 82, 83
  Soviet trade with, 2, 15, 19

Libya, 19, 25

Malaysia, 15
Mali, 6, 8, 14, 32, 77
Mexico, 16, 83
Morocco, 3, 15
  phosphate deal, 33
Mozambique, 138

Nigeria, 6, 15, 19

Pakistan, 6, 75
Philippines, 15, 19, 75
Poland
  economic research, 60-61
Portugal, 83, 98

Réunion, 139

Singapore, 15, 19
Syria, 3, 8

Turkey, 75

Uganda, 18
United Arab Republic, *see* Egypt
United States
  economic aid, 4, 8, 9, 11
  and Egypt, 4
  and India, 142
  policy recommendations for, 149-50
  reaction to Soviet threat, 9-10
Uruguay, 3

Vietnam, 99

West Germany, 30, 142

Yemen, People's Democratic Republic
  of, 103
Yugoslavia, 19, 31

NAME INDEX

Amin, S., 135-36
Andreasian, R., 28, 29 *quoted*
Avakov, R. M., 91

Ben Bella, A., 77, 86
Berliner, J., 9
Bogomolov, O. T., *quoted*: 25, 29, 55, 120, 123
Bohr, N., 53
Bragina, E., 95
Brandt Commission Report, 61-62, 89
Brandt, W., 62, 89
Brezhnev, L., 13, 25, 46, 49, 89
  and academic research, 45ff, 58, 127, 134, 148
  on colonialism and imperialism, 57, 81
  on global problems, 53-54, 58, 63
  on LDCs, 49, 56, 57, 64-65
  on socialist orientation, 98-99, 101
Brutents, K., 57, 93, 140 *quoted*
Bulganin, N., 3, 5

Dillon, D., 9
Dobozi, I., 127-128 *quoted*
Dulles, J. F., 4

Elianov, A., 95
Engels, F., 102

Frolov, I., 63-64, 67, 126
Furtado, C., 136

Gafurov, B. G., 57-58
Gromyko, A., 111

Gromyko, A. A., 99

Harbison, F., 82

Inozemtsev, N. N., 67
Ivanov, I., 94-95

Kalecki, M., 60
Khrushchev, N. S., 38, 39, 40-41
  and academic research, 40-45, 148
  Asian tour (1955), 3-4
  economic policies, 3ff, 17, 39
  ouster of, 12-13
Kiva, A., 101
Kleer, J., 61, 136 *quoted*
Kollontai, V. M., 77 *quoted*
Kosygin, A., 13, 16, 17, 47-48, 57
Kovalevsky, A. A., 94
Krylov, V., 91 *quoted*
Kuusinen, O., 5

Lange, O., 2
Lenin, V. I., 47, 48-49
  on colonialism, 64, 81
  on NEP, 79, 80, 85
  on transition to socialism, 79, 86, 103
Levkovsky, A., 75, 85, 96
Lowenthal, R., 21

Maksimova, M., 47, 48-49, 55 *quoted*, 128
Malenkov, G., 5
Marx, K., 87, 92
Mikoyan, A., 11-12, 41, 53
Mirsky, G., 56, 57

187

Molotov, V., 5
Myrdal, G., 61

Nayyar, D., 143
Nesterov, M. V., 1

Obminsky, E., 83-84 *quoted*
Ostrovitianov, K., 5

Paszynski, M., 131 *quoted*, 132-33
 quoted
Patolichev, N. S., 15, 54
Ponomarev, B., 88-89, 100, 137-38
Prebisch, R., 135
Primakov, E., 57-58, 93, 94, 100
 quoted, 101, 121 *quoted*

Reisner, L. I., 53 *quoted*, 88, 89
Rummel, R., 82
Rymalov, V., 44 *quoted*, 46, 84

Shmelev, N. P., 114 *cited*, 121 *quoted*
Simoniya, N. A., 86-87
Skachkov, S. A., 19, 25
Skorov, G., 91
Stalin, J., 1, 37, 38, 43

on two world markets, 39-40, 46
Starushenko, G. B., 102 *quoted*,
 103 *quoted*
Sukarno, 6
Szentes, T., 61, 130 *quoted*

Tiagunenko, V. L., 44, 84
Tinbergen, J., 89
Tuzmukhamedov, R., 59

Ulianovsky, R. A., 57, 75, 78, 84
 quoted

Varga, E., 41-2
Vernon, R., 94
Volkova, N., 94

Wiles, P., 97 *cited*

Yashkin, V., 121, 137 *quoted*

Zagladin, V., 63, 67, 88 *quoted*,
 126
Zevin, L., 48, 122 *quoted*, 125 *quoted*
Zurawicki, L., 132 *quoted*

ABOUT THE AUTHOR

ELIZABETH KRIDL VALKENIER is Resident Scholar at the W. A. Harriman Institute for Advanced Studies of the Soviet Union at Columbia University. She has taught Russian history and Soviet policy at Hunter College, Manhattanville College, and currently at Columbia. Since 1967 she has done extensive research in the Soviet Union on several extended stays, twice as a senior scholar on the official U.S.-Soviet cultural exchange program. Her studies of Soviet policies toward the developing countries have appeared in many U.S. and European journals, such as *Problems of Communism*, *World Politics*, *Survey* and *Europa-Archiv*. She has contributed to various symposia on Soviet foreign policy and has commented on Soviet activities in Asia and Africa in the *New York Times* and *The Christian Science Monitor*. She is also author of *Russian Realist Art: The State and Society* (1977).

This book inaugurates the **Studies of the Harriman Institute**, successor to:

Studies of the Russian Institute

ABRAM BERGSON, *Soviet National Income in 1937* (1953)

ERNEST J. SIMMONS, JR., ed., *Through the Glass of Soviet Literature: Views of Russian Society* (1953),

THAD PAUL ALTON, *Polish Postwar Economy* (1954)

⟶DAVID GRANICK, *Management of the Industrial Firm in the USSR: A Study in Soviet Economic Planning* (1954)

ALLEN S. WHITING, *Soviet Policies in China, 1917-1924* (1954)

GEORGE S. N. LUCKYJ, *Literary Politics in the Soviet Ukraine, 1917-1934* (1956)

MICHAEL BORO PETROVICH, *The Emergence of Russian Panslavism, 1856-1870* (1956)

THOMAS TAYLOR HAMMOND, *Lenin on Trade Unions and Revolution, 1893-1917* (1956)

DAVID MARSHALL LANG, *The Last Years of the Georgian Monarchy, 1658-1832* (1957)

JAMES WILLIAM MORLEY, *The Japanese Thrust into Siberia, 1918* (1957)

ALEXANDER G. PARK, *Bolshevism in Turkestan, 1917-1927* (1957)

HERBERT MARCUSE, *Soviet Marxism: A Critical Analysis* (1958)

CHARLES B. McLANE, *Soviet Policy and the Chinese Communists, 1931-1946* (1958)

OLIVER H. RADKEY, *The Agrarian Foes of Bolshevism: Promise and Defeat of the Russian Socialist Revolutionaries, February to October, 1917* (1958)

RALPH TALCOTT FISHER, JR., *Pattern for Soviet Youth; A Study of the Congresses of the Komsomol, 1918-1954* (1959)

ALFRED ERICH SENN, *The Emergence of Modern Lithuania* (1959)

ELLIOT R. GOODMAN, *The Soviet Design for a World State* (1960)

JOHN N. HAZARD, *Settling Disputes in Soviet Society: The Formative Years of Legal Institutions* (1960)

DAVID JORAVSKY, *Soviet Marxism and Natural Science, 1917-1932* (1961)

MAURICE FRIEDBERG, *Russian Classics in Soviet Jackets* (1962)

ALFRED J. RIEBER, *Stalin and the French Communist Party, 1941-1947* (1962)

THEODORE K. VON LAUE, *Sergei Witte and the Industrialization of Russia* (1962)

JOHN A. ARMSTRONG, *Ukrainian Nationalism* (1963)

OLIVER H. RADKEY, *The Sickle under the Hammer: The Russian Socialist Revolutionaries in the Early Months of Soviet Rule* (1963)

KERMIT E. McKENZIE, *Comintern and World Revolution, 1928-1943: The Shaping of Doctrine* (1964)

HARVEY L. DYCK, *Weimar Germany and Soviet Russia, 1926-1933: A Study in Diplomatic Instability* (1966)

(Above titles published by Columbia University Press.)

HAROLD J. NOAH, *Financing Soviet Schools* (Teachers College, 1966)

JOHN M. THOMPSON, *Russia, Bolshevism, and the Versailles Peace* (Princeton, 1966)

PAUL AVRICH, *The Russian Anarchists* (Princeton, 1967)

LOREN R. GRAHAM, *The Soviet Academy of Sciences and the Communist Party, 1927-1932* (Princeton, 1967)

ROBERT A. MAGUIRE, *Red Virgin Soil: Soviet Literature in the 1920's* (Princeton, 1968).

T. H. RIGBY, *Communist Party Membership in the U.S.S.R., 1917-1967* (Princeton, 1968)

RICHARD T. DE GEORGE, *Soviet Ethics and Morality* (University of Michigan, 1969)

JONATHAN FRANKEL, *Vladimir Akimov on the Dilemmas of Russian Marxism, 1895-1903* (Cambridge, 1969)

WILLIAM ZIMMERMAN, *Soviet Perspectives on International Relations, 1956-1967* (Princeton, 1969)

PAUL AVRICH, *Kronstadt, 1921* (Princeton, 1970)

EZRA MENDELSOHN, *Class Struggle in the Pale: The Formative Years of the Jewish Workers' Movement in Tsarist Russia* (Cambridge, 1970)

EDWARD J. BROWN, *The Proletarian Episode in Russian Literature* (Columbia, 1971)

REGINALD E. ZELNIK, *Labor and Society in Tsarist Russia: The Factory Workers of St. Petersburg, 1855-1870* (Stanford, 1971)

PATRICIA K. GRIMSTED, *Archives and Manuscript Repositories in the USSR: Moscow and Leningrad* (Princeton, 1972)

RONALD G. SUNY, *The Baku Commune, 1917-1918* (Princeton, 1972)

EDWARD J. BROWN, *Mayakovsky: A Poet in the Revolution* (Princeton, 1973)

MILETON EHRE, *Oblomov and his Creator: The Life and Art of Ivan Goncharov* (Princeton, 1973)

HENRY KRISCH, *German Politics Under Soviet Occupation* (Columbia, 1974)

HENRY W. MORTON and RUDOLPH L. TÖKÉS, eds., *Soviet Politics and Society in the 1970's* (Free Press, 1974)

WILLIAM G. ROSENBERG, *Liberals in the Russian Revolution* (Princeton, 1974)

RICHARD G. ROBBINS, JR., *Famine in Russia, 1891-1892* (Columbia, 1975)

VERA DUNHAM, *In Stalin's Time: Middleclass Values in Soviet Fiction* (Cambridge, 1976)

WALTER SABLINSKY, *The Road to Bloody Sunday* (Princeton, 1976)

WILLIAM MILLS TODD, III, *The Familiar Letter as a Literary Genre in the Age of Pushkin* (Princeton, 1976)

ELIZABETH VALKENIER, *Russian Realist Art. The State and Society: The Peredvizhniki and their Tradition* (Ardis, 1977)

SUSAN SOLOMON, *The Soviet Agrarian Debate* (Westview, 1978)

SHEILA FITZPATRICK, ed., *Cultural Revolution in Russia, 1928-1931* (Indiana, 1978)

PETER SOLOMON, *Soviet Criminologists and Criminal Policy: Specialists in Policy-Making* (Columbia, 1978)

KENDALL E. BAILES, *Technology and Society under Lenin and Stalin: Origins of the Soviet Technical Intelligentsia, 1917-1941* (Princeton, 1978)

LEOPOLD H. HAIMSON, ed., *The Politics of Rural Russia, 1905-1914* (Indiana, 1979)

THEODORE H. FRIEDGUT, *Political Participation in the USSR* (Princeton, 1979)

SHEILA FITZPATRICK, *Education and Social Mobility in the Soviet Union, 1921-1934* (Cambridge, 1979)

WESLEY ANDREW FISHER, *The Soviet Marriage Market: Mate-Selection in Russia and the USSR* (Praeger, 1980)

JONATHAN FRANKEL, *Prophecy and Politics: Socialism, Nationalism, and the Russian Jews, 1862-1917* (Cambridge, 1981)

ROBIN FEUER MILLER, *Dostoevsky and the Idiot: Author, Narrator, and Reader* (Harvard, 1981)

DIANE KOENKER, *Moscow Workers and the 1917 Revolution* (Princeton, 1981)

PATRICIA K. GRIMSTED, *Archives and Manuscript Repositories in the USSR: Estonia, Latvia, Lithuania, and Belorussia* (Princeton, 1981)

EZRA MENDELSOHN, *Zionism in Poland: The Formative Years, 1915-1926* (Yale, 1982)

HANNES ADOMEIT, *Soviet Risk-Taking and Crisis Behavior* (George Allen & Unwin, 1982)

SEWERYN BIALER and THANE GUSTAFSON, eds., *Russia at the Crossroads: The 26th Congress of the CPSU* (George Allen & Unwin, 1982)

ROBERTA THOMPSON MANNING, *The Crisis of the Old Order in Russia: Gentry and Government* (Princeton, 1982)

ANDREW A. DURKIN, *Sergei Aksakov and Russian Pastoral* (Rutgers, 1983)